LET US SEARCH OUR WAYS

Let Us Search Our Ways

A Commentary on the Book of Lamentations

Evan and Marie Blackmore

DeWard
for your journey

Let us Search Our Ways: A Commentary on the Book of Lamentations
© 2015 by DeWard Publishing Company, Ltd.
P.O. Box 6259, Chillicothe, Ohio 45601
www.deward.com

Case laminate cover concept by Jonathan Hardin, designed by Eric Wallace. Dust jacket design by Barry Wallace.

Opposte Page: a coin authorized by the Roman senate—*S(enatus) C(onsulto)*—to celebrate the Roman emperor Vespasian's conquest of Jerusalem. It shows a humiliated woman seated on the ground mourning, with the inscription *IUDEA CAPTA* ("Judea captured"). The opening verses of Lamentations describe the earlier Babylonian conquest of Jerusalem in similar terms: "How she has sat alone, the city that was great with people; she has become like a widow.... There is no comforter for her among all of her lovers" (Lam 1.1–2).

Reasonable care has been taken to trace original sources for any excerpts and quotations appearing in this book and to document such information. For material not in the public domain, fair-use standards and practices were followed. Should any attribution be found to be incorrect or incomplete, the publisher welcomes written documentation supporting correction for subsequent printings.

Printed in the United States of America.

ISBN: 978-1-936341-76-4 (case laminate)
978-1-947929-36-4 (dust jacket)

"Let us search our ways, and let us search them out,
and let us return to the Lord"

Lamentations 3.40

CONTENTS

PREFACE

In most commentary series, Lamentations shares a volume with Jeremiah. Jeremiah is one of the very longest books in the Bible (by some reckonings, it is the longest of all), so this does not leave much room for its shorter companion. Many commentators have written well on Lamentations under those conditions—C. F. Keil, Payne Smith, Theo Laetsch, R. K. Harrison, John Humphries, and others—but inevitably they have been able to deal with only a proportion of the questions that an ordinary Bible reader might want discussed.

Certainly there are some full-length separate-volume commentaries on Lamentations, which examine the book in more detail. But nearly all of them have been written by authors who do not fully accept that all Scripture is the word of God (2 Tim 3.16) and that all His word is truth, without error or inconsistency (John 17.17; cf. Titus 1.2; Num 23.19; Rom 3.4). Most of them assume that the book of Lamentations contradicts certain other Scriptures, such as parts of Deuteronomy and Jeremiah. A few, more cautiously, maintain that the book of Lamentations *may* contradict Jeremiah or other Scriptures, but that this is not certain.

Clearly, explanations offered by commentators who assume the existence of contradictions in Scripture, or who allow at least the possibility of such contradictions, will not always satisfy readers who regard the Scriptures as the inerrant word of God.

This commentary is designed to fill the gap. It is designed to supplement the classic commentaries that may already be on readers' shelves. It aims to provide more detailed phrase-by-phrase information than they were able to do, while preserving the classic view that every part of Scripture is consistent with every other part, and is to be understood in the light of every other part.

The Translation

The English translation of Lamentations in this volume has been newly prepared, but most of its policies will be familiar from standard English versions of the Scriptures:

- As in the KJV, ASV, and NASB, *italics* mark material that does not correspond to anything in the original, but has been added by the translators for the sake of clarity.
- Pronouns referring to Deity are capitalized ("He," "You").
- Capitalization is also used to distinguish a few words that might otherwise be confusing or ambiguous. The word "Law" is capitalized when it refers generically to the Law of God, but is printed in small letters, "law," when it refers to specific laws. The word "Man" is capitalized when it refers generically to both male and female (Hebrew *'dm*, Greek *anthrōpos*), but is printed in small letters, "man," when it refers specifically to males (Hebrew *'yš* or *gbr*, Greek *anēr*).
- The unique name of the true God (Hebrew *YHWH*) is translated "Lord" in small capitals.
- Words and phrases addressed to one person (KJV "thou" or "thee") are marked with a superscript dagger thus: you[†]. Words and phrases addressed to two or more people (KJV "you" or "ye") are marked with a superscript [pl] thus: you[pl]. Where the English rendering of a verb includes an English pronoun, the superscript is attached to that pronoun (e.g., "You[†] commanded"). Where it does not, the superscript is attached to the last of whatever English words are used to render it (e.g., "Deal severely[†] with them").

The Commentary

In the commentary sections of this volume, **boldface print** marks a quotation from the passage under discussion, whereas quotations from other sources are cited in quotation marks.

Some paragraphs of commentary are inset and printed in a smaller font size than others. Those paragraphs may be omitted by readers who wish to follow the main line of discussion without diversion. The use of a smaller font does not imply that those paragraphs are less "important," or that they are less relevant to the gospel of Christ. The difference in font size is intended solely as a visual aid, helping the reader to distinguish different lines of discussion.

In supplementing the classic commentaries on Lamentations, we have aimed to include two kinds of material in particular:

- The book of Lamentations was not written only for Israelites who lived in the distant past. It was also "written for our instruction" during the present new covenant era (Rom 15.4; cf. 1 Cor 10.11). Therefore, we have related the book more closely to the New Testament Scriptures, and have cited New Testament passages more frequently, than most commentators on Lamentations have had room to do. The God who punished Jerusalem so severely, more than 2000 years ago, is the same God before whose judgment seat we must all one day stand; and if we do not learn from the things that happened then to the holy city, we ourselves must expect to suffer no less severely than she did (Luke 13.1–5; Heb 2.1–4).

- Scripture readers are often puzzled by the different translations that they hear other people reading, and/or by the alternate renderings printed in the margins of their own Bibles. Therefore, where there are significant variations between the standard Bible versions (in English and other Western languages), or where variant readings are given in the margin of those versions, we have sought to explain the reasons for them. Again, relatively little information of this kind can be found in most of the classic Lamentations commentaries.

More generally, we have aimed to provide material suitable for three types of believers: those who are reading the book of Lamentations individually, those who are discussing it in groups, and those who are seeking sermon material from it.

Chapter and verse numbers are always cited according to the system used in standard English Bible versions (e.g., KJV, ASV, NASB, and ESV)—even when the reference is to a foreign language edition that normally uses a different numbering system.

It should be noted that all the chapter numbers, verse numbers, and book titles in standard editions of the Bible were inserted by uninspired people, and are not parts of the word of God. What the KJV calls "The First Epistle of Paul the Apostle to the Corinthians" was certainly not Paul's first epistle to the Corinthians; he had already written at least one other epistle to them (cf. 1 Cor 5.9). What the KJV calls "The Second Book of Samuel" is not about Samuel at all, and never even mentions him; he had already died before the events recorded in it (cf. 1 Sam 25.1;

28.3). Therefore, all references in the present commentary to "1 Cor," "2 Sam," etc., should be regarded merely as nominal symbols for sections of Scripture, not as abbreviated descriptions of their content.

Foreign-language commentaries are quoted in our own English translations, but we have supplied page references both to the original editions and to previously published English versions (if any). So, for instance, "Keil 573/378" refers to a statement on page 573 of Keil's German commentary and page 378 of its published English version. The previously published English version will of course differ in wording (and occasionally in meaning) from our own rendering.

Readers of this book are urged to search the Scriptures to determine what is so (Acts 17.11), and by that standard to test all things in the following pages, holding fast whatever is good, but rejecting whatever is evil (1 Thes 5.21–22).

ABBREVIATIONS AND OTHER SYMBOLS

†	second person singular (KJV "thou" or "thee"); contrast ^{pl}
§	section (e.g., of a reference grammar or lexicon entry)
≡	corresponds to
4QLam^a	Qumran manuscript 4QLam^a
Aalders	Aalders, *Klaagliederen* (Korte Verklaring)
Adeney	Adeney, *Song of Solomon and the Lamentations* (Expositor's Bible)
Albertus	Albertus Magnus, *In Threnos… commentarii*
Albrektson	Albrektson, *Studies in… Lamentations*
Assan-Dhôte	Assan-Dhôte and Moatti-Fine, *Baruch, Lamentations, Lettre de Jérémie* (Bible d'Alexandrie)
ASV	American Standard Version
ATD	Otto Kaiser, "Klagelieder" (Alte Testament Deutsch)
BAe	Bibliotheca Aegyptiaca
Bar	Baruch
BDB	Brown, Driver, and Briggs, *Hebrew and English Lexicon*
Blayney	Blayney, *Jeremiah and Lamentations*
Böttcher	Böttcher, *Ausführliches Lehrbuch der hebräischen Sprache*
Brenton	*Septuagint Version,* tr. Brenton
BTX	Biblia Textual
Calvin	Calvin, *Praelectiones in Lamentationes*
Castro	Castro, *Commentariorum in Ieremiae prophetas, Lamentationes…*
CH	Code of Hammurabi

Costa	a Costa de Andrada, *Commentarii in Threnos*
del Rio	del Rio, *Commentarius litteralis in Threnos*
Diodati	Bibbia Diodati (2nd ed., 1641)
Dobbs-Allsopp	Dobbs-Allsopp, *Lamentations* (Interpretation)
Donne	"Lamentations of Jeremy," tr. Donne
DRCV	Douai-Rheims-Challoner Version (1749–1750)
EA	El-Amarna tablets
ed.	edition; edited by
Eighteen Psalms	Eighteen Psalms of the Roman period ("Psalms of Solomon")
ELB	Revidierte Elberfelder Bibel (3rd ed., 2006)
ESV	English Standard Version
Ewald	Ewald, *Die Psalmen und die Klaglieder* (3rd ed., 1866)
Fuerst	Fuerst, *Hebrew and Chaldee Lexicon*, tr. Davidson
GCS	Griechischen Christlichen Schriftsteller der ersten drei Jahrhunderte
Geneva	Geneva Bible
Gerlach	Gerlach, *Klagelieder*
GKC	Kautzsch, *Gesenius' Hebrew Grammar*, revised by Cowley
Gordis	Gordis, *Song of Songs and Lamentations*
HALOT	Koehler, Baumgartner, and Stamm, *Hebrew and Aramaic Lexicon of the Old Testament*
HCSB	Holman Christian Standard Bible
HDB	*Dictionary of the Bible*, ed. Hastings
Hillers	Hillers, *Lamentations* (Anchor Bible; 2nd ed., 1992)
Hornblower	Hornblower, additions to the American edition of Nägelsbach
House	House, "Lamentations" (Word Biblical Commentary)
Hrabanus	Hrabanus Maurus, *Commentaria in Jeremiam*
Humphries	Humphries, *Jeremiah and Lamentations* (Truth Commentaries)
IBHS	Waltke and O'Connor, *Introduction to Biblical Hebrew Syntax*
Ibn Ezra	Ibn Ezra's commentary on Lamentations (Lewin-Epstein, 1924)

JB	Jerusalem Bible (1966)
JM	Joüon and Muraoka, *Hebrew Grammar*
Joosten	Joosten, *Verbal System of Biblical Hebrew*
JPS	Jewish Publication Society Version
K	Kᵉtîb (the reading in the text of MT)
Kaiser	Walter C. Kaiser, Jr., *Grief and Pain in the Plan of God*
Keil	Keil, *Jeremia und die Klagelieder* (Keil and Delitzsch)
KJV	King James Version
König 1–3	König, *Lehrgebäude der hebräischen Sprache*, vols. 1–3
König 4	König, *Stilistik, Rhetorik, Poetik*
Laetsch	Laetsch, *Bible Commentary: Jeremiah*
Lapide	Cornelius a Lapide, *Commentarius in Ieremiam prophetam, Threnos, et Baruch*
LBLA	La Biblia de las Américas
LSJ	Liddell and Scott, *Greek-English Lexicon*, revised by Jones, with revised Supplement (1996)
Luther	Lutherbibel (1545)
LXX	Old Greek (including Septuagint)
Mackay	Mackay, *Lamentations* (Mentor Commentary)
Martin	Version Martin, revised by Roques (1744)
mg	marginal note
MLB	Modern Language Bible (New Berkeley Version)
MT	Masoretic text
NAB	New American Bible (1st ed., 1970)
Nägelsbach	Nägelsbach, *Jeremia und dessen Klagelieder* (Lange's Bibelwerk)
NASB	New American Standard Bible (1st ed., 1971)
NBG	Nederlands Bijbelgenootschap-vertaling 1951
ND	Nuova Diodati (1991)
NEB	New English Bible
NIDOTTE	VanGemeren, *New International Dictionary of Old Testament Theology and Exegesis*
NIV	New International Version
NJB	New Jerusalem Bible
NJPS	New Jewish Publication Society Version
NKJV	New King James Version
NRSV	New Revised Standard Version

NSR	Nouvelle Version Segond Révisée (1978)
NZB	Neue Zürcher-Bibel (2007)
Ostervald	Version Ostervald (2nd ed., 1744)
Parry	Parry, *Lamentations* (Two Horizons Old Testament Commentary)
Payne Smith	Payne Smith, "Lamentations" (Speaker's Commentary)
pl	second person plural (KJV "you" or "ye"); contrast †
Provan	Provan, *Lamentations* (New Century Bible Commentary)
Q	Qerê (a reading in the margin of MT)
Quarles	Quarles, *Sions Elegies*
Rashi	Rashi's commentary on Lamentations
REB	Revised English Bible
Renkema	Renkema, *Klaagliederen* (Commentaar op het Oude Testament)
Rotherham	Emphasized Bible, tr. Rotherham
RST	Russian Synodal Version
RSV	Revised Standard Version
S21	Version Segond 21
Salters	Salters, *Lamentations* (International Critical Commentary)
Sanctius	Sanctius, *In Ieremiam*
Sandys	Sandys, *Paraphrase upon the Divine Poems*
Sir	Ben Sira (Jesus son of Sirach)
SL	Sokoloff, *Syriac Lexicon*
Smith	*Holy Bible*, tr. Julia Smith
Stone	Stone Tanach
Streane	Streane, *Jeremiah… Lamentations* (Cambridge Bible for Schools and Colleges)
SV	Statenvertaling
Syr	Syriac
TDOT	Botterweck, Ringgren, and Fabry, *Theological Dictionary of the Old Testament*
Tg	Targum
Theodoret	Theodoret, *Explanatio in Threni*

TLOT	Jenni and Westermann, *Theological Lexicon of the Old Testament*
tr.	translated by
TWOT	Harris, Archer, and Waltke, *Theological Wordbook of the Old Testament*
v, vv	verse, verses
VDF	Version Darby Française
Vg	Latin Vulgate
VRV 1602	Versión Reina-Valera (1602)
VRV 1909	Versión Reina-Valera (1909)
VRV 1960	Versión Reina-Valera Revisada (1960)
Westermann	Westermann, *Klagelieder*
Wis	Book of Wisdom (of Solomon)
Wordsworth	Wordsworth, *Holy Bible*

INTRODUCTION

The Babylonian Destruction of Jerusalem

Six hundred years before Christ, the people of Judah appeared to be flourishing.

They were living in the land that the Lord had given to them, "a land flowing with milk and honey... the splendor of all lands" (Ezek 20.6). They were worshiping at the place that the Lord had chosen: the city of Jerusalem (Zion), "the gladness of all the earth... the city of the great King" (Psa 48.2; cf. Jer 7.2; 26.2). Traders with loads of merchandise were passing through Jerusalem's gates every day (Jer 17.19–22, 27; cf. Neh 13.15–18). "The sound of joy and the sound of gladness, the sound of the bridegroom and the sound of the bride, the sound of the millstones and the light of the lamp," were heard and seen in its streets (Jer 25.10; 7.34; 16.19). The people were living just like the other nations of the world, worshiping in the same ways, indulging in the same deeds (Ezek 20.32; Jer 3.6–10).

True, they were doing many things that the Lord had forbidden. They were neglecting His worship, committing fornication, making money by means of deceit, and failing to care for the poor among them (Ezek 22.6–13). But they had been living that way for many years, and no harm had happened; they "had plenty of food, and were well off, and saw no evil" (Jer 44.17). Besides, their religious leaders (with few exceptions) told them that no evil would come upon them for living like that (Jer 23.17). Most of the people felt that they had nothing to fear from the Lord (Jer 44.10; 36.24). In their hearts they secretly believed that He would do neither good nor evil (Zep 1.12).

Yet the Lord had warned them repeatedly that a terrible punishment would befall them if they persisted in disobeying Him: "If you will not hearken to Me, and will not do all these commandments… I will scatter you among the nations, and I will unsheathe the sword after you; and your land will be a desolation, and your cities a dried up place" (Lev 26.14–15, 31–39; Deut 28.15, 49–57, 63–65).

The Lord is "a God merciful and compassionate, slow to anger, and abounding in lovingkindness and faithfulness, keeping lovingkindness for thousands, forgiving iniquity and transgression and sin" (Exod 34.6–7; Psa 86.5, 15; 103.8–13; 145.8; Mic 7.18; Neh 9.17; 2 Chr 30.9). "He does not afflict from His heart and grieve the sons of Man" (Lam 3.33; Ezek 33.11). When His people sinned against Him, "many times He turned back His anger, and did not rouse up all His fury" (Psa 78.38; 106.43–45; Neh 9.28). Again and again He sent them prophets, generation after generation, exhorting them to return to Him, and warning them of the terrible punishment that would happen if they persisted in their disobedience (Lev 26.14–38; Deut 28.15–68; Josh 24.20; 1 Kgs 9.6–9; 2 Kgs 17.13; Neh 9.30–37; Jer 5.11–19; 25.3–11). But most often the people did not listen (2 Kgs 17.13–17; Jer 7.25–27; 25.4–7; Neh 9.30; Matt 21.34–36).

Although the Lord is merciful, He "will not justify the wicked," because it would not be right to do so (Exod 23.7). When the nation ignored His warnings and continued in their disobedience, eventually they reached a point where "there was no healing" any more, and the prophesied punishment had to come (2 Chr 36.15–21; Dan 9.11–14; Zec 7.9–14). In the end, "a man who hardens his neck from many corrections will suddenly be broken, and there will be no healing" (Prov 29.1).

After many generations, and many warnings, the Lord removed the ten northern tribes of Israel, leaving only the southern kingdom of Judah (2 Kgs 17.18–23). But Judah did not take warning from the example of its brethren. It followed the same path as the northern kingdom, and brought upon itself a similar punishment (Jer 3.8–10; Ezek 23.31–32; cf. 2 Chr 36.15–17; Jer 44.2–6).

The Lord raised up Nebuchadnezzar king of Babylon, and gave him authority over the nations (Dan 2.37–38; 4.22). The Lord commanded Judah and the surrounding nations to serve Nebuchadnezzar (Jer 27.5–15). But the people of Judah, under three successive kings—Jehoiakim, Jehoiachin, and Zedekiah—disobeyed the Lord and rebelled against Nebuchadnezzar.

- When **Jehoiakim** rebelled, Nebuchadnezzar besieged Jerusalem, took the king and some of the nobles captive to Babylon, and took away some of the precious vessels from the temple (2 Chr 36.5–8; 2 Kgs 24.1–4; Dan 1.1–4; Jer 35.11).

- When **Jehoiachin** rebelled, the consequences were similar but more severe. Again Nebuchadnezzar besieged Jerusalem, took the king and many of the people captive to Babylon, and took away the precious vessels from the temple (2 Kgs 24.10–16; 2 Chr 36.9–10; Ezek 1.2–3).
- When **Zedekiah** rebelled, the consequences were most terrible of all. Yet again Nebuchadnezzar besieged Jerusalem. This time the siege lasted for almost a year. Many of the people in Jerusalem died of starvation or were slain by the Babylonians. The king and most of the remaining people were taken captive to Babylon. Only "some of the poor people, who had nothing," were left. The temple was completely despoiled and burned, and many other important buildings were also destroyed. For seventy years the land remained desolate (Jer 39.1–10; 52.3–27; 2 Kgs 24.20–25.21; 2 Chr 36.13–21).

The Book of Lamentations

The book of Lamentations mourns over the condition of Jerusalem after that final Babylonian siege.

- The book mourns over the condition of the **people.** Many of them have been dispersed among the nations (1.3, 5, 18; 2.9; cf. 4.22). Even the king, the LORD's anointed, has been captured and taken away (2.9; 4.20). Other people have been slain (1.20; 2.20–21, 4; 3.43; 4.9, 13; 5.12) or have died of starvation (1.19; 2.11–12, 19; 4.9–10, 4). Those who remain are harshly oppressed and enslaved (5.1–13; 3.1–20, 45–63; 4.14–16).
- The book also mourns over the condition of the holy **city.** Its walls and gates have been destroyed (2.7–9). The inhabitants' houses have been taken over by foreigners (5.2). Even the holy place, the temple, has been entered by foreigners (1.10) and destroyed (2.6).
- The book freely confesses the **cause** of these troubles: the sins of the people ("The LORD has grieved [Jerusalem] because of the abundance of her transgressions," 1.5, 18; 3.42; 4.13; 5.7, 16).
- The book exhorts the **people** to repent of their sins and return to the LORD ("Let us search our ways, and let us search them out, and let us return to the LORD; let us lift up our heart to our hands to

God in the heavens," 3.40–41), acknowledging the justice of His punishment: "The LORD—He is righteous; for against His mouth I have rebelled" (1.18; 3.26–27, 33–39).

- The book requests the LORD to look on the sufferings of His people ("See, LORD, my affliction," 1.9, 11, 20; 3.55–63; 5.1), to restore them ("Return us, LORD, to Yourself... renew our days as before," 5.20), and to do what is just and right, both for them ("You have seen, LORD, the crooked dealing done to me; judge my judgment," 3.55–59) and for their oppressors ("You will give back to them for their dealing, LORD, in accordance with the work of their hands," 3.60–66; 1.21–22; 4.21–22).

After the Babylonian Destruction

The prayers in the book of Lamentations, asking the Lord to look on His people and restore them, were indeed heard and answered.

Many centuries before the Babylonian destruction, Moses had prophesied that if the Israelites persisted in disobeying the Lord, they would be besieged and afflicted and taken away from their land into exile (Deut 28.15–68). But he also prophesied that if "you return to the LORD your God and hearken to His voice... with all your heart and with all your soul, then the LORD your God will restore your restoration and have compassion on you, and He will return and gather you from all the peoples where the LORD your God has scattered you... and the LORD your God will put all these curses on your enemies, and on those who hated you, who persecuted you" (Deut 30.1–10).

The Lord had repeated that promise through Jeremiah: "When you seek Me out with all your heart... I will gather you from all the nations... and return you to the place from which I exiled you" (Jer 29.10–14).

Nevertheless, the nation could not be restored instantly. The people of Judah would have to serve the king of Babylon for 70 years. During that time, because of their sins, the land would remain desolate. But when the 70 years ended, the Lord would set free the exiles in Babylon. They would return to their home in Judah, and the nation would be restored (Jer 25.8–12; 29.10; 2 Chr 36.20–21; Dan 9.2; Zec 1.12).

After 70 years of Babylonian rule, these promises were fulfilled, and the prayers in the book of Lamentations were answered. King Cyrus of Persia conquered the city of Babylon, placed the Babylonians in subjection, and authorized the exiles from Judah to return to their homeland (2 Chr 36.22–23; Ezra 1.1–2.70).

Lamentations and the World Today

Like everything in the Scriptures, the book of Lamentations is not merely a document recording events that happened thousands of years ago. It was "written for our instruction" (Rom 15.4; 1 Cor 10.11; 2 Tim 3.16–17).

Like the people of Judah in early Babylonian times, we have been blessed by the Lord in many ways. He has given us the Scriptures to teach us how to live. He has given us abundant food, clothing, and everything we need to live happily and comfortably. People are eating and drinking, buying and selling, planting and building, marrying and giving in marriage (cf. Luke 17.26–30). But most of us do not acknowledge that it is God who has given to us our "grain, and wine, and oil, and multiplied [our] silver and gold" (Hos 2.8), and do not give Him thanks. We live in the midst of people who set aside the Law of the Lord, and are not ashamed of greed, drunkenness, all kinds of sexual immorality and indecency, hatred and malice, lying, and blasphemy of the name of God. They say in their hearts that "there is no God" (Psa 14.1), or that if there is, He will not punish anyone.

Like the people of Judah in those days, our leaders "have broken the yoke; they have torn off the bonds" (Jer 5.5) and "decree unrighteous decrees" (Isa 10.1). Even many preachers of the gospel "speak to us smooth things" (Isa 30.10). They "have caused many to stumble at the Law" (Mal 2.8) by assuring them that they will have peace even if they continue in sin. They "have healed the wound of the daughter of My people slightly, saying, 'Peace, peace,' and there is no peace" (Jer 6.14).

Like the people of Judah in those days, we have plain and repeated warnings of the punishment that will come on all sinners who do not repent, from which none will escape (Matt 24.35–25.46; Acts 17.15; Rom 2.5–10; 1 Thes 5.3; 2 Thes 1.6; 2 Thes 1.6–10; 2 Pet 3.7–14). Like them, we have repeatedly seen people around us suffering and being destroyed, sometimes unexpectedly, sometimes in large numbers all at one time. Like them, we know for certain that the city we live in will one day be destroyed. The Scriptures tell us that "the present heavens and earth… are treasured up, being kept for a day of judgment in fire and destruction of the irreverent people…. All these things being thus broken, what sort of people is it necessary for you to be, in holy conduct and reverence" (2 Pet 3.7–14).

Therefore, when we today read the book of Lamentations, considering the world in which we live, we find that many of its statements are true of the present day as they were true of Jerusalem of old times. God's holy temple, the church, is desecrated by unbelievers, who mock at the Lord, His word, His church, and everything that is holy. The pathways to the gospel are deserted, few faithful worshipers walk along them, and the enemies of God rejoice to see it so. Little children are growing up in this world being starved for lack of nourishment from God's word. There are young men and young women in every street, lying dead in their trespasses and sins. They rejoice, but we cannot rejoice with them. Like the prophet, we sit alone and keep silence, and we pray to God to see, and to hear, and not to delay to save.

Causes of Suffering

The sufferings of Jerusalem, recorded in the book of Lamentation, happened because of sin. This is clearly taught in the book itself and in other Scriptures.

- Many of the inhabitants were suffering because they themselves had sinned against the LORD by disobeying Him (Lam 1.5, 18; 3.42; 4.13; 5.16).
- The infants in the city, who were too young to know the evil that their parents had done (cf. Deut 1.34), were not suffering for their own sins, but they were suffering as a result of the sins of their fathers (Lam 5.7).
- There were also adults like Jeremiah and Baruch, who had opposed the sins of the people around them, and had not shared in their evil deeds. Nevertheless they too had to suffer as a result of the people's sins (Jer 20.7–18; 43.3–5).

However, the book of Lamentations does not teach that *all* sufferings occur because of sin. In fact, the Scriptures clearly teach that only *some* sufferings are the result of sin. When Jesus was asked about a man born blind, "Who sinned, this one or his parents, that he should be born blind?"—He replied: "It was neither that this one sinned nor his parents, but it was in order that the works of God might be revealed in him" (John 9.2–3). James instructs the elders of the church to pray for the sick, and adds: "if he may be in a situation of having done sins, they will be forgiven to him" (Jas 5.15). Paul's thorn in the flesh was not to punish sin but to prevent Paul from sinning. It was bestowed on him "so that I should not exalt myself" (2 Cor 12.7). Job suffered greatly, but not because of sin (Job 2.3). His friends incorrectly told him that he had sinned (Job 4.7–8; 22.5–11) and encouraged him to repent (Job 11.13–20; 22.23). But when the LORD appeared, He revealed that they had not spoken what was right (Job 42.7–8).

Sometimes the LORD makes the reason for sufferings apparent to people. The people of Jerusalem could know the cause of their sufferings, because the LORD's prophets had revealed to them that their sufferings were punishments for their sin (Jer 7.13–34; Ezek 7.2–27). But the LORD does not always reveal to people the cause of their sufferings. Job was never told why the LORD allowed him to suffer. Even when the LORD spoke to Job directly (Job 38.1–41.34), He never explained the reason for Job's sufferings. He declared only that His ways are not to be questioned.

We today have no prophets to reveal the reasons for the particular events in our lives, so we are often in Job's situation when we suffer. We must be content not to know. When serious accidents, severe illnesses, and natural disasters occur, no prophet will come and declare from God the reason for these afflictions, as prophets did to the people of Jerusalem in the days leading up to its destruction. Of course, if anyone should "suffer as a murderer or a thief or an evildoer" (1 Pet 4.15), then they could certainly know that their own sins caused their sufferings. But usually, the reasons for suffering are unknown. Has it been caused by sin, or has it happened to prevent somebody from sinning, or is there some other reason for it? Very often, in this life, we will not know.

Sometimes people may *feel* that they know the reason for their own sufferings or for other people's sufferings. But feelings and uninspired human opinions are not to be trusted. "He who trusts in his own heart is a fool" (Prov 28.26). "The way of a fool is right in his own eyes" (Prov 12.15). "I know nothing against myself, but I am not justified by this: but the one who judges me is the Lord" (1 Cor 4.4). Many a time, people have been thoroughly convinced in their heart that something is so before God, and have been wrong (Prov 14.12; 30.12; Matt. 7.21–23; John 16.2; Acts 26.9; Rev 3.17). Job's friends felt that they could explain the cause of Job's sufferings; but they were wrong (Job 42.7–8).

The only trustworthy guide in these matters is the word of God. And if the word of God has not revealed the cause of sufferings in any particular case, then the cause of those sufferings cannot be known. There are things that it is not for us to know (Acts 1.7)—"hidden things," which "belong to the LORD your God" (Deut 29.29). In such situations we can only submit and accept our ignorance, as Job finally did (Job 42.2–3).

Structure

Lamentations is perhaps the most tightly patterned book in the whole of the Scriptures. It consists of five distinct lamentations, each of which has exactly 22 parts. This aspect of its patterning can be seen even in modern English Bibles, because the five lamentations are printed as five chapters, and their parts are printed as separate verses. (Notice that chapters 1, 2, 4, and 5 have 22 verses each; chapter 3 has 22 × 3 = 66 verses.)

Each of the five lamentations has two main components:

- It begins with an extended description of the **current sufferings** of the people (1.1–19; 2.1–19; 3.1–54; 4.1–20; 5.1–18). This description occupies by far the largest part of the lamentation. It circles around its subject like a bird of prey, mentioning one point, then moving on to another, then moving to a third, then returning to the first point, and so on. By the end of the description, a vividly detailed, insistently repetitive picture of inescapable affliction has built up.

- It ends with a short conclusion that seeks some **future change,** ending Jerusalem's sufferings and/or overturning her persecutors. In four of the five lamentations, this conclusion is an appeal addressed directly to the LORD (1.20–22; 2.20–22; 3.55–66; 5.19–22). In the other lamentation, it is a prophecy addressed to the nearest of the persecutors, Israel's neighbor Edom (4.21–22).

The description and the conclusion are not simply placed side by side, but are interlinked in ways that vary from chapter to chapter. For instance, in the first chapter, the extended description itself contains brief anticipatory appeals to the LORD (1.9, 11); in the last chapter, the whole description is embedded within and framed by the appeal (5.1, 19–22). The central chapter (chapter 3) has the most intricate design (see its headnote).

Like most of the Psalms, the Song of Songs, and many passages in other books (especially the prophets), the text of the Lamentations is arranged in groups of matching lines. In modern editions of the Bible, these lines are usually printed as verse so that the correspondence between them can be seen more easily:

> The Lord is good to those who are waiting for Him,
>> to the soul that is seeking Him;
> it is good that he is hoping and in stillness
>> for the salvation of the Lord;
> it is good for a man that he bears
>> a yoke in His youth (3.25–27).

Here the first line ("The Lord is good to those…") corresponds to the second ("it is good that he is hoping…") and to the third ("it is good for a man…"). Moreover, each line can itself be subdivided into two halves, as indicated above.

In the first three lamentations (chapters 1–3), nearly all of the matching lines are grouped in **threes** (as in the above example). In the fourth (chapter 4), the matching lines are grouped in **pairs:**

> The ones who were eating delightful things
>> have been made desolate in the streets;
> the ones who were nursed on scarlet
>> have embraced the dirt (4.5).

The final lamentation (chapter 5) consists only of **single lines,** although each line can still be subdivided into two halves:

> Our inheritance has been turned over to strangers,
>> our houses to aliens (5.2).

The first four lamentations have another remarkable feature. In the original Hebrew, they are alphabetic acrostics—that is, each verse begins with one of the 22 successive letters of the Hebrew alphabet. This feature is not usually imitated in translations, because it could not be done in most languages without twisting the sense. Nevertheless, the following may give some idea of the effect:

Ah, how alone she has sat,
>the city that was great with people!
She has become as a widow,
>the great one among the nations;
the princess among the provinces,
>she has been put to menial tasks.

Bitterly she is weeping in the night,
>and her tear is on her cheek;
there is no comforter for her
>among all of her lovers;
all of her companions have acted treacherously with her;
>they have become her enemies.

Coming from affliction, and coming from great slavery,
>Judah has gone into exile;
she has dwelt among the nations;
>she has found no rest;
all of her pursuers have reached her
>in between the oppressive places.

Dejected are the roads of Zion,
>because none are coming to the appointed assembly;
all of her gates are desolate;
>her priests are groaning;
her virgins are grieved;
>and she—it has been bitter for her.

Enemies have become the head over her;
>those who oppress her have been at ease;
for the Lord has grieved her
>because of the abundance of her transgressions;
her young children have gone
>in captivity before the face of the oppressor.

From the daughter of Zion,
>all of her honor has gone out;
her leaders have become like stags;
>they have not found any pasture,
and they have gone without strength
>before the face of the pursuer (1.1–6).

The middle Lamentation (chapter 3) is the most elaborately structured, because it is a triple acrostic: it has three lines beginning with the first letter of the Hebrew alphabet *('alep)*, three lines beginning with the second letter *(bet)*, three lines beginning with the third letter *(gimel)*, and so on throughout the alphabet:

> **A**s for me, the man who has seen affliction
> by the rod of His fury,
> **A**way He has led me, and made me walk
> in darkness, and not light;
> **A**ll the day surely He is turning,
> He is turning back His hand against me.
>
> **B**ody and skin, He has worn me away;
> He has crushed my bones;
> **B**esieging me, He has surrounded me
> with poison and weariness;
> **B**lack places He has made me inhabit,
> like those who have been dead from lasting time.
>
> **C**onfining me so that I cannot go out,
> He has made my bronze chain heavy;
> **C**ry out and cry for help as I may,
> He has shut out my entreaty;
> **C**losing up my roads with hewn stone,
> He has made my paths crooked (3.1–9).

Alphabetic acrostics are also found in eight of the Psalms (Psa 9–10; 25; 34; 37; 111; 112; 119; 145) and in Proverbs 31.10–31. The exact arrangement of the letters varies: in some cases certain letters are omitted, or the order of them is rearranged. In each of the four alphabetic lamentations all the letters are present, but only the first one (chapter 1) has the letters in the order nowadays familiar, with *'ayin* (v 16) before *pe* (v 17). The other three alphabetic lamentations (chapters 2–4) place the *pe* verses (2.16; 3.46–48; 4.17) before the *'ayin* ones (2.17; 3.49–51; 4.17).

Often, the alphabetic acrostic format tends to keep each segment of a psalm separate from its neighbors. The extreme example of this is Psalm 119, where the alphabetic segments are simply strung side by side like a row of perfectly matching pearls; every one of them is self-contained and makes complete sense in itself, even if read in isolation. The same "string of pearls" design is seen in some of the extended descriptions of suffering in the Lamentations (e.g., most of 1.1–19): matching self-contained vignettes are set side by side in successive alphabetic segments, without any connecting link between them. Here again, the central chapter has a more complex design: in it, there are often connections of sense between one alphabetical segment and the next. Placement in darkness appears in the first two segments (3.2, 6); being walled up in the second and third (3.5, 7); disrupted paths in the third and fourth (3.9, 11); wounding with arrows in the fourth and fifth (3.12, 13); and so on. The chapter's most crucial turn of thought is introduced in one alphabetic segment ("This I am bringing back to my heart...", 3.21) but completed only in the next ("... the lovingkindnesses of the LORD", 3.22)—a spilling over of thought (enjambment) unique in the whole of Biblical Hebrew poetry.

The final lamentation (chapter 5) has the simplest and plainest design. It is not an acrostic, even though it has the same number of verses as the letters of the Hebrew alphabet (22). Psalms 38 and 103 also have 22 verses but are not acrostics.

Thus no two of the lamentations have the same pattern. The following table summarizes the differences:

Chapter 1	Chapter 2	Chapter 3	Chapter 4	Chapter 5
3–line stanzas	3–line stanzas	3–line stanzas	2–line stanzas	1–line stanzas
Acrostic with *'ayin* before *pe*	Acrostic with *pe* before *'ayin*	Acrostic with *pe* before *'ayin*	Acrostic with *pe* before *'ayin*	Not acrostic
1 acrostic line per stanza	1 acrostic line per stanza	3 acrostic lines per stanza	1 acrostic line per stanza	Not acrostic

Some ancient manuscripts in Greek and other languages indicated the difference between the acrostic chapters 1–4 and the non-acrostic chapter 5 by marking the latter with a separate heading, "Prayer" (or, sometimes, "Prayer of Jeremiah"). The same policy can be seen in some English editions of the Bible, such as the Geneva Bible, where chapter 5 is set apart with a special subheading, "The Prayer of Jeremiah."

Most ancient translations also showed the acrostic form of chapters 1–4 by writing the successive letters of the Hebrew alphabet at the start of the various sections: *'alep* at the start of 1.1, *bet* at the start of 1.2, *gimel* at the start of 1.3, and so on. This too can be seen in some English Bibles, including the HCSB and Scrivener's Cambridge Paragraph edition of the KJV.

Names

Like the sections of the Law of Moses, the book of Lamentations has traditionally been named in two ways:

- By its first word, *'êkāh* ("How!"). This has been a common Hebrew name for the book at least since the early centuries after Christ (Babylonian Talmud, *Bᵉrākôt*, 57*b*; *Bābā' Batrā'*, 15*a*), and is the name given to it in all the standard Masoretic Hebrew manuscripts.
- By a description of its contents, *Qînôt* ("Dirges"). This method of naming the book was also used in Hebrew during the early centuries after Christ (Epiphanius, PG 43.280; Babylonian Talmud, *Bābā' Batrā'*, 14*b*). Today this name is less often employed in Hebrew than *'êkāh*, but translations of *Qînôt* have become the book's usual name in most other languages, including English *(Lamentations)*.

Authorship

Like the rest of Scripture, Lamentations is "breathed by God" (2 Tim 3.16): "No prophecy of Scripture comes about by one's own interpretation, for no prophecy was ever brought about by a man's will, but men who were borne along by the Holy Spirit spoke from God" (2 Pet 2.20–21).

In style and subject matter, the book of Lamentations strongly resembles the prophecies of Jeremiah. Some of the verbal similarities are obvious even in translation:

Jeremiah	Lamentations
all of your lovers have forgotten you [Israel] (30.14)	there is no comforter for her [Zion] among all of her lovers (1.2)
the virgin daughter of my people (14.17)	the virgin daughter of Judah (1.15)

weeping, my eye will weep and go down with tears (13.17)	I am weeping; my eye, my eye is going down with waters (1.16)
terror from round about (6.25; 20.10)	those who terrify me from round about (2.22)
those whose judgment was not to drink of the cup—drinking, they will drink… drinking, you [Edom] will drink (49.12)	daughter of Edom… against you also the cup will pass; you will be filled with strong drink (4.21)

Therefore it has often been suggested that the book of Lamentations was written by Jeremiah. The idea goes back at least as far as the preface added to Lamentations in the earliest Greek version of the book: "And it came about, after Israel was taken captive and Jerusalem was made desolate, Jeremiah sat weeping, and he lamented this lamentation over Jerusalem." That preface was probably already in existence shortly before the time of Christ. During the first few centuries after Christ, the view that Jeremiah was the author of the Lamentations was repeated in the headings to the Peshitta Syriac version and the Aramaic Targum, in the Babylonian Talmud (*Bābā' Batrā'*, 15a), and in the earliest known commentary on Lamentations (by Origen, GCS 6.235).

Nevertheless, the similarities between Lamentations and the known writings of Jeremiah need not mean that they were written by the same person. The psalms of Asaph and Solomon are very similar in style and subject matter to those of David—not because they were written by the same person, but because they were written by people of the same mind (Php 2.2; 1 Cor 1.10; Rom 15.5) under the guidance of the same Spirit (1 Cor 12.4–11). Again, the praises uttered by Mary, Zechariah, and Simeon (Luke 1.46–55, 68–79; 2.29–32) are very similar to one another in style and subject matter. Like the book of Psalms, or the praises in the opening chapters of Luke, the five lamentations might have been written by different people sharing the same mind and the same inspiration. And even if all five were written by the same person, that person need not have been Jeremiah. The Spirit who came on Jeremiah could at any time have come on any one of Jeremiah's faithful associates—such as Baruch or Ebed-melech (cf. Jer 39.16–18), or a member of the family of Shaphan (cf. Jer 26.24; 29.3; 36.10; 39.14)—just as the Spirit came on Eldad and Medad in the days of Moses (Num 11.26–29).

The person or people who were "borne along by the Holy Spirit" to write the Lamentations are never named in the Scriptures. In that respect, the book resembles (for instance) Hebrews, and differs from the Law of Moses, the prophecies of Isaiah and Daniel, and the psalms of David. We have the repeated testimony of God's word that the Law was indeed given through Moses at Mount Sinai and in the wilderness (Lev 26.46; 27.34; Num 36.13; Deut 1.1; 29.1; 2 Chron 34.14; John 1.17; 5.46–47; 7.19). We have the repeated testimony of God's word that David, Isaiah, and Daniel did indeed write the psalms and prophecies attributed to them (2 Chron 29.30; Isa 1.1; Dan 7.1–2; 12.4, 9; Mark 12.35–37; Matt 15.7–9; 24.13; John 1.23; 12.38–41; Acts 1.16; 2.25, 34; Rom 4.6–7; 9.27, 29; 10.16, 20; 15.12). But the human writers of Lamentations and Hebrews are never revealed in the Scriptures. While it is an error to refrain from teaching any truth that God has revealed (Acts 20.26–27), it is equally an error to teach as truth anything that God has not revealed (Matt 15.9; Prov 30.5–6). The human authorship of Lamentations is therefore among the many "hidden things" that "belong to the LORD our God" (Deut 29.29), and that we humans must be content not to know (cf. Acts 1.7; Mark 13.32; Rom 11.33).

Text

Several fragmentary copies of the **Hebrew** text of Lamentations were found among the Dead Sea Scrolls, in manuscripts probably written before the time of Christ. The surviving fragments contain much of the first chapter (1.1–18) and smaller portions of the other four chapters.

Complete Hebrew copies exist in numerous medieval and later manuscripts written by Masoretic scribes.

The most important surviving ancient translations of the book of Lamentations include:

- The earliest **Greek** version (prepared some time during the last two centuries before Christ, and included in modern editions of the Septuagint).
- The **Syriac** Peshitta version (prepared during the first or second century after Christ).
- The **Latin** Vulgate version (prepared by Jerome about 400 years after Christ).

Lamentations is a small book with few textual variants of any kind. The only substantial variant occurs at the very start, where the Greek version prefaces the book with a statement attributing its authorship to Jeremiah (see the previous section of this introduction). Most other texts of Lamentations do not contain that prefatory statement.

The few other textual variants that have any bearing on the meaning of the book are discussed in the commentary below.

Concluding Reflections

Jesus told a parable about two men who went to the temple to pray. Both of them, like all of us, had sinned (1 Jn 1.8–10; Ecc 7.20; Rom 3.23). One of them did many good deeds and told God about them in his prayer. But he did not remember that he had sinned. Because of this, he regarded himself with pride and others with scorn. The other man was deeply ashamed of his sins and prayed, "God, be merciful to me a sinner." Jesus tells us that God accepted the man who humbled himself, and did not accept the other (Luke 18.9–14).

This parable shows that without a broken spirit and contrite heart over our sins (Psa 51.17) even the best of us cannot find favor in God's eyes. Our sin must be ever before us (Psa 51.3; cf. 2 Pet 1.9). The fear of the most holy God who abhors and punishes sin must be ever before us (Luke 12.5).

Of all books in the Bible, Lamentations is the one that is most totally concerned with sin and its consequences. It is valuable in giving us a right understanding of sin and the punishment we deserve when we sin.

It shows us Jerusalem, not when she was "the perfection of beauty," "the joy of the whole earth" (Psa 50.2; 48.2), but in her humiliation and nakedness, with all her sin and shame uncovered and laid out before the eyes of this unforgiving world, as one day everyone's sins will be (Ecc 12.14; 1 Cor 4.5). It shows her people living in poverty, in hunger, in constant fear of their lives, in dishonor, and in reproach, because of their sins and the sins of their forefathers. The LORD has become like an enemy and has brought all these punishments upon His people for their sins. And with the LORD against them, they look in vain for help anywhere else.

The book of Lamentations teaches us to regard sin and the punishment of sin with the utmost abhorrence and horror. Any suffering is better than to suffer punishment for sin. Any reproach is better than to be justly reproached for having sinned. Any enemy is better than to have the LORD as our enemy.

When we do sin and He chastens us to turn us back from sin (1 Cor 11.32), or when He afflicts us for any reason, the book of Lamentations teaches us to accept it with patience. He chastens us for our good (Heb 12.10). He punishes us less than our iniquities deserve (Ezra 9.13). He wants us to accept His chastening with humility and patience, and wait eagerly for Him to lighten His hand from us and show favor to us, as He will most certainly do to all who seek refuge in Him. And when He does this, "O the blessednesses of the one whose transgression is lifted, whose sin is covered!" (Psa 32.1). The LORD's "lovingkindness is better than life" (Psa 63.3).

Though she has sinned, Jerusalem is presented in the book of Lamentations with great compassion. She is like a princess who has been brought low and bereaved (Lam 1.1). She is like "a wife forsaken and grieved in spirit, even a wife of youth, when she is rejected" (Isa 54.6). She has no friends, no helpers. She sits alone and desolate. The speaker in Chapter 3 cannot overcome his grief at seeing her in such distress (Lam 3.38–39). This book teaches us to regard the sufferings of all sinners with compassion. It teaches us never to mock at suffering, no matter how much it may seem to be deserved, and to comfort those who are in any affliction. Vengeance belongs to the Lord; our task is to do good even to those who have done evil (Rom 12.19–21), and not to be like Jerusalem's enemies who rejoiced and mocked at her.

The sufferings of Jerusalem described in this book inevitably recall the sufferings of the One who never sinned but who suffered for the sins of the whole world and was mocked, reproached, and hated, but without cause. All who follow in His steps must expect to share in some degree with His sufferings. The book of Lamentations teaches us to think with compassion on the experiences of suffering endured by our brethren in the world, to comfort them as we have opportunity, and to pray for them constantly. It teaches us to be friends who love our brethren in Christ at all times (Prov 17.17), rather than fair weather friends who cluster to them in prosperity and flee from them when they are in adversity.

The book of Lamentations shows how one generation's sins afflict the next generation. "Our fathers have sinned; they are not; we ourselves have borne the burden of their iniquities" (Lam 5.7). Infants who have not shared in Jerusalem's sins suffer from thirst; little children ask for food and receive none (Lam 4.4). If we sin, our sins will afflict not only ourselves but also our children and they will suffer (Exod 34.7). And if they choose to follow our sinful examples, they will suffer not only in this life but also in the next (Matt 23.31–33).

The book shows the evil influences that led to the sins of Jerusalem and her great punishment: "It was because of the sins of her prophets, the iniquities of her priests, those who have shed in her midst the blood of the righteous ones" (Lam 4.13). The very ones who should have been leading the people in the way of righteousness led them instead into destruction. "Your prophets have seen for you worthlessness and whitewash, and they have not uncovered what is over your iniquity to restore your restoration, and they have seen for you worthless uplifted oracles and misleading things" (Lam 2.14). False teaching is destructive to the people of God, as Paul repeatedly warned in his late letters (1 Tim 4.1, 7; 6.3–5, 20–21; 2 Tim 2.14–18; 3.13; 4.3–4; Titus 1.10–14; 3.9–11). If we have ears that itch for soft and flattering doctrines, or if we think that false teachers can't really do much harm in the church, the book of Lamentations will prove us wrong.

Shortly before the time of the Lamentations, the prophet Ezekiel was shown a vision of the sins committed in the temple at Jerusalem and the consequent departure of the glory of the Lord from the temple (Ezek 8–10). The book of Lamentations shows what happened to the temple after the glory of the Lord had departed from it. "The Lord has cast away His sacrificial altar; He has repudiated His holy place; He has delivered into the hand of the enemy the walls of her citadels" (Lam 2.7), so that Gentiles who should never even have entered the holy place were seizing its treasures (Lam 1.10). This book teaches us to dread the desecration of God's holy temple on earth. Nowadays His temple consists of the holy people among whom He dwells, namely the church of God (1 Cor 3.16; 2 Cor 6.16). If we dishonor the temple of God, He will depart from it and give it over to the unbelievers to tread underfoot. This is no distant possibility. He has actually done this in the past. And He will do it to any church that does not abide in the truth (Rev 2.5).

The book of Lamentations teaches us where to put our trust and where not to put it. It teaches us that prosperity in this world is temporary. Jerusalem had been so prosperous that nobody would ever have believed that an enemy could enter her gates (Lam 4.12). Nevertheless, an enemy did enter her gates and even her temple, and all her gold and precious things were taken away. Those who trusted in her king and princes were also disappointed because they had all been exiled, put to death, or ended up wandering the streets of Jerusalem unrecognizable. They could not help themselves, let alone their people. Confidence in them was "like a tooth that is evil and a foot that has slipped" (Prov 25.19). The help that comes from humans or from riches is shown to be unreliable and worthless. Only God can help us in trouble.

Like the Psalms, the Lamentations are God-breathed prayers, and therefore inspired models for our own prayers of confession of sin. They are appeals to God to do justice at a time when His word is mocked or suppressed, and when His holy name is blasphemed by the nations. When we are in distress over our own sins or the sins of our people, we can pour out our hearts to God in the words of this book and know that He will take notice of the afflictions of His people and act in righteousness.

The book of Lamentations provides comfort and hope for those who seek the Lord in the depths of their affliction. Though He dealt severely with the people of Jerusalem, the LORD did not make a full end of them. They were chastened and cast down but not utterly destroyed. Therefore, the book expresses hope that "if He causes grief, then He will have compassion, in accordance with the abundance of His lovingkindnesses" (Lam 3.32), if we wait patiently for it. And the prophecies of Isaiah, Jeremiah, and Ezekiel indeed promised that he would turn and again have compassion on His people (Isa 54; Jer 30–33; Ezek 34; 36; 37; 40–48). The book of Lamentations therefore gives us a strong anchor for our hope that God will deliver His people from every trial and affliction. The darkest periods of the history of the people of God have been and always will be followed by the fulfillment of His great and precious promises. "Though it tarries, wait for it, because, coming, it will come; it will not delay" (Hab 2.3).

LAMENTATIONS 1

Summary

Verses 1–19 mourn over the afflictions of Jerusalem. Once a great city, she has become an outcast. The LORD has grieved her in His anger because of the abundance of her transgressions. Her people have fallen into the hand of an oppressor, and have gone into exile. In the city, even her priests and elders perish for lack of food. Forbidden nations have come into her holy place. Her gates are desolate. She has no helper; those who used to love her have become her enemies.

The description does not tell us in logical sequence what has happened to Jerusalem and why. To learn that, we must go to other sections of Scripture (especially 2 Kgs 24–25; 2 Chr 36; Jer 39; 52). Instead, this Lamentation puts us down directly in the midst of the suffering city. It piles up detail after detail, circling around and coming back repeatedly to the same points: Jerusalem has sinned against the LORD (vv 5, 8, 14, 18); she has no comforter (vv 2, 7, 16, 17); her people have gone into captivity and exile (vv 3, 5, 18); those who remain in the city are starving (vv 11, 19). The description also shifts repeatedly between speaking about Jerusalem in the third person ("How she has sat alone, the city...") and presenting Jerusalem's utterances directly in the first person ("See, LORD, my affliction..."). The third-person sections are mainly, but not entirely, in the earlier stages of the chapter (vv 1–9b, 10–11b, 17); the first-person sections are mainly, but not entirely, in the later stages (vv 9c, 11c–16, 18–22).

In the final verses (20–22) Jerusalem asks the LORD to see how greatly she is oppressed. She acknowledges that she has received severity from Him because of all her transgressions. Now she entreats Him to deal similarly with her oppressors because of their own evildoing.

The other four Lamentations follow the same basic pattern: an extended, repeatedly circling description of the sufferings of the city, followed by a shorter final appeal to the Lord. Chapter 3 has the most complex design, but even there the pattern is fundamentally the same.

1.1 How she has sat alone, the city
  that was great *with* people;
she has become like a widow,
  the great *one* among *the* nations;
the princess among *the* provinces,
  she has been *put* to menial tasks.

The city will be named soon ("Zion," 1.4, 6; "Jerusalem," 1.7–8). For the moment, however, the Lord asks us to contemplate not her name, but her situation.

She is pictured here as a woman, like many cities in the Scriptures (Isa 54.1–17; 62.1–5; Ezek 23.2–49), including the heavenly city (Rev 21.2, 9–10). In former times, she was **great** (Hebrew *rbty*) in two ways:

- She was **great with people** (for a similar phrase, cf. "great with sons," 1 Sam 2.5). Many inhabitants lived in her; many travelers visited her ("there gathered at Jerusalem a great number of people... an extremely great assembly," 2 Chr 30.13).

- She was also **great among the nations.** She was a city of high status among the surrounding **nations** and **provinces** (districts of an empire: Est 1.1, 22). She was "glorified" (1.8). She was called "the whole of beauty, the gladness of all the earth" (2.15). That was what God had promised her: "If, hearkening, you will hearken to the voice of the Lord your God, to be watchful to do all his commands... the Lord your God will set you high above all the nations of the earth" (Deut 28.1).

Her greatness among the nations is further described by the term **princess** *(śrh)*. A **princess** was a woman of high rank, someone fit to be the wife of a king (1 Kgs 11.3), someone in a position of authority—a *souveraine* (Segond), a *señora* (VRV 1602–1960) in the fullest sense of the term. Indeed the word **princess** is simply a feminine form of *śrr*, "rule" (Prov 8.16; Isa 32.1). Abraham's wife was given that very word as her name, "Sarah" *(śrh)*, because her descendants would be rulers of nations (Gen 17.15–16). Jerusalem is described as a **princess** because she was a royal city—like ancient Gibeon ("a great city, like one of the royal cities," Josh 10.2), Nineveh (Jnh 3.2–3; 4.11), Babylon (Dan 4.30), and Rome ("the great city that rules over the kings of the earth," Rev 17.18). She was the city of "mighty kings… who ruled over all the region beyond the River; and tribute, duty, and toll, was paid to them" (Ezra 4.20), especially in the time of Solomon (1 Kgs 4.21). Indeed her greatness went even beyond that. She was the most royal of all cities, "the city of the great King" (Psa 48.2; Matt 5.35).

But **great** cities, royal cities, can be brought low. The great cities of Nineveh and Babylon were made desolate (Zep 2.13–15; Jer 50.9–18). The great city of Gibeon was enslaved (Josh 9.23–27). The great city of Rome fell (Rev 18.1–24).

That also happened to Jerusalem. Her fall is described in three ways:

- Whereas she used to be **great with people,** now she **has sat alone,** like a leper forced to live outside the camp (Lev 13.46), or like Jeremiah rejected by his persecutors (Jer 15.17). "None are coming to the appointed assembly; all her gates are desolate" (1.4). Her former inhabitants have either perished (1.20) or gone into captivity (1.5, 18).

- Whereas she used to be **great… among the nations,** now she **has become like a widow**—in other words, she has suffered great loss: like a widow, she has been left alone and desolate. The fall of both Babylons is depicted in the same way. The Babylon of Old Testament prophecy, who was formerly the "sovereign of kingdoms," suffered "widowhood," "loss of children," and "desolation" (Isa 47.5, 7–11). The Babylon of New Testament prophecy, who formerly said, "I am sitting as queen, and I am no widow, and I shall not at all see mourning," was likewise "made desolate," bereaved of all that she had (Rev 18.7–8). All three cities possessed great blessings (they were "sovereign of kingdoms," "queen," **great… among the nations**) but lost everything (like someone "who is a widow indeed, and left alone," 1 Tim 5.5; cf. Ruth 1.5; Acts 6.1; Exod 22.22; Mal 3.5; Mark 12.40; Luke 21.2–4). When Jerusalem was captured, much of what was valuable was either taken (2 Kgs 25.13–17) or destroyed (2 Kgs 25.9), and the people were carried away into exile. Only some of the "poorest ones of the land" were left (2 Kgs 25.12).

• Whereas she used to be a **princess** ruling others, now she **has been put to menial tasks. Menial tasks** (Hebrew *ms*) were the very opposite of ruling (Prov 12.24); they were obligations imposed on a "vassal" (RSV) by a ruler (Est 10.1). When she was a **princess,** foreign peoples were in subjection under her—such as the Canaanites, who "became slaves to do menial tasks" under her rule (Josh 16.10; 17.13; Jdg 1.28). But now she herself is in subjection under a foreign master, under a "yoke of iron" (Jer 28.14). Her inhabitants say: "Slaves have ruled over us; there is none delivering from their hand" (5.8). They are back in the lowly situation of their ancestors in Egypt, who were "enslaved with severity" under taskmasters (*śry msym,* "masters of menial tasks," Exod 1.11–14). The exact nature of their **menial tasks** is not specified in this verse; either tribute (cf. KJV) or forced labor (cf. NASB; a *corvée,* NSR)—or both—might possibly be in view here.

No position, no status, no eminence on earth is secure. "Here we have no enduring city" (Heb 13.14). "Not to the swift is the race, and the battle is not to the strong… but time and occurrence happen to them all" (Ecc 9.11). We are merely vessels in the hand of our Potter (Isa 64.8), and He has the power to raise or lower each one of us at any moment, as He pleases (Jer 18.3–10; Rom 9.21; 1 Sam 2.7).

Contrast the earthly Jerusalem described in this verse with the spiritual Jerusalem, which God's people enter even in this life (Heb 12.22) and more fully after the final judgment (cf. Rev 3.12). The earthly Jerusalem **sat alone,** but the spiritual Jerusalem is eternally thronged with many thousands, "a great multitude, which no one could count" (Rev 7.9). The earthly Jerusalem suffered loss **like a widow,** but the spiritual Jerusalem knows no suffering at all, "neither mourning nor crying nor pain" (Rev 21.2–4). The earthly Jerusalem was subjected to **menial tasks,** but the spiritual Jerusalem is eternally glorious, "having the glory of God" (Rev 21.10–11).

> **How** *('ykh).* The word is used to "ask" (Deut 12.30) and/or to "mourn" (Jer 48.17). In the present passage, it "does not express surprise or ignorance, but is prompted by mercy and compassion" for the sufferings of the fallen city (Albertus 250)—as is made clear by the context, which repeatedly la-

ments over her grief (1.2, 4, 8, 12, 16, 22) and over her lack of comforters (1.2, 9, 16, 17, 21).

She has sat *(yšbh)*. This is a Qaṭal verb-form, which would usually be rendered by an English past tense. However, if an English past tense is used, care must be taken not to misunderstand it. It indicates that Jerusalem has been reduced to a seated position in the past—but it does not imply that she is no longer in that position in the present (cf. JM §112*a*). Qaṭal verb-forms are also used to describe the Lord's sitting on His throne (Psa 47.8), which is certainly present (and future) as well as past: "The LORD has sat at the Flood; the LORD has sat as King to lasting time" (Psa 29.10). Jerusalem *est... assise* (Ostervald), *está sentada* (VRV 1909); cf. "is seated" (Rotherham).

Great one *(rbty)*. The parallel with the next clause shows that **great one,** like **princess,** functions here as a noun followed by the preposition *b-* (**among**). In this part of the verse, **great** is a name for the city's status (like **princess**); in the earlier part, **great** was an adjective describing the city's population size.

1.2 Weeping, she is weeping in *the* night,
>and her tear *is* on her cheek;
there is no comforter for her
>among all of her lovers;
all of her companions have acted treacherously with her;
>they have become her enemies.

Weeping, the city **is weeping** (*llorando llorará,* VRV 1602). Such repetitions are frequent in the Scriptures, and can be used for many different reasons. In the present passage, the context emphasizes not only that the weeping is intense ("she weeps bitterly," NASB) but also, and especially, that it is persistent ("she weepeth continually," Geneva); it "does not cease" and has "no slackening" (3.49; 2.18; cf. Jer 9.1). Even **in the night,** when others would be asleep and at rest, she continues to weep. **Her tears** have never stopped; they are **on her cheek** at this very moment. Her groanings are many (1.22), and there is no pain like hers (1.12).

Jerusalem's **lovers** and **companions** had been the surrounding nations in whom she trusted (1.19; Ezek 23.22–23; Jer 22.20–22) and the false gods whom she worshiped (Hos 2.5–13). In fact, trust in those nations and worship of those gods were closely linked (Jer 2.20, 23, 36; 3.1, 9). In the present passage, the reference is principally to the nations (1.19). Those who love Jerusalem ought to rejoice with her (Isa 66.10), pray for her peace, and seek what is good for her (Psa 122.6, 9). But in her current distress, her so-called **lovers** and **companions** are not merely no help (there is no **comforter** among them) but actually a harm to her (they are **her enemies**). They have counted her worthless (1.8), deceived her (1.19), and **acted treacherously with her** (a term that is applied elsewhere to the betrayal of allies, Jdg 9.23, or family members, Jer 3.20; 12.6). God told her, "All your lovers have forgotten you" (Jer 30.14). It is a common story: people are popular while they prosper, yet are shunned when they need help most desperately. "The poor person is hated even by his companion, but those who love the rich one are many" (Prov 14.20).

> **Weeping, she is weeping** *(bkw tbkh)*. Similar constructions in this book are "rebelling, I have rebelled" (1.20); "being mindful, she is mindful" (3.20); "rejecting, You have rejected" (5.22). "It is only from the context that the nuance added [by the extra word] can be deduced in each case" (JM §123*d*; IBHS §35.3.1e). This is especially true when (as here) the repetition plainly does not have any of its usual meanings (JM §123*k*). Some nineteenth century grammarians maintained that "weeping, she weeps" must mean "she weeps bitterly," whereas "she weeps continually" would have to be "she weeps, weeping"; but Scripture usage shows that the meaning of such clauses is not necessarily determined by word order (JM §123*d*; IBHS §35.3.1d). In the present case, "weeping" *(bkw)* is placed before "she weeps" *(tbkh)* simply because the verse is to start with the letter *b*.
>
> **Lovers** *('hb)* are people who love—in almost any sense of the term. The same form of the word is applied to those who love the Lord (Exod 20.6), His word (Psa 119.165), wisdom (Prov 8.17), Jerusalem (Isa 66.10), one's child (Prov 13.24), one's king (1 Sam 18.16), evil (Mic 3.2), money (Ecc 5.10), wine (Prov 21.17), sleep (Isa 56.10), etc. The opposite of loving is hating (Prov 13.24; Mic 3.2; etc.).
>
> The point of calling the surrounding nations **lovers** of Jerusalem is that they had once loved Jerusalem (they were *ceux*

qui l'aimaient, Segond)—not that Jerusalem had loved them (*ceux qu'elle aimait,* Ostervald), although no doubt that was true too. (Similarly, when Hiram of Tyre is called a "lover of David" [1 Kgs 5.1], the point is that he loved David—not that David loved him.) But their love had not endured. It had now turned to enmity (like Amnon's love for Tamar, 2 Sam 13.15). Jerusalem had rejected the One who loves with an everlasting love (Jer 31.3), preferring those who loved her only while she was prosperous (Prov 19.7).

Companions *(r')* is a much broader term, which can be applied not only to "friends" (KJV) but to anyone nearby (*Nächsten,* Luther)—from the closest friend (Deut 13.6) to the most mortal enemy (Deut 19.11). While the Israelites lived in Egypt, they were **companions** of the Egyptians (Exod 11.2). **Lovers** refers principally to affection regardless of proximity; **companions** refers principally to proximity regardless of affection. This is the word used in the great commandment "You shall love your neighbor [*r'*] as yourself" (Lev 19.18 ≡ Greek *plesion,* Matt 22.39 ≡ Rom 13.9 ≡ Jas 2.8).

1.3 Judah has gone into exile from affliction,
    and from *the* abundance of *her* slavery;
she—she has dwelt among *the* nations,
    she has not found rest;
all of her pursuers have reached her
    in between the oppressive places.

Judah has gone into exile. God had chosen Israel from among the nations to be His people, worshiping in His holy city at His holy temple, in accordance with all His commandments (Deut 7.6–8; 26.18–19). But His people turned away from Him and mocked at His prophets, "even until there was no remedy" and they had to go **into exile** (2 Chr 36.16): first the ten tribes of the northern kingdom (2 Kgs 17.6–23), and finally the southern kingdom of **Judah** (2 Chr 36.17–21).

    She has dwelt among the nations. God had given her a land of her own to dwell in (Deut 8.10; Josh 21.43). He had told her that other nations should "not dwell in your land" (Exod 23.33). But now, because of her disobedience, she is forced to dwell in theirs. Many of the people of

Judah had been carried away to Babylon: some in the time of Jehoiakim (2 Chr 36.6; Dan 1.1–4); more in the time of Jehoiachin (2 Kgs 24.14–16); more still in the time of Zedekiah (2 Kgs 25.11; 2 Chr 36.20); and some others even later (Jer 52.30). Others fled to Moab, Ammon, Edom (Jer 40.11–12), and Egypt (2 Kgs 25.26; Jer 41.16–18; 43.4–7). That is what He had warned: "If you will not take care to do all the words of this law... the Lord will scatter you among all peoples, from the end of the earth and to the end of the earth" (Deut 28.58–64; 4.27; Neh 1.8; Ezek 12.15; cf. Acts 2.5, 9–11). They would be forced to live "in the lands of their enemies" (Lev 26.33–39).

She has not found rest. When Judah dwelt in her own land, she had **rest** from all her enemies ("so that you dwell in safety," Deut 12.10; Josh 21.44; 23.1; 1 Chr 22.18; 1 Kgs 8.56). Moreover, He promised her a still greater rest in the future (Isa 11.10), a promise that is now made available through Jesus: "we who have believed enter into that rest" (Heb 4.3–11). But the Lord had also warned Israel that, if she disobeyed Him and was scattered in foreign nations, "among these nations you will find no relief, and there will be no rest for the sole of your foot, but the Lord will give you there a trembling heart, and failing of eyes, and sorrow of soul; and your life will hang in doubt before you, and you will be afraid night and day, and will have no confidence of your life. In the morning you will say, 'Who will give me evening?' and in the evening you will say, 'Who will give me morning?' from the fear of your heart that you will fear" (Deut 28.65–68). That terrible warning was fulfilled: Judah could find **no rest** among the nations where she had gone (just as "the dove found no rest for the sole of her foot" while the waters of the flood were covering the earth, Gen 8.9).

All of her pursuers have reached her in between the oppressive places. While Israel was faithful to God, she herself had been able to pursue *(rdp)* and overtake her enemies (Lev 26.7–8; Josh 23.10), whereas none of those who tried to pursue her could overtake her (Neh 9.11; cf. Psa 18.37). But when she disobeyed Him, the Lord warned her that her enemies would "pursue you until you are destroyed" (Deut 28.22). Even "the sound of a driven leaf will pursue them; and they will flee, as one flees from the sword; and they will fall when no one is pursuing... and you will have no power to stand before your enemies" (Lev 26.36–37). That is what had now happened. When Jerusalem was captured by the Babylonians, "Zedekiah the king of Judah and all the men of war... fled and went out of the city at night, by the road of the king's garden, through the gate in between the two walls… but the army of the Chaldeans pursued after them, and reached Zedekiah in the plains of Jericho" (Jer 39.4–5).

Oppressive places. The Hebrew word *(mṣrym)* is an *m*-prefixed form of *ṣrr*, "oppress" (the term applied to Jerusalem's enemies in 1.5, 7, etc.; cf. BDB 864–65; TDOT 12.455–64). **Oppressive places** are "straits" (KJV), "narrow places" (HCSB), like the "oppressive place [*ṣr*] where there was no way to turn to the right or the left," in which the angel trapped Balaam (Num 22.26; cf. 2 Kgs 6.1). Judah has been oppressively hemmed in—cornered—by her pursuers/oppressors, in a place "where she is narrowly confined" (NAB), a place "where there is no way out" (NJB; cf. 1 Sam 13.6); she is "between a rock and a hard place" (Humphries 534). The Spanish rendering *estrechuras* (VRV 1602–1960) perhaps expresses this idea more succinctly than any English term. By contrast, those who remain faithful to the Lord have His promise that "when you walk, your steps will not be oppressed [*ṣrr*]; and when you run, you will not stumble" (Prov 4.12). They have been taken "from the mouth of oppression into a wide place where there is no constraint" (Job 36.16), and they praise Him because "You have not delivered me into the hand of the enemy; You have set my feet in a wide place" (Psa 31.8; 118.5; 18.19).

> From a geographical viewpoint, **Judah** was the territory within which Jerusalem (Zion) was located (Josh 15.1, 8, 63). Nevertheless, the prophets often grouped the two names together and applied the same terms to both, for what was true of the city was generally true also of the whole region (Jer 4.3; 7.17; 13.9; 14.2; etc.). So the suffering people in Lamentations are called both Judah (1.3) and Jerusalem (1.7) or Zion (1.17), both "the virgin daughter of Judah" (1.15) and "the virgin daughter of Zion" or "the daughter of Jerusalem" (2.13).
>
> **Judah has gone into exile from affliction, and from the abundance of her slavery.** The prefix **from** (Hebrew *m*-) is very common and can have various meanings. The main options here are the following:
>
> 1. *M*- can mean "out of," describing a change from one place or condition or time to another: "I will bring you up out of [*m*-] the affliction of Egypt" (Exod 3.17); "Israel was carried away into exile out of [*m*-] its own land to Assyria" (2 Kgs 17.23; other Scripture examples are listed in BDB

577–78, §§1a–b; 581, §4a). If that is the meaning here, then the passage is saying that the nation has gone from a bad situation to a worse one: "From affliction and servitude Judah has now gone into exile" (MLB). However, in Scripture usage a person who goes "out of" [*m-*] a place or condition does not generally remain in it—whereas Judah continued to suffer both **affliction** and **slavery** when she went into exile.

2. *M-* can mean "because of": "my people have gone into exile because of [*m-*] lack of knowledge" (Isa 5.13; other Scripture examples are listed in BDB 579–80, §§2e–f; and cf. GKC §119z). That would leave two possible ways of construing the clause:

   2a. Judah has gone into captivity in Babylon because of the **affliction** and **slavery** that the Jews had imposed on their own servants, contrary to the Law of Moses. This is indeed stated in Jeremiah 34.8–17 to have been one of the causes of the captivity (cf. also Isa 3.14–15). In the present context, however, **affliction** and **slavery** should surely refer to the affliction and slavery that have just been mentioned ("alone... a widow... menial tasks," 1.1–2): the affliction and slavery that Judah herself is suffering, not the affliction and slavery that she has imposed on others.

   2b. Judah has fled into exile in the surrounding countries (Moab, Ammon, Edom, Egypt) because of the **affliction** and **slavery** that she has been suffering from the Babylonians. However, it is not clear that the term **gone into exile** (Hebrew *glh*) can refer to a journey undertaken in a state of freedom. (In 2 Sam 15.19 and Ezek 12.3 the meaning "go freely to another place" is possible; but in neither passage is that meaning required by the context.)

3. Finally, some translations assume that *m-* in this passage has a meaning not clearly found anywhere else in the Scriptures, such as "with" ("Judah has gone into exile with suffering and hard servitude," NRSV) or "under" ("Judah has gone into exile under affliction, and under harsh servitude," NASB).

Even in ancient times, readers were not of one mind about the meaning of this clause (the Targum favored option 2a, the Vulgate option 2b).

If option 2b is correct, then the final line of this verse might possibly contain a play on words (Lapide 294): the word *mṣrym* might mean not only *mᵉṣārîm* (**oppressive places**), but also *miṣrāyim* ("Egyptians"), as in 5.6. Adopting that view, Joüon ("Notes de critique textuelle (suite)," 209–10) paraphrased the verse as follows: "Judah has gone into exile to flee from affliction and severe slavery; she has settled [*elle s'est établie*] among the nations, but without finding rest there; all her pursuers have overtaken her among the Egyptians."

Pursuers. Hebrew *rdp* can describe anyone who pursues, whether physically or metaphorically. (In the present passage, KJV chooses to refer specifically to metaphoric pursuers— "persecutors.") Physically, Pharaoh pursued the Israelites at the Red Sea (Exod 14.8–9) and Saul pursued David in the Judean wilderness (1 Sam 23.28). Metaphorically, Job was "pursued" (hunted down, assailed) by his friends (Job 19.22) and Jeremiah by his opponents (Jer 20.10–11; 15.15).

1.4 *The* roads of Zion *are* mourning,
    because none *are* coming to *the* appointed *assembly;*
all of her gates *are* desolate;
    her priests *are* groaning;
her virgins *are* grieved;
    and She—it has been bitter for her.

None are coming to the appointed assembly. The term **appointed assembly** ("solemn assembly," ASV; "appointed feast," ASV mg), describes the occasions when Israel assembled at appointed times every year to worship the Lord in accordance with His commands: at the Passover, the Feasts of First Fruits (including Pentecost), and the assemblies of the seventh month, including the Feast of Tabernacles (Lev 23.2–44; Num 28.2–29.39). Those assemblies were appointed for rejoicing (Lev 23.40; Deut 12.7, 12, 18; 16.11–15; 26.11; 27.7). From the time of Solomon until the death of Christ, there was only one place on earth where they could be celebrated (Deut 16.2; 26.2; 12.5–7, 10–14). That place was the

Jerusalem temple (1 Kgs 8.29; Psa 78.68–69; 132.13). Therefore, Jerusalem (**Zion**), and no other place on earth, was the city "where the tribes have gone up… to give thanks to the name of the LORD" (Psa 122.1–4). Sometimes a whole "throng," a "multitude," would travel there together (Psa 42.4; 55.14).

But when Zion's temple was destroyed, the people who should have rejoiced at the feasts were mourning, and the assemblies that should have been attended by multitudes were deserted. A few weeks after the destruction of the temple, "men came from Shechem, from Shiloh, and from Samaria, eighty men, having their beards shaved and their clothes torn, and having cut themselves, and with offering and incense in their hand, to bring them to the house of the LORD" for the next appointed assemblies, those of the seventh month (Jer 41.5). Those men never reached Jerusalem; most of them were slain on the way (Jer 41.6–9), and the remainder fled to Egypt (Jer 41.16–18).

Everything involved in the appointed assemblies is pictured as grieving: the routes that led to them (the **roads** and **gates**), the people who served at them (the **priests** and **virgins**), and in fact the whole city (**she**).

- **The roads of Zion are mourning.** "The road [*drk*] of the tree of life" (Gen 3.24) is the road leading to the tree of life; "the road [*drk*] of the sea" (Isa 9.1) is the road leading to the sea. Similarly, the **roads** [*drk*] **of Zion** are the roads leading to Zion—the roads that would previously have been traveled by throngs **coming to the appointed assembly.**

- **All of her gates are desolate.** Just as people coming to the assembly would pass along Zion's **roads** to reach the temple, so they would pass through Zion's **gates** (2.9; Neh 1.3). But now, that is no longer happening. All of those gates are **desolate** *(šmm)*, a term that describes both a condition ("deserted," as in 5.18; Isa 49.19; 61.4) and a response to that condition ("appalled," as in Ezek 26.16; 27.35; Isa 52.14). Those two aspects are closely linked in the Scriptures: "I will make the land desolate [deserted, *šmm*]; and your enemies that dwell therein shall be desolated [appalled, *šmm*] at it" (Lev 26.32; cf. TDOT 15.238–48; TLOT 3.1372–75). In this verse, both aspects are present. The gates are not only deserted (**none are coming** through them), but also distressed (just as the roads **are mourning**)—in accordance with Isaiah's prophecy: "her gates will lament and mourn" (Isa 3.26).

- **Her priests are groaning.** Under the old covenant, sacrifices could be presented at Jerusalem during the appointed assemblies only by **priests** descended from Aaron (Lev 17.5; Num 18.7; 16.40). Those priests would have had many reasons to **groan** (as also did the city, 1.8, 21, and "all of her people," 1.11). "Many of the priests" were now captives in Babylon (cf. Ezra 3.12; Ezek 1.1–3). Some had died of starvation (1.19); others had been slain in the sanctuary (2.20); still others, including both the high priest and the second priest, had been taken from the temple and later executed in the presence of Nebuchadnezzar (2 Kgs 25.18–21). The temple itself had been burned, and all its furnishings had been broken in pieces and taken away (2 Kgs 25.9, 13–17). Whatever offerings may have been presented afterwards (cf. Jer 41.5; Baruch 1.10, 14), they must have been presented amid desecrated ruins, and by very small numbers of priests.
- **Her virgins are grieved.** This statement is placed in parallel with **her priests are groaning;** therefore, it evidently refers not to all the **virgins** in Zion, but specifically to those who served, like the priests, at the **appointed assembly,** when "the singers went in front, the players of music afterwards, between them the virgins who play the tambourine" during the procession to the holy place (Psa 68.24–25). While the women played their tambourines, they danced (cf. Exod 15.20; Jdg 11.34; 21.19, 21; 1 Sam 18.6; Jer 31.4, 13). The playing and the dancing were not optional, and were not done to entertain visitors: both were specifically commanded under the old covenant, and were acts of worship to the Lord (Psa 149.3; 150.4). Such acts were expressions of joy (Jdg 11.34; 1 Sam 18.6; Psa 30.11; Jer 31.4, 13). But now that the temple had been destroyed, those who should have been rejoicing were **grieved.**
- **It has been bitter for her.** Not only the roads and gates leading to the temple, and the priests and virgins serving at the temple, but the whole city (Zion) was suffering. Her situation was **bitter,** like the bitterness of Israel's oppression by hard bondage in Egypt (Exod 1.14).

> **Appointed assembly.** The Hebrew term *(mw'd)* is an *m*-prefixed form of the word "appoint" *(y'd;* BDB 416–18; TLOT 2.551–54). It can refer either to an appointed time (as in Gen 17.21; Jer 8.7) or to an appointed gathering (Num 16.2). Often,

as here, both of those aspects are involved: the Lord appointed both the time and the gathering that took place at it.

Grieved (*ygh*, as in 1.5, 12; 3.32; Zep 3.18). The particular form used here is *nwgwt*, a Niphʻal feminine participle (a masculine equivalent, *nwgy*, appears in Zep 3.18). The LXX has "her virgins have been dragged away" (ESV mg), apparently construing the word as equivalent to *nhwgwt* (a form of *nhg*). But that would lose the parallel with the priests who are **groaning.**

1.5 Her oppressors have become *the* head;
  her enemies have been at ease;
for *the* Lord has grieved her
  because of *the* abundance of her transgressions;
her young children have gone
  in captivity before *the* face of *the* oppressor.

Her oppressors have become the head, her enemies have been at ease. The Lord had promised Israel that, if she obeyed Him, "The Lord will set you for the head, and not for the tail; and you will be above only, and will not be underneath" (Deut 28.13). In the days when the nation had been faithful to the Lord, that had indeed happened: she had been a "princess"—a ruler—"among the provinces" (see the notes on 1.1), and she had prospered (Zec 7.7). But the Lord had also warned Israel that, if she departed from Him, "those who hate you will rule over you" (Lev 26.17); the foreigner "will be the head, and thou will be the tail" (Deut 28.44). So, because of the **abundance of her transgressions,** the Lord had exalted her **oppressors** and **enemies** high above her (2.17; Psa 89.42). Now she suffers the grief and deprivation described in verses 1–4, while **her enemies have been at ease** (Hebrew *šlh*)—that is, they have strength, peace, and wealth (Job 21.23; Psa 73.12; Ezek 16.49). The Aramaic form of the word is applied to Jerusalem's conqueror Nebuchadnezzar, "at ease [*šlh*] in my house and flourishing in my palace" (Dan 4.4).

For the Lord has grieved her because of the abundance of her transgressions. Jerusalem has suffered because **the Lord** has caused her to suffer (**grieved her**—the same word as in 1.4). "God is the judge: He makes this one low, and He raises that one aloft" (Psa 75.6–8). No harm can happen to a city (Amos 3.6), or a sparrow (Matt 10.29), or His own

Son (John 19.11), unless it is part of His will (3.38; Isa 45.7; Job 2.10). In this case He willed the affliction because of the **abundance** of Jerusalem's **transgressions.** She had sinned against Him not once, but over and over again, generation after generation, sometimes even "more than the nations whom the LORD had destroyed from before the sons of Israel" (2 Chr 33.9). Even so, "because He had compassion on His people," He did not destroy them instantly; He "sent to them by the hand of His messengers, rising early and sending... but they mocked at the messengers of God, and despised His words, and scoffed at His prophets, even until the LORD's anger went up against His people, even until there was no remedy" and the judgment eventually came (2 Chr 36.15–17).

Her young children have gone in captivity before the face of the oppressor. The Lord had warned His people that, if they persisted in disobedience, He would bring against them "a nation of fierce countenance, who will not show favor to the face of the old, and will not show mercy to the young" (Deut 28.49–50). That warning was accomplished. "He brought against them the king of the Chaldeans... and he had no compassion on young man or virgin, old man or aged; He gave them all into his hand" (2 Chr 36.17). Even those with **young children** were taken (cf. Ezra 3.12). Young children with no knowledge of good and evil will not be held guilty of a community's sin (Deut 1.39; Ezek 18.20); but they may nevertheless suffer the consequences of that sin (Num 14.33; Jer 44.7).

> **Have gone [in] captivity** *(hlkw šby).* **Captivity** is an adverbial accusative, describing the state **in** which they went: they have gone "as captives," NASB (cf. "you will not go [in] haughtiness [*tlkw rwmh*]," Mic 2.3; other examples are listed in GKC §118*q*; IBHS §10.2.2d). Contrast 1.18, where the preposition *b-* describes the state "into" which they went: they "have gone into captivity" *(hlkw bšby,* as in Isa 46.2; Amos 9.4).

1.6 And *there* has gone out from *the* daughter of Zion
　　　all of her honor;
her leaders have become like stags;
　　　they have not found *any* pasture,
and they have gone without strength
　　　before *the* face of *the* pursuer.

There has gone out from the daughter of Zion all of her honor. In this context, the **daughter of Zion** is a figure representing Zion itself (see the small print notes below). **Honor** (Hebrew *hdr* ≡ Greek *timē:* Heb 2.7, 9 ≡ Psa 8.5) is a characteristic of God Himself (Psa 96.6; 104.1; 145.5; Isa 2.10), which He has bestowed on His Son (Psa 21.5; 45.3–4; Heb 2.9) and on His people (Ezek 16.14; Deut 33.17). The people of Zion had previously been honored by the surrounding nations (1.8, 1), but that was no longer so (5.12).

Her leaders have become like stags; they have not found any pasture, and they have gone without strength before the face of the pursuer. The term **leaders** (Hebrew *śr*) includes people in various positions of authority—"princes" (KJV) in the sense of principal people, *príncipes* (VRV 1602–1960)—such as army commanders (Gen 21.22; 37.36; Jdg 4.2; 1 Sam 14.50; 2 Kgs 25.19, 23), kings (Dan 10.20), chief priests (Ezra 8.24; 1 Kgs 4.2, 4), and city governors (2 Kgs 23.8; 2 Chr 18.25). When Jerusalem was captured, "Zedekiah the king of Judah and all the men of war fled, and went out of the city at night" (Jer 39.4–5). Jerusalem's leaders were like **stags** (deer) that are starving (**they have not found any pasture**) and have no **strength** to keep ahead of their **pursuer.** "Upon our neck we have been pursued; we have wearied ourselves; no rest has been given to us" (5.5; cf. 4.19). "The army of the Chaldeans pursued after the king, and reached Zedekiah in the plains of Jericho; and all his army was scattered from him." Then "all the leaders [*śr*] of Judah" were slain; Zedekiah himself was bound in chains and kept in prison till he died (Jer 52.8–11).

> **The daughter of Zion** (also at 2.1, 4, 8, 10, 18; 4.22) is described more fully in these Lamentations as "virgin daughter of Zion" (2.13), and is also called "the daughter of Jerusalem" (2.13, 15), "the daughter of my people" (2.11; 3.48; 4.3, 6, 10), "the daughter of Judah" (2.2, 5), and "the virgin daughter of Judah" (1.15). The people of foreign nations are described similarly ("daughter of Edom," 4.21–22; "daughter of Babylon," Jer 50.42; 51.33; Psa 137.8; "virgin daughter of Babylon," Isa 47.1; "daughter of Tarshish," Isa 23.10; "virgin daughter of Sidon," Isa 23.12; "daughter of Tyre," Psa 45.12). The Bible often pictures cities and countries as women (see the comments on 1.1), so it is natural to speak of them as "daughters." Such turns of phrase are flexible ones (cf. König 3, §§337*f*–*g;* JM §129*f.*7; IBHS §9.5.3h). The "land of Zuph" (1 Sam 9.5) can mean both

the land named "Zuph" and the land belonging to the person Zuph (1 Sam 1.1). Similarly, the **daughter of Zion** can be either a figure representing the city Zion itself (the **daughter** named **Zion**) or a figure representing all the young women of Zion (the **daughter** belonging to **Zion**). In the present verse and 2.10, **the daughter of Zion** possesses **leaders** and "elders," so in these verses the term stands for Zion itself. Yet in 1.15, "trodden a winepress for the virgin daughter of Judah" refers specifically to the young women belonging to Judah (it is parallel to "crush my young men"). The term is a picture, and in the Bible a picture can be used to illustrate different points in different contexts.

Stags *(ylym).* The Hebrew word could theoretically be vocalized either *'ayālîm* (**stags,** as in Song 2.9; BDB 19; HALOT 1.40) or *'ēlîm* ("rams," as in Gen 32.14; BDB 17–18; HALOT 1.40). Some ancient translations (LXX and Vg) chose the second option here, but the context shows the first option to be correct: deer, not rams, are hunted and flee **before the face of the pursuer.** In the Scriptures, rams are used rather to depict strength and defiance (Dan 8.3–4).

1.7 Jerusalem has called to mind
　　in the days of her affliction and of her strayings
all of her desirable things that were
　　from days of beforehand;
as her people *were* falling into *the* hand of *the* oppressor,
　　and there was no helper for her,
the oppressors saw her;
　　they laughed over her cessations.

Jerusalem has called to mind… all of her desirable things that were from days of beforehand. Under both the old and the new covenants, the Lord's people are exhorted never to forget Him and the blessings that He has bestowed. Under the old covenant, He gave Israel the blessings of salvation from Egypt, a good land to live in, righteous laws to obey, and the promise of the Messiah (Deut 4.7–8, 34; 8.7–9; Psa 147.19–20; Rom 3.1–2; 9.4–5). What more could have been done, that He did not do for her (Isa 5.4)? She was to be mindful constantly of **all of her desir-**

able things that He had given her, and never to forget them (Deut 5.15; 8.18; 15.15; 16.3, 12; 24.18, 22; Psa 103.2–5; 105.5–6; 143.5; Isa 46.9; Mal 4.4). Yet in her prosperity she forgot the God of her salvation, and was not mindful of the days of her youth (Isa 17.10; Ezek 16.43; Psa 106.7; 78.42). Only in **the days of her affliction and of her strayings** did she "call to mind the LORD from far away" (Jer 51.50; Psa 137.1; Deut 4.30; 30.1–2) and say to herself, "I will go and return to my first husband, for then was it better for me than now" (Hos 2.7). The lost son in Jesus' parable similarly came to his senses in the days of his affliction, when he called to mind the pleasant things provided by his father ("an abundance of bread," Luke 15.17).

Her people were falling into the hand of the oppressor, and there was no helper for her. Among all the "lovers" and "companions" in whom Jerusalem had trusted, there was "no comforter for her" (1.2). **Help** comes only from the Lord (Gen 49.25; Deut 32.38; 2 Chr 32.8; Psa 121.1–2; 94.17). Those who trust in Him will be helped (Psa 18.6; 28.7; 37.40; Heb 13.5–6; 4.16); but help from any mere human source is vain (Psa 60.11; Isa 30.5–7; 31.1–3; Ezek 30.8).

The oppressors saw her; they laughed. Jerusalem's enemies had no compassion on her. Instead of mourning over the sufferings of their fellow humans—as Jeremiah did (Jer 9.1), as Jesus did (Luke 19.41–44), and as we are commanded to do (Rom 12.15; Heb 13.3)—they mocked (2.15–16; Psa 79.4).

> **Jerusalem has called to mind in the days of her affliction and of her strayings all of her desirable things that were from days of beforehand.** Most English versions construe the phrase **the days of her affliction and of her strayings** as describing the time when the act happened: Jerusalem called to mind, **in** those days, all of her desirable things. Such constructions are very common in Hebrew, e.g., "I have made you [in] this day a fortified city" (Jer 1.18; further examples are given in GKC §118*k*; JM §126*i*). Other translations construe **the days of her affliction and of her strayings** as among the things called to mind: "Jerusalem remembered the days of her affliction, and of her rebellion, and all her pleasant things" (Geneva; similarly VRV 1602–1960). But in that case, Hebrew would almost always insert an "and" *(w-)* before the final item in the list (GKC §154[1]*a*). No such *w-* is present in this instance.

Her strayings. The Hebrew word *(mrwd)* occurs also in 3.19 and Isa 58.7. It has been construed in various ways, depending on whether the *m-* is taken to be a prefix or part of the root word. The two main suggestions are the following:

1. *Mrwd* could be an *m*-prefixed form of *rwd,* "roam about" (as in Jer 2.31; Gen 27.40; Psa 55.2; BDB 923–24). If so, it would mean "wanderings" (ASV mg), referring to the fact that "Judah has gone into exile… she has dwelt among the nations" (1.3). However, nowhere else in the Lamentations does **Jerusalem** wander. In every other instance, those who wander are the people of the nation, leaving **Jerusalem** herself behind (see, e.g., 1.3, 5, 18).

2. *Mrwd* could be a form of *mrd,* "rebel" (the opposite of "serve," 2 Kgs 18.7). It might be an active form (cf. GKC §84ᵃ*m;* JM §88E*c*), describing Jerusalem's "rebellion" (Geneva). Certainly Jerusalem had rebelled *(mrd),* both against the Lord (Neh 9.26) and against His appointed king, Nebuchadnezzar (2 Chr 36.13; Jer 52.3), but this sense would not fit well in 3.19 or Isa 58.7. Alternatively, it might be a passive participle, describing Jerusalem as "rebelled against" (or even possibly "suffering" [cf. Fuerst 866], although no clear example of that sense can be found in the Scriptures). But nowhere else do the Scriptures say that any nation had "rebelled against" Jerusalem at this time; she herself is always presented as the rebel.

Desirable things. The Hebrew term *(mḥmd)* is an *m*-prefixed form of *ḥmd,* "desire" (as in Exod 20.17; Psa 19.10; 68.16; Isa 1.29), which is translated into Greek as *epithumeō* by the Spirit of God (Exod 20.17 ≡ Deut 5.21 ≡ Rom 13.9; 7.7).

Her cessations. The Hebrew term *(mšbt)* is an *m*-prefixed form of *šbt,* "cease" (as in Gen 8.22; 2 Chr 16.5). The Lord had warned Jerusalem: "I will cause to cease [*šbt*] from the cities of Judah, and from the streets of Jerusalem, the voice of joy and the voice of gladness, the voice of the bridegroom and the voice of the bride; for the land shall become a desolation" (Jer 7.34; 16.9). All of that had now happened; Jerusalem was now suffering from the **cessation** (*disparition,* NSR; *final,* BTX) of all those things: "elders have ceased [*šbt*] from the gate… the gladness of our heart has ceased [*šbt*]" (5.14–15). The term *šbt* is also applied to God's "ceasing" or "resting" on the seventh day (Gen 2.2), and to the Sabbath day appointed for Israel (Exod 20.8–11)—hence the KJV translation in the present verse: "the adversaries... did mock at her sabbaths."

1.8 Jerusalem has sinned a sin,
　　　　therefore she has become an outcast;
all of *those* who glorified her have counted her worthless,
　　　　for they have seen her nakedness;
also she herself has groaned,
　　　　and she has turned away backward.

Jerusalem has sinned a sin. The wording does not necessarily imply that Jerusalem has sinned in an unusually "great" (NASB) or "grievous" (KJV) way, but simply that she has committed sin (*pecado cometió*, VRV 1909–1960). Whenever we disobey any "one of the commands of the Lord," we have **sinned a sin** (Lev 4.27–28; cf. Deut 19.15). Everyone has done that (Rom 3.9–23; 1 Jn 1.8, 10; Ecc 7.20), and everyone deserves a punishment at least as great as Jerusalem's (Luke 13.1–3; Rom 11.17–22). We are no less guilty than she (Jas 2.10–11). None of us can look on her and think in our hearts that we are better (cf. Luke 18.11).

All of those who glorified her have counted her worthless, for they have seen her nakedness. In the past, Jerusalem had been **glorified** by the surrounding nations (see the comments on 1.1). But now her secret self is exposed; and, seeing it, those who used to honor her **count her worthless** (see the comments on 1.11). In ancient times, people might be punished or degraded by having their nakedness exposed, so that they were shamed and humiliated (Isa 20.4; cf. Gen 3.10). That was what the Lord had now done to Jerusalem because of her sins: "Because of the abundance of your iniquity your skirts have been taken away.... I Myself will uncover your skirts over your face, and your shame will be seen" (Jer 13.22, 26; Ezek 16.37–39; 23.27–29). The same thing happened to other nations that sinned (see on 4.21; Nah 3.5; Isa 47.3), and will happen under the new covenant to those who disobey their Lord: "I counsel you to buy from Me... white garments, in order that you may be clothed, and that the shame of your nakedness may not be visible" (Rev 3.17–18). "Blessed is the one who remains alert, and who keeps his garments, lest he should walk naked, and they should see his shame" (Rev 16.15).

She herself has groaned, and she has turned away backward. Jerusalem's utter humiliation not only causes her to suffer (she **has groaned,** 1.4, 11, 21), but also causes her to retreat in embarrassment from the onlookers. In the past it was Jerusalem's enemies that retreated: "my enemies turn away backward, they stumble, and they are destroyed from Your face" (cf. Psa 9.3; 56.9). But now she is the one who turns back (Psa 44.10).

Has sinned a sin. Two forms of the same word *(ht' ht'h)*, somewhat as in 1.2 (see the notes there; cf. König 3, §329*d;* GKC §117*k;* JM §125*q;* IBHS §10.2.1g).

An outcast. The Hebrew term *(nydh)* occurs only here. It is clearly a form of *ndd, ndh,* or *nwd,* which are basically three subgroups of the same Hebrew word (the Scripture evidence for this is summarized in TDOT 9.232, §I.1; 9.271, §I). However, the meaning of the particular form *nydh* is remarkably difficult to establish.

1. It could be a feminine form of *nwd.* Indeed, the only surviving Dead Sea Scroll of the passage (4QLam^a) spells it *nwd* here. *Nwd* generally means "move to and fro," but that still leaves two possible translations:

   1a. "A wanderer" (Stone). Compare "I will never again cause the foot of Israel to wander [*nwd*] out of the land that I gave to their fathers" (2 Kgs 21.8); "fleeing and wandering [*nwd*] you will be" (Gen 4.12). Most of the ancient translations (including LXX, Vg, and Tg) evidently took the word in this sense.

   1b. "An object of scorn" (HCSB). This takes the term "move to and fro" to describe the shaking of head in derision, as in "You have set us as a byword among the nations, a shaking of the head [*mnwd*] among the peoples" (Psa 44.14). In the present passage, that would fit well with the immediately preceding and following lines: **They laughed over her cessations.... All those who glorified her have counted her worthless** (1.7–8).

2. *Nydh* could be a fuller spelling of the noun *ndh,* which occurs in 1.17 (just as *btwlt,* 2.10, is a fuller spelling of *btlt,* 5.11). Indeed, various Masoretic Hebrew manuscripts spell it *ndh* here. The noun *ndh* has been translated in two different ways:

2a. A "removed" person (KJV); cf. the Dutch translation *een afgezonderde vrouw* (SV). This rendering suits the usage of the corresponding verb ("your brothers who hate you, who cast you out [*ndh*] for My name's sake," Isa 66.5; cf. Amos 6.3), but it does not fit some of the passages where *ndh* occurs as a noun (see the next paragraph).

2b. "An unclean thing" (ASV). The Hebrew Scriptures apply the noun *ndh* to anything unclean (Ezra 9.11; Zec 13.1), ranging from uncleanness of the flesh under the old covenant Law (e.g., menstrual uncleanness, Lev 15.19–20) to spiritual uncleanness (e.g., fornication, Lev 20.21). "When the house of Israel dwelt on their own land, they defiled it by their way and by their doings; their way before Me was like the uncleanness of a woman in her impurity [*ndh*]" (Ezek 36.17).

All four of the above undoubtedly describe facets of this word-group's meaning, and therefore all may contribute to the sense here. *Nydh* would be a particularly appropriate description of people who are all four of those things: wandering, an object of scorn, removed, and unclean (cf. Gordis 155).

1.9 Her uncleanness *was* in her skirts;
    she was not mindful of her end;
and she has gone down marvelously;
    there is no comforter for her.
See†, Lord, my affliction,
    for *the* enemy has made himself great.

Her uncleanness was in her skirts. The **skirts** are the fringes of a robe (Exod 28.33–34). Even the outermost fringes of Jerusalem's garments were tainted by the uncleanness of her transgressions (Ezek 24.13). Sin corrupts every part of a person, "from the sole of the foot even to the head" (Isa 1.4–6); it leaves nothing pure (Titus 1.15; Rom 7.18; Isa 64.6).

She was not mindful of her end. Like Babylon (Isa 47.7), Jerusalem had not thought about what would happen in the future (the **end**). She had indulged in **uncleanness** without considering the future consequences of her deeds. "Because the sentence against an evil deed is not done quickly, therefore the heart of the sons of Man is filled within them to do evil"; but even when "a sinner is doing evil a hundred times, and it is prolonged for him" (Ecc 8.11–12), his **end** will be destruction (Psa 73.17–19) unless he calls to mind his Creator before the evil days come (Ecc 12.1) "when your flesh and your inner flesh are brought to an end, and you say, 'How I have hated discipline, and my heart has despised correction, and I have not hearkened to the voice of my teachers, and I have not turned my ear to those who instructed me!'" (Prov 5.11–13).

She has gone down marvelously. Jerusalem has **gone down** from being a princess in majesty to being a forced laborer in desolation (1.1, 4, 6). She is completely forsaken; she has **no comforter** (1.2, 7). Abasement and exaltation, making poor and making rich, killing and making alive—all are the work of the Lord (1 Sam 2.6–8; Luke 1.51–52). **Marvelously** does not just mean "greatly" or "amazingly"; the same Hebrew word *(pl')* is applied to all the "marvelous things" that God has done (Isa 25.1; Psa 136.4)—including the abasement of nations (Exod 3.20; Deut 28.59) as well as the redemption of nations (Exod 15.11; Psa 77.11–20; 78.12–16).

See, LORD, my affliction. Here Jerusalem herself speaks (as in most of 1.11–22). As in other Scriptures (e.g., Psalm 2, especially in the original Hebrew, and the Song of Songs), the change of speaker is indicated only by the context; it is not marked by any preliminary words (such as "She says"). Jerusalem prays to the Lord, asking Him to **see** her **affliction,** as He saw the affliction of His people in Egypt (Exod 3.7; 4.31; Deut 26.7; Neh 9.9), and as He saw the affliction of persecuted Hannah (1 Sam 1.11: in all these passages the Hebrew words are the same). Her plea is not based on any claim that she is righteous, or that she deserves to be helped, or that she has a "right" to be helped (cf. Dan 9.18; Jer 14.7). It is based solely on God's own justice. An **enemy** has **made himself great,** has attributed to himself the greatness that should be attributed only to God (Isa 10.13–15; Ezek 35.13). The Judge of all the earth will always do justice (Gen 18.25; Deut 32.4; Psa 94.2); He will put an end to the oppressive rule of all those who magnify themselves against Him and against His people (Zep 2.8–10; Jer 48.26, 42; Obad 12, 15).

1.10 *The* oppressor has spread out his hand
over all of her desirable *thing*s;

for she has seen *the* nations
> come *into* her holy place,
the ones that You† commanded
> they should not enter Your† assembly.

The oppressor has spread out his hand over all of her desirable things.
Jerusalem had been given many **desirable things** by God (see the comments on 1.7), but during the Babylonian onslaught, **all of** them were touched and either destroyed (2 Chr 36.19) or else taken away by the **oppressor** (2 Kgs 25.13–17).

Among the **desirable things** that had been touched by the oppressor's **hand** was the Jerusalem temple (Ezek 24.21)—the **holy place**. God had **commanded** the foreign **nations** not to **enter** the temple. Only descendants of Aaron could enter it, or even approach the altar in front of it; "the stranger who comes near shall be put to death" (Num 18.7; 3.10, 38). Indeed, people from the nearby nations—Moabites, Ammonites, Edomites, and Egyptians—were forbidden to enter even the courtyard surrounding it (Deut 23.3, 7–8). But now the Lord had permitted the **nations** to enter the **holy place** itself (2.7), and even to destroy it (2 Chr 36.19; cf. Psa 74.3–7; 79.1; Isa 64.11).

1.11 All of her people *are* groaning,
> seeking bread;
they have given their desirable *thing*s for food
> to restore *the* soul.
See†, Lord, and look†,
> for I have become worthless.

All of her people are groaning, seeking bread. The Lord had warned His people repeatedly that, "because you did not serve the Lord your God with joy and with goodness of heart from the abundance of all things, then you will serve your enemies whom the Lord will send against you, with hunger and with thirst and with nakedness and with lack of all things" (Deut 28.47–48; Jer 14.6; 16.3–4; 18.21; 21.7, 9). His prophets told them that those who remained in Jerusalem would be besieged, and a large proportion of them would die of famine (Ezek 6.12; 7.15) "because you have defiled My holy place with all of your detestable things and with all of your abominations" (Ezek 5.11–17). The Babylonian siege of Jerusalem lasted for six months, by which time "the hunger was powerful in the city, and there was no bread for the people of the land" (Jer 52.6; 38.9), as the Lamentations repeatedly describe (2.11–12; 4.4–5, 9–10; 5.9–10). After the fall of the city, its remaining inhabitants would have been able to go out and seek **bread** in the surrounding regions, but by that time "the fruit of your livestock and the fruit of your land… grain, new wine, and oil, the offspring of your livestock and the young ones of your flock" had been consumed by the invaders (Deut 28.49–51). **Food** of any kind commanded a high price (5.4; cf. 2 Kgs 6.25): to obtain it, people had to give up the very things that they would least wish to lose—the things that were **desirable** to them (1.7; their "precious things," NASB; their "treasures," ESV).

See, Lord, and look; for I have become worthless. As in 1.9 (see the comments there), Jerusalem herself speaks the last line, again asking the Lord to **see** her affliction. To be **worthless** *(zll)* is the opposite of being honored (1.8) and precious (Jer 15.19). Those who are **worthless** are shunned by the world (Prov 19.4); but if they turn for refuge to the Lord, He will deliver them (Zep 3.12; Isa 25.4; Psa 116.6; 2 Tim 4.16–18).

> **Worthless** *(zll)*. Compare also *dll*, which has a similar meaning (it is the opposite of "rich," Exod 30.15, and "mighty," Lev 19.15) and appears to be a kindred form (cf. HALOT 1.223, 272).

1.12 *It is* not for you^{pl},
>   all of *you* who are passing over *the* road;
look^{pl} and see^{pl} if there is *any* pain like my pain,
>   which has been severely dealt out to me,
with which *the* Lord has grieved *me*
>   in *the* day of *the* fierceness of His anger.

Now Jerusalem speaks to **all of** those who are in the neighborhood (those **who are passing over the road**), the surrounding nations (see 2.15–16, where the same expression is used). She asks them to **see** whether there is any **pain like** the **pain** that she is now suffering. God punishes sinners who know His will more severely than sinners who are ignorant of His will (Luke 12.47–48; Matt 11.20–24). Therefore the Babylonian destruc-

tion of Jerusalem was "a great evil, which has not been done beneath all of
the heavens, as it has been done in Jerusalem" (Dan 9.12; Ezek 5.9). And
hundreds of years later, when Jerusalem again rejected Him by crucifying
His Son, again she suffered an exceptionally severe punishment (Matt
24.21). God had revealed much more of His will to her than to other nations, and therefore He punished her disobedience more severely (Amos
3.2). He has revealed even more of His will today under the new covenant
(Col 1.26–27; Rom 16.25–26; 1 Pet 1.10–12); so if we today depart from
His new covenant, we will suffer even more severely than Jerusalem suffered for departing from the old covenant (Heb 10.28–30). It would be
better for us never to have known the way of righteousness at all, than to
know it and then turn away from it (2 Pet 2.20–21).

> **It is not for you.** The Hebrew phrase is exceptionally concise,
> *lw' 'lykm*, and has been construed in a variety of different ways.
>   1. Treating the first word as *lō'* ("not"):
>   1a. The phrase has been read as a simple statement, "[It is]
>   not for you." This suffering is not for you other nations.
>   It is only for me; **look and see if** any other nation has
>   suffered such punishment as Israel. Compare Ezra
>   4.3: "[it is] not for you and for us to build a house for
>   our God [together], but we ourselves only will build"
>   it; 1 Sam 23.20: "[it is] for us to deliver him into the
>   hand of the king."
>   1b. The phrase has been read as a wish, "[May it] not [be]
>   for you." May you other nations never suffer as I am
>   suffering. This is the traditional view of the phrase (it
>   goes back at least as far as Babylonian Talmud, *San-
>   hedrin* 104b), although many have felt uneasy with it,
>   since it is not easy to see how it fits in with the imme-
>   diate context. Whether or not the idea is expressed in
>   the present passage, it is certainly consistent with the
>   teaching of Scripture (see the comments on 1.21).
>   1c. The phrase has been read as a question, "[Is it] not
>   for you?" Jerusalem's suffering has been inflicted not
>   only for her own sake, but also for the sake of other
>   nations (Provan 48), who may **see** that her punish-
>   ment is just (1.18) and learn to avoid sin themselves
>   (otherwise, they will be punished as well: 4.21–22).

This view too is consistent with the Scriptures (see the comments on 1.18). However, in Hebrew a question would normally be marked by an interrogation marker (GKC §150*c*). Such a marker is not required if the context itself shows that the passage is a question (GKC §150*a*)—but in the present passage the context contains nothing of that kind.

1d. The phrase has been read as a different kind of question, "[Is it] nothing to you?" Do you other nations care nothing about my suffering? (In fact, many of the other nations actually rejoiced at Jerusalem's sufferings: see 2.15; 4.21.) This too is consistent with the Scriptures. To be touched by the sight of suffering is an attribute of God Himself: "The Lord has looked from the heavens to the earth to hear the groaning of the person in bondage, to set free the sons of death" (Psa 102.19–20). Our Lord is not "a high priest who is unable to sympathize with our weaknesses" (Heb 4.15). And as He is, so we are to be. "Be mindful of those who are imprisoned, as if you are imprisoned together with them; and those who are mistreated, as being also in the body yourselves" (Heb 13.3). "But whoever… may see his brother having a need, and may shut up his inner parts from him—how does God's love abide in him?" (1 Jn 3.17). We are not to be like those who "passed across on the other side" when they saw a man wounded and half dead, but like the Samaritan whose "inner parts were moved" and who "acted mercifully with him" (Luke 10.30–37). In the present passage, the main difficulties with this view are: (i) There are none of the customary indications that the phrase is a question (see the discussion of 1c above). (ii) In Hebrew, such a thought would be expressed by *b'ynykm*, "in your eyes," rather than *'lykm*, "for you" (cf. Hag 2.3; 1 Sam 18.23; Num 13.33; Est 1.17; 3.6).

2. Treating the first word as *lû'* ("O that," "if only," as in Isa 48.18):

2a. The phrase has been read as a wish: "O that, among you," there were people who would **look and see** how I suffer (Blayney 380–81).

2b. The phrase has been read as an exclamation adding urgency to an imperative: "Oh, [as for] you," all of you, **look and see** (Renkema 109/154). However, it is notoriously difficult to recognize places where *l-*, *lû*, or *lû'* is used in such a sense (HALOT 2.510–11, §II; 2.521, §5). Perhaps the most likely Scripture examples are in Gen 23.13 and Isa 38.20.

Even in ancient times, readers had trouble understanding this phrase. Some of the ancient translators construed the first word as an exclamatory *lû'* (*oi*, most LXX manuscripts [cf. LSJ 1200]; *O*, Vg), but others construed it as a negative *lō'* (*ou*, Antiochene Greek manuscripts 62 and 407; *l'*, Syr). Nearly all modern English translations conform to the traditions of their respective denominations: the Judaic versions adopt view 1b, following the Talmud; the Roman Catholic versions adopt view 2b, following the Vulgate; the Protestant versions adopt view 1d, following Calvin.

Pain (*mk'[w]b*; "sorrow," KJV). Forms of *k'b* are applied to the pain of circumcision (Gen 34.25), the pain of being stabbed by a thorn (Ezek 28.24), the painful toil of the Israelites under their Egyptian taskmasters (Exod 3.7), and the pains borne by Christ on our behalf (Isa 53.3–4).

This pain **has been severely dealt out** (*'ll*) to Jerusalem. Forms of *'ll* are applied to the plagues inflicted on Egypt by the Lord (Exod 10.2; 1 Sam 6.6), the injuries inflicted on the Levite's concubine by her molesters (Jdg 19.25), and the treatment that Kings Saul and Zedekiah feared from their conquerors (1 Sam 31.4; Jer 38.19), as well as to the act of gleaning a crop field so thoroughly that it is left virtually bare ("desolate," Isa 24.12–13; Mic 7.1; Lev 19.10; Jer 6.9). Fuerst (1056–57) suggests that the term is applied only to "constant, repeated" actions. The form used in Lamentations, the verb, "always has a negative connotation or denotation" (NIDOTTE 3.423–25; BDB 759–60; TWOT 2.670–71); indeed, in 3.51 a neutral rendering would make no sense. It is usually assumed that related nouns can be used without any negative implication, although this is doubtful (even *'lylh* in Isa 12.4 and *'lylyh* in Jer 32.19, often translated simply "deeds," may specifically describe God's terrifying works in judgment).

1.13 From *the* height, He has sent fire into my bones,
  and He has had mastery over it;
He has spread out a net for my feet;
  He has turned me away backward;
He has made me desolate,
  ill all of *the* day.

Jerusalem's sufferings have left her **desolate** (deserted and appalled: see on 1.4). The city is a hunted animal whose **feet** have been caught in a **net** (Hos 7.12; Psa 66.10–11; Ezek 12.13). The city is a person who has been stricken **ill** (*dwh*, a term for infirmities or illnesses of all kinds: 1.22; 5.17; Lev 15.33; Isa 1.5; Deut 7.15). She has been **turned... backward** (see the comments on 1.8).

Like all human troubles, these things did not just happen by chance. They were **sent** from on high—from the **height** where God is (Isa 57.15). **He** is the One who has power to send **illness** (Deut 28.27, 59–61) and to heal illness (Exod 15.26; 3 Jn 2), to trap in a **net** (Psa 66.11; Ezek 12.13) and to deliver from a net (Psa 25.15; 31.4), to make **desolate** (Ezek 32.15; 33.28) and to relieve from desolation (Ezek 36.34–36). He is totally in control of all these things—He has **mastery over** them (*rdh*, "dominion," like a mighty king, 1 Kgs 4.24, or a powerful overlord, Ezek 34.4). His **mastery** has no limits (cf. Psa 72.8). Who can oppose it? Who can stop Him from sending us whatever He decrees (Dan 4.35; Isa 43.13)? And He had warned the Israelites plainly beforehand that, if they persisted in disobeying Him, He would send them illness (Deut 28.60), and a net (Ezek 17.20), and desolation (Lev 26.32). He has done to them simply what He said He would do.

"Our God is a consuming fire" (Heb 12.29). His judgment on Jerusalem was a **fire**—both physically (Jer 34.22; 52.13) and spiritually (Jer 15.14; 4.4)—and it was so devastating that it consumed even the innermost parts, the **bones** (cf. Prov 16.24), as His prophets had foretold it would do: "Increase the wood, kindle the fire... and let the bones be burned" (Ezek 24.10; cf. Sanctius 1066–67). Yet His final judgment on sinners will be an even greater fire (2 Pet 3.7; Heb 10.27), one that is eternal and unquenchable (Matt 3.12; 18.8; 25.41; Mark 9.43, 48).

> **The height.** This does not describe God's physical situation (1 Kgs 8.27; Psa 139.7–10) but His spiritual situation: He is

superior to all those on earth and has authority over them all (Psa 113.4; 99.1–2; Dan 4.34–35).

And He has had mastery over it *(wyrdnh)*. Some translations construe this clause as saying that the fire **had mastery over** the bones ("prevaileth against them," KJV). That would not be impossible in Hebrew, but it is doubly improbable, because (i) the verb **had mastery over** is masculine whereas **fire** is feminine, and (ii) the suffix **it** *(-nh)* is singular whereas **bones** is plural. Other translations (e.g., NIV and ESV) emend the text to *ywrdnh*, "He has made it go down." (No existing Hebrew manuscript has that reading, but the LXX was probably translated from such a manuscript.)

1.14 My transgressions have been formed into a yoke;
　　by His hand they are intertwined;
they have come up on my neck;
　　He has made my strength stumble;
the Lord has given me into *the* hands of
　　those before whom I am not able to stand.

Yokes are bars (Lev 26.13) set on the necks of oxen (Num 19.2; 1 Kgs 19.19, 21) in order to force them to serve their master (cf. 1 Kgs 12.4; Jer 27.12). A yoke might be either heavy or light (2 Chr 10.4, 10–11; Matt 11.30).

Now God has **intertwined** Jerusalem's **transgressions** into a **yoke** on her **neck**. He has **made** her **stumble**—like someone bearing too heavy a burden (5.13; Neh 4.10) or forced to labor too hard in slavery (Psa 107.10–12)—so that she is **not able to stand** in the presence of her enemies (cf. Josh 7.11–12). "His own iniquities capture the wicked one, and he is held in the cords of his sin" (Prov 5.22). "Everyone who is doing sin is the slave of the sin" (John 8.34; cf. 2 Pet 2.19), and the burden of that slavery is never light. "My iniquities have passed over my head; like a heavy burden, they are too heavy for me" (Psa 38.4). "My strength has stumbled because of my iniquity" (Psa 31.10). "Those who do iniquity have fallen… and they have not been able to stand" (Psa 36.12). We have no strength to lift this burden from ourselves; only God has the power to do that (Psa 32.5).

Have been formed into *(nśqd)*. No form of *śqd* is found anywhere else in the Scriptures, but the general sense is clear from the context: Jerusalem's **transgressions** have become a **yoke** on her **neck**. Some translators, following the LXX, construe the verb as an otherwise unknown *n*-prefixed (Niphʻal) form of *šqd* ("keep watch") and the next word, *ʻl,* as "over" rather than **yoke**—so that the first clause becomes "watch has been kept over my transgressions" (cf. NAB). However, the meaning **yoke** for *ʻl* is confirmed by the phrase **on my neck** later in the verse.

Stumble *(kśl)*. Not only "fail" (ASV), but more specifically, "stagger" or "totter" (HALOT 2.502–03; BDB 505–06; TDOT 7.353–60; NIDOTTE 2.733–35)—in Spanish, *tropiecen* (LBLA mg). The word is applied to people who trip over obstacles (Jer 6.21; Lev 26.37; Nah 3.3) because they cannot see where they are going (Prov 4.19; Isa 59.10) or are walking on crooked ground (Jer 18.15; 31.9) or, as here, are bearing heavy burdens (5.13; Neh 4.10) and lack the strength to remain standing (Isa 40.30). Jerusalem has been "overswayed" by the "weight of sin" (Quarles).

1.15 *The* Lord has heaped up all of my mighty *one*s
　　　in my midst;
He has called against me an appointed *assembly*,
　　　to crush my young men;
the Lord has trodden a winepress
　　　for *the* virgin daughter of Judah.

Under the old covenant, the Lord had commanded His people to hold a series of "appointed assemblies… which you shall proclaim in their appointed times" during the year (Lev 23.2–44; Num 28.1–29.39), such as the Passover, Pentecost, the Day of Atonements, and the Feast of Tabernacles. But when the Israelites disobeyed God's word, their appointed assemblies were no longer acceptable to Him (Isa 1.14–17). Therefore He punished them by proclaiming an **appointed assembly** of a different kind—an appointed assembly **against** Jerusalem, **to crush** her **young men.** Some of them were killed by the sword (2.21); others were carried away captive (1.18). So He crushed "this people and this city, as one crushes a potter's vessel that cannot be healed again" (Jer 19.10–11). They were **trodden** under His feet like grapes in a **winepress** (Isa 63.3). And indeed anyone who persists in sin and does not repent will ultimately receive the same punishment: "he will be crushed suddenly, and there will be no healing" (Prov 6.12–15; Psa 37.17); he will be trampled underfoot by the King of kings in "the winepress of the fierceness of the anger of God" (Rev 19.15; 14.19–20).

> **Has heaped up.** This particular word form, *slh*, is extremely rare (its only other apparent occurrence is in Psa 119.118, again describing the punishment of those who disobey the Lord). However, a very similar form undoubtedly means "heap up," and is used in a similar context in relation to the destruction of Babylon: "Heap her up [*slwh*] like sheaves, and devote her to destruction" (Jer 50.26). The Scriptures often portray the Lord's judgments on nations as a harvest, in which He cuts off and heaps up the crops (either grain, Matt 13.30, or grapes, Isa 18.5): "Send out the sickle, for the harvest is ripe; come, tread down, for the winepress is full" (Joel 3.13; Rev 14.14–20). Two other renderings of *slh* have been proposed: (i) "Trodden under foot" (KJV) derives from Rashi's suggestion that *slw* means "tread down" in Isa 62.10. (In that passage, however, the meaning is surely "heap up"—as even the KJV translators concluded.) (ii) "Rejected" (NASB) derives from comparison with Job 28.16, where *tslh* is usually translated "valued." (However, on this view it is hard to explain the point of the additional phrase **in my midst** [Hillers 74–75; Salters 81]; and even in Job 28.16, "heaped up" [in a balance] would fit the context well.) The basic sense of the clause is not in dispute: whether we say that Jerusalem's **mighty ones** are **heaped up,** "trodden under foot," or "rejected," we are saying that they are no longer acceptable to the Lord.
>
> **The virgin daughter of Judah.** Terms of this kind are used flexibly in the Scriptures, sometimes describing the whole nation, sometimes specifically the nation's young women (see the comments on 1.6). Here it must refer to the young women in particular, because **trodden a winepress for** Judah's **virgin daughter** stands parallel to **crush** Jerusalem's **young men** ("my virgins and my young men have gone into captivity," 1.18; "my virgins and my young men have fallen by the sword," 2.21). Similarly, in Jer 31.4 the "virgin of Israel" is not Israel

itself but the virgins belonging to Israel (as verse 13 of the same chapter makes clear).

1.16 Because of these *thing*s I *am* weeping;
>my eye, my eye *is* running down with waters;
for a comforter has been far from me,
>*one* who restores my soul;
my sons *are* desolate,
>for *the* enemy has been mighty.

Jerusalem is **weeping** constantly (see the comments on 1.2; cf. 2.11; 3.48–49), because there is no **comforter** (1.2) and no one who **restores** her **soul** (1.11; Psa 23.3; cf. Ruth 4.15). When the Lord's people are shunned by everyone else, they still have their Master with them to comfort them (John 16.32; 2 Tim 4.16–17). "Neither death, nor life, nor angels, nor rulers, nor things present, nor things to come, nor powers, nor height, nor depth, nor any other created thing, will have the power to separate us from the love of God, which is in Christ Jesus our Lord" (Rom 8.38–39). But if we make the Lord our enemy—as Jerusalem had done (2.4–5)—what source of comfort do we have left (Hos 9.12; Jer 17.5–6)? As a result, Jerusalem's inhabitants (her **sons**) were **desolate**: that is, they had nobody (Jer 33.10).

>**My eye, my eye.** The Scriptures use exact repetition mainly to draw additional attention to a key point ("Turn aside, turn aside," 4.15; "She has fallen, she has fallen, Babylon," Isa 21.9 ≡ Rev 14.8; 18.2; "Amen, amen, I say to you," John 1.51, etc.; cf. König 4.155–57).

1.17 Zion has spread out with her hands;
>there is no comforter for her;
the LORD has commanded for Jacob
>*that those* round about him *would be* his oppressors;
Jerusalem has become an outcast
>in between them.

Zion has spread out with her hands. The **hands** can be **spread out** in entreaty to God (Psa 143.6), in entreaty to people (Isa 65.2), or for other reasons (1.10; Isa 25.11). Here (as in Jer 4.31) there is no indication that the city is seeking help in any specific direction, or even that she sees any hope of finding any; there is **no comforter** anywhere in sight (1.16). This is no accident: it is part of the punishment that **the LORD has commanded for** Israel (**Jacob**). At His own good pleasure, He may arrange that people will find favor with those around them (Gen 39.21; Prov 16.7; cf. Neh 1.11), or else He may arrange that people will be opposed by those around them (Psa 105.25; Deut 2.30; Josh 11.19–20). In the situation described here, He ordained that the surrounding nations would be Israel's **oppressors** (see on 1.5) and would treat Jerusalem as an **outcast** (see on 1.8). Those who reject God will be delivered into the hand of **oppressors;** those who seek Him will be delivered from their oppressors (Neh 9.27; Deut 4.30; Psa 60.12).

> **Zion has spread out with her hands.** The preposition *b-* (**with**) adds emphasis to the act by stressing the instrument **with** which it is done: cf. "He gave forth with His voice" (Psa 46.6); "they separate with the lip" (Psa 22.7; further Scripture examples are listed in GKC §119*q;* JM §125*m*).

> **Jacob.** The names **Jacob** and **Israel** are used interchangeably, sometimes to describe the patriarch (Gen 32.28), sometimes— as here—to describe the nation descended from him (2.3; Gen 49.7; Num 23.10; Psa 78.71).

> **In between** [*byn*] **them.** The oppressors are all around Jerusalem, and she is *en medio de ellos* (LBLA), "in their midst" (Rotherham). For the meaning of *byn,* cf. "all of her pursuers have reached her in between [*byn*] the oppressive places" (1.3); "they went out of the city… by the gate in between [*byn*] the two walls" (Jer 39.4; 52.7); "they cut the calf in two and passed in between [*byn*] its pieces" (Jer 34.18–19; Gen 15.17); see also Jdg 16.25; 1 Sam 17.3; 2 Sam 14.6; 1 Kgs 22.34; 2 Kgs 9.24; Psa 104.10.

1.18 The LORD—He *is* righteous,
     for against His mouth I have rebelled;
hear[pl] now, all of *the* peoples,
     and see[pl] my pain;

my virgins and my young men
    have gone into captivity.

"The Lord is righteous in all His ways" (Psa 145.17)—that is, "He does no injustice; morning by morning He gives forth justice; at daylight He never fails" (Zep 3.5; Deut 32.4). All His judgments are **righteous** judgments (Rev 16.7; Psa 119.137). Even when He punished Jerusalem so severely for her sins, He was doing a **righteous** thing: "the Lord our God is righteous in all His works that He has done; but we have not hearkened to His voice" (Dan 9.14, 7; Neh 9.33; Ezra 9.15). And even in the great judgment on the last day, when He condemns to eternal punishment all those of us who have persisted in our sins, no one will have valid grounds for objection: it will be a **righteous** thing for Him to impose that terrible punishment (2 Thes 1.6–9).

Jerusalem had rebelled **against His mouth**—that is, against His command (the same expression is applied to Israel's earlier rebellions against the Lord in the time of Moses: Num 20.24; 27.14; Deut 1.26, 43; 9.23). The term "rebellion" is not limited only to supposedly "severe" sins. On the contrary, God told Joshua that "every man who… does not hearken to your words in all that you command him" "rebels against your mouth" (Josh 1.18). Every time we disobey any part of God's word, we **have rebelled against** it (Exod 23.21; 1 Sam 12.14–15). The **mouth** of the Lord had repeatedly warned Israel—by the hand of all His prophets, from Moses to Ezekiel—that He would punish them if they continued to rebel (Deut 31.27–29; Ezek 12.25). But they ignored those warnings, and now the punishment had come. "If they did not escape when they rejected the One who warned on earth, how much more we, who turn away from the One who warns from heaven?" (Heb 12.25).

Again Jerusalem urges the other nations (**all of the peoples**) to **hear** and **see** her **pain** (see the comments on 1.12). We are to contemplate her punishment and learn from it. When God "made a city into a heap, a fortified city into a ruin," He did so in order that "a strong people will glorify You, a city of ruthless nations will fear Your name" (Isa 25.2–3). Otherwise, they too would suffer punishment (4.21–22). "Behold, I am beginning to bring evil on the city on which My name is called; and will you, going unpunished, go unpunished? You will not go unpunished" (Jer 25.29). All the punishments that God has imposed on sinners in the past have been imposed not merely for their own sake, but also for ours. "These things came about as examples for us, so that we may not be desiring evil things, just as they also desired" (1 Cor 10.6, 11; 2 Pet 2.6; Heb 4.11).

My virgins and my young men have gone into captivity. See the comments on 1.5.

1.19 I have called to my lovers;
>they—they have deceived me;
my priests and my elders
>in *the* city have perished
when they sought food for themselves
>and they would restore their soul.

"The LORD is near to all those who call on Him" (Psa 145.18; 86.5; Joel 2.32). But those who look in any other direction cannot expect help. "There is no salvation in any other one" (Acts 4.12). When the priests of Baal opposed Elijah at Mount Carmel, they called on their god all day, "and there was no voice, and there was no one who answered, and there was no one who paid attention" (1 Kgs 18.26–29). Jerusalem, in her distress, **called to** her **lovers** (see on 1.2)—the foreign nations in whom she had trusted (including her northern and eastern neighbors, Lebanon, Bashan, and Abarim, Jer 22.20–23, and Babylonia and Assyria further away, Ezek 23.22–23). But they had **deceived** her; there was no help in them. The LORD had warned her: "There is no one to judge your judgment.... All your lovers have forgotten you; they will not seek you" (Jer 30.13–14). Worse still, "your lovers have despised you; they seek your life" (Jer 4.30). "Do not be confident... in a son of humanity, in whom there is no salvation" (Psa 146.3; Jer 17.5–6).

Even those who should have been in positions of honor—Jerusalem's **priests** (Deut 21.5; Acts 23.5) and **elders** (Lev 19.32)—**perished** for lack of **food** to **restore their soul** (see the comments on 1.11).

1.20 See[†], LORD, for *there is* oppression to me;
>my inner parts have been churning over;
my heart *has been* turned around in my inside,
>for, rebelling, I have rebelled;

out on *the* street *the* sword has bereaved;
in *the* house *it is* like death.

The LORD is the only one to whom Jerusalem can call for help (see the comments on 1.19), as Jesus also did in the time of His oppression (Luke 22.41–42). "Grant help to us from the oppressor; but salvation from humanity is worthless" (Psa 60.11).

Jerusalem is suffering **oppression** *(ṣr)*, the condition that is caused by "oppressors" (Neh 9.27), a condition of being hemmed in ("in straits," Donne; see the comments on 1.3). Her **heart has been turned around** *(hpk)*. This word can mean simply "overturned" (NASB—like the overthrow of Sodom, 4.6); but in relation to the **heart,** it describes a mental change of direction (either for good, 1 Sam 10.9, or for evil, Psa 105.25). So Jerusalem is saying not only that her heart has been "wrung" (ESV), but also that her heart has been changed ("I know how wrong I was," NJPS), as the next clause makes clear: she confesses that she had gone astray, that she had **rebelled** (see the comments on 1.18).

In the time of Moses, God had warned the Israelites that, if they persistently disobeyed Him, "**out on the street** the sword will bereave, and **in** the inner rooms will be terror" (Deut 32.25). That warning had recently been repeated by both Ezekiel and Jeremiah: "The one who is in the countryside will die by the sword, and the one who is in the city— hunger and disease will devour him" (Ezek 7.15; Jer 14.18). Now it had all come to pass. If Jerusalem's inhabitants go **out** to the **street,** they are slain by the **sword;** if they remain **in the house,** it is **like death** there too. There is no escape from God's judgment in any direction (Amos 9.1–4; Psa 139.6–12).

> **My inner parts have been churning over.** Hebrew *m'h* (**inner parts**) is a general term for the abdominal regions, including the digestive tract (Job 20.14; Ezek 3.3; Jnh 1.17; 2.1) and the womb (Gen 25.23; Ruth 1.11; Isa 49.1). The term *hmr* (**have been churning over;** "in ferment," NASB mg) is applied to turbulent waves (Psa 46.3) and wine that has been shaken thoroughly to mix it (Psa 75.8). To say that Jerusalem's **inner parts have been churning over** is to say that they are "like seas with storms oppressed" (Sandys). Some other languages can express this picture more easily than English: *mis entrañas hierven* (VRV 1960); *mes entrailles bouillonnent* (Ostervald).

Here (and in 2.11) we have a reduplicated (Pe'al'al) form of the verb—*ḥmrmr* (GKC §55e)—suggesting repeated and perhaps failing or waning action (in 2.11, it stands parallel to "have come to an end" and "has been poured out").

Like death could mean either (i) "equivalent to death" ("at home there is the like of death," JPS) or possibly (ii) "death itself" ("inside, there is only death," NIV; *dentro non vi è stato altro che morte,* Diodati), if the prefix *k-* (**like**) is regarded as simply a mark of emphasis (cf. GKC §118x).

1.21 They have heard that I *am* groaning;
     there is no comforter for me;
all of my enemies have heard of my evil;
     they have been glad that You† Yourself† have done *it.*
You† have brought *the* day You† have called,
     and let them be like me.

All of Jerusalem's **enemies have heard of** the **evil** that has happened to her. They are aware that she is in distress—that she is **groaning** (1.4, 8, 11)—but there is no one who provides her with any comfort (1.2, 9, 16, 17). On the contrary, **they have been glad that** the Lord has **done** this to Jerusalem. The fall of Jerusalem brought great joy to the surrounding regions of Edom (4.21; Psa 137.7), Moab (Jer 48.27; Ezek 25.8), Ammon (Ezek 25.3, 6), Tyre (Ezek 26.2), and Babylonia (Jer 50.11). The Lord is therefore asked that they too may suffer punishment: **let them be like** Jerusalem (4.21–22). Justice requires that everyone who sins be punished by the Lord sooner or later, except those who repent. We too have sinned (Rom 3.23; 1 Jn 1.8, 10); we too deserve to suffer a terrible punishment (Rom 6.23; Matt 10.28; Rev 20.15; 21.8). "Unless you repent, you will all likewise perish" (Luke 13.1–5).

The people of this world rejoice when troubles happen to their enemies (Jdg 16.23; John 16.20; Rev 11.10). But under both the old and the new covenants, God commanded His people not to behave like that (Prov 24.17). Instead, we are to love our enemies, seek good for them, and pray for their good (Exod 23.4–5; Matt 5.44; Rom 12.14–21), as Jesus did (Luke 23.34).

Evil *(r')*. In the Scriptures, the term is applied sometimes to things that are unpleasant, sometimes to things that are sinful (see the comments on 3.38). Here it is used in the former sense ("trouble," KJV); in the next verse it is used in the latter sense ("wickedness," KJV).

You have brought the day You have called. What **day** is being discussed here?

1. According to one view, this **day** was the day when God punished Jerusalem (as described in the previous clauses of 1.20–21). The word *hb't* (**You have brought**), is a Qaṭal (perfect) verb-form, which would usually refer to an action in the past—exactly like *'śyt* (**You have done**) in the preceding clause. If so, **You have brought** and **You have done** would both refer to the same act: the Lord's judgment on Jerusalem (Renkema 139–40/195–97). He has **called** that judgment (appointed and summoned it, 1.15; 2.22); now He has **brought** it and **done** it.

2. According to another view, this **day** was the day when God would punish the enemies of Jerusalem (as described in the following clauses of 1.21–22). This view fits the structure of the verse better: a new topic would be much more likely to start at a major structural break (**You have brought...**) than at a subordinate break (**and let them be...**). But the punishment of Jerusalem's enemies was still future when the Lamentations were written. Why then would the passage use the Qaṭal verb-form *hb't* (**You have brought**)?

2a. The Qaṭal verb-form might indicate that the event was "as good as done already" in the mind of God (Keil 573/378; cf. Rogland, *Alleged Non-Past Uses of Qatal in Classical Hebrew*, §3.4.5). There are many similar Qaṭal forms in Isaiah's prophecy of Christ's death (e.g., "He poured out [*h'rh*] his soul to death," Isa 53.12). Christ's death was still in the future when Isaiah wrote, but it had already been fixed in the past in God's determination (Eph 1.4). This view is the basis for the KJV rendering "Thou wilt bring the day that thou hast called."

2b. Alternatively, some have argued that the Qaṭal form might possibly express a wish: "Oh, that Thou wouldst bring the day which Thou hast proclaimed" (NASB).

There may be no conclusive evidence in the Scriptures that Qaṭal verb-forms can express wishes. Advocates of this view suggest that such forms exist also in 3.56–66 and 4.22 (Hillers 78); other possible examples are listed in JM §112*k*; Joosten 211–12.

And let them be *(wyhyw)*. This verb and the next (**let… come**, v 22) are Yiqṭol forms. If the context were set aside, they could be treated as simple future tenses ("They shall be like me. All their evil shall come before thee," Smith), but in this context, the following imperative (**deal severely with them**, v 22) shows that they function as jussives (JM §48*g*, n. 3; IBHS §34.2.1a); Jerusalem is not simply making a statement, but is uttering a plea to the Lord. Compare the similar Yiqṭol next to an imperative in Psa 69.25, which the Holy Spirit renders in Acts 1.20 as a plea, not a simple statement.

1.22 Let all of their evil come before Your† face,
> and deal severely† with them,
as You† have dealt severely with me
> because of all of my transgressions;
for many *are* my groanings,
> and my heart *is* ill.

Under both the old covenant and the new, God's people are to pray for their enemies (see the comments on 1.21); but, under both the old covenant and the new, they are also to pray that those who persist in doing **evil** may be punished. Faithful brethren who were slain for the word of God have prayed both "Lord, do not count this sin against them" (Acts 7.60) and "How long, O Master, holy and true, will You not judge and avenge our blood on those who dwell on the earth?" (Rev 6.10—a prayer that is explicitly approved by Jesus Himself, Luke 18.7–8). God desires all people to be saved (1 Tim 2.4; 2 Pet 3.9), but He cannot abide those who do wickedness (Hab 1.13; Psa 5.4–6). Whenever we pray for His will to be done (Matt 6.10), we are inescapably praying for His will to be done in all respects. We are praying for His will to be done not only with those who repent of their sins, but also with those who persist in their sins.

Just as Jerusalem had committed **transgressions,** so her enemies had also done **evil.** God had **dealt severely** with Jerusalem **because of** those transgressions, and it had been a righteous and desirable thing for Him to do so (1.18). Therefore, it was also a righteous and desirable thing for her enemies to "be like" her in suffering punishment (1.21).

Many are my groanings (see 1.4, 8, 11, 21), **and my heart is ill** (see 1.13).

LAMENTATIONS 2

Summary

Verses 1–17 mourn over the afflictions of Jerusalem. The Lord has done what He planned: He has swallowed up Israel, delivered Jerusalem into the hand of the enemy, and repudiated His temple. Her prophets have seen worthless things; now her people are lamenting, and her enemies are joyful.

While the first Lamentation concentrated mainly on the sufferings themselves ("she has sat alone... she is weeping..."), this one stresses primarily the fact that the Lord is causing them ("the Lord is clouding in His anger... He has put down... He has not been mindful..."). Indeed, the Lord is the subject of almost every clause throughout verses 1–8 and 17; He is the one who is "doing" everything.

The final verses (18–22) urge Jerusalem to pour out her heart before the Lord, pleading with Him to see her sufferings, and asking Him whether these things should be permitted to continue.

2.1 How *the* Lord has been clouding in His anger
    the daughter of Zion;
He has put down from *the* heavens *to the* earth
    the splendor of Israel,
and He has not been mindful of *the* footstool of His feet
    in *the* day of His anger.

Formerly, "in [His] great compassions," the Lord had provided His people with a cloud that guided them and revealed His glory to them (Exod 16.10; 34.5; 40.34–38; 1 Kgs 8.10–11). But now, **in His anger,** He has sent them a different kind of **cloud**—a cloud of darkness and gloom (Zep 1.15), so that the people can no longer see the way to go (Jer 13.16) and their entreaties can no longer reach Him (3.44). The prophets had warned that this would happen if the Israelites persisted in disobeying Him: "they will cry to the LORD, and He will not answer them, and He will hide His face from them, because they have done evil in their deeds" (Mic 3.4); "your iniquities have separated between you and your God, and your sins have hidden His face from you, so that He does not hear" (Isa 59.2). We cannot approach God in a state of sin; we must be cleansed of our sins first, and then He will hear our prayers (Prov 15.8; 28.9).

Formerly, **Israel,** and particularly its temple, had been a place of **splendor** (Israel: Deut 26.19; Jer 13.11; the temple: 1 Chr 22.5; Isa 64.11). But now, the Lord has cast **down** that **splendor,** like a star that has fallen **from the heavens to the earth** (compare the casting down of Babylon, Isa 13.19; 14.12–15; Jer 51.53; and of Edom, Obad 3–4). There is a King even over the **heavens**—and "those who walk in pride He is able to bring low" (Dan 4.37; Luke 14.11).

Formerly, the temple had been the **footstool of** God's **feet** (Psa 99.5 ≡ 99.9; 132.7; 1 Chr 28.2). But now, **in the day of His anger,** He has **not been mindful of** His footstool. God has always been mindful of those who are faithful to Him—that is, He has thought on them and granted them His help (Noah, Gen 8.1; Hannah, 1 Sam 1.19). "To lasting time He is mindful of His covenant" (Psa 111.5). Even if we are not mindful of Him, He will be longsuffering toward us (Neh 9.17; Psa 106.7–8). But if we persist in that disobedience, we will ultimately provoke His **anger** (Ezek 16.43; Psa 78.40–42, 56–64).

> **Has been clouding** (*y'yb*, a Yiqtol form: see the comments on 2.22). This particular word-form appears nowhere else in the Scriptures, but it is evidently a Hiph'il derivative of a verb *'yb* or *'wb*, corresponding to the noun *'b* ("cloud," Psa 18.11–12; Jdg 5.4; etc.; cf. BDB 728; HALOT 2.794). *Nubló* (LBLA) is a good Spanish equivalent. McDaniel ("Philological Studies in Lamentations," 34–35) and Hillers (96–97) construed it as a Hiph'il derivative of a verb *y'b* or *w'b*, corresponding to the noun *tw'bh* ("abomination," Psa 88.8; Jer 2.7; etc.); but elsewhere in the Scriptures, the verb corresponding to that noun is always *t'b* (Deut 7.26; Psa 106.40; etc.).

> **The daughter of Zion.** The inhabitants of Jerusalem (see on 1.6).

> **Splendor** *(tp'rt)* The term includes both "beauty" (KJV), as in Isa 3.18, and "honour" (REB), as in Jdg 4.9.

2.2 *The* Lord has swallowed up; He has not spared
　　　any of the settlements of Jacob;
He has demolished in His fury
　　　the inaccessible places of *the* daughter of Judah;
He has made *them* touch down to *the* ground;
　　　He has defiled *the* kingdom and her leaders.

Formerly, the Lord had provided Israel (**Jacob,** 1.17) with **settlements** *(n'wt)*—places where a flock could both graze and reside (Psa 23.2; Isa 65.10; cf. TDOT 9.273–77; HALOT 2.678). But now, He had **swallowed up** (2.5, 8) all of those **settlements** (Jer 25.35–37; 23.10; cf. Amos 1.2), as the fish swallowed up Jonah (Jnh 1.17), and as the earth swallowed up Korah and his companions (Num 16.32; Psa 106.17). For generations the Lord had been merciful to Israel; He had "sent to them, rising early and sending, by His messengers, because He **spared** His people and His dwelling place"; but because they kept disobeying Him, eventually "He brought up against them the king of the Chaldeans... and he did not spare young man or virgin, old or aged; He gave them all into his hand" (2 Chr 36.15–17; Jer 13.14; 21.7; Lam 2.17, 21; 3.43). "Is it a light thing for the house of Judah to do the abominations that they have done here, that they have filled the land with violence, and have kept returning to provoke Me to anger?... Then I also will act in anger: My eye will not pity, nor will I spare; and they will call out in My ears with a great voice, and I will not hear" (Ezek 8.17–18).

　　Formerly, the people of Judah (the **daughter of Judah:** cf. 1.6) had been living in **inaccessible places** ("strongholds," KJV; "fortified cities," HCSB; Hebrew *mbṣrym*, an *m*-prefixed form of *bṣr*, "inaccessible," "impossible" to reach, Gen 11.6; Jer 33.3; cf. BDB 130–131; HALOT 1.148–49; 2.542–43; TWOT 1.123). Those places had been given into their hands by God, when the Israelites first entered the land of Canaan (Deut 9.1–3; Neh 9.25). But the **daughter of Judah** had put her trust in the **inaccessible places** themselves, not in the One who had given them

(Jer 5.17; Hos 8.14), and therefore He had **demolished** them (2.5), just as He had warned (Deut 28.52; Mic 5.11; Jer 5.17). Even if its defensive fortifications extend upward as high as heaven, no place in the world can be made inaccessible to God (Jer 51.53).

Formerly, the **kingdom** of Israel had been "a holy nation" to the Lord (Exod 19.6 ≡ 1 Pet 2.9; Deut 14.2; Jer 2.3). But now, it and its **leaders** (1.6) had been **defiled** (*ḥll*)—made unclean (*contaminó*, VRV 1602; *deslustró*, VRV 1909), the exact opposite of holy (Lev 10.10; Ezek 22.26; 44.23).

> **He has made them touch down to the ground.** Grammatically, this line looks both backward and forward:
>
> 1. It can be connected with the previous lines: **the Lord… has demolished** Judah's **inaccessible places** and **made them touch down to the ground,** bringing the strongholds' high walls (Psa 89.40) all the way **down to the ground** (2.1; cf. Isa 25.12: "the inaccessibility of the height of your walls He will bring down, make low, make touch to the ground, as far as the dust").
> 2. It can also be connected with the line that follows: the Lord has **defiled the kingdom and her leaders,** humbling them and making them **touch to the ground** (cf. Dan 4.37: "those who walk in pride He is able to bring low").
>
> **He has made them touch [*ngʿ*] down to the ground.** *Ngʿ* can be used of the lightest possible contact (cf. Psa 88.3; Num 4.15; "skim, graze, reach," JM §125*b*). Therefore, it stands out in this context as a remarkably "gentle" word (Salters 117). Several English translators have felt it to be too light, and have replaced it by something more intense ("razed," Stone). But even when the Lord acts in **anger** (2.1), **fury** (2.2), and **fierceness** (2.3), He remains perfectly controlled; He never loses His temper, as a human might do. Therefore His deeds can be described either in violent-sounding words (He has **swallowed up** and **demolished**) or in perfectly calm-sounding words (He has **made them touch down to the ground**).
>
> **Down to [*l-*] the ground.** As often elsewhere (many examples are listed in BDB 511, §1g*(a)*), the preposition *l-* indicates the direction of the act (it could be approximately represented as an arrow: "He has made them touch → the ground"). Compare "sitting → the ground" (v 10), "poured out → the

ground" (v 11), "lain down → the ground" (v 21), all with
l- and the same Hebrew noun.

2.3 He has cut off in *the* fierceness of His anger
      all of *the* horn of Israel;
He has turned away backward His right hand
      from *the* face of *the* enemy;
and He has burned in Jacob as a flame of fire;
      it has eaten up round about.

The **horn** of a nation was its power (Deut 33.17; cf. 1 Sam 2.10, 1; Psa 18.2), and the nation's **horn** was **cut off** when its power was destroyed (Jer 48.25; Zec 1.18–21; Dan 8.8, 22). Formerly, Israel's **horn** had been strong (Deut 33.17). But when the Lord cast down her splendor (2.1), defiled her leaders (2.2), and killed all her desirable things (2.4), He **cut off… all of the horn of Israel:** the nation was left powerless (1.14, 6). "God is the Judge; He makes this one low, and He raises this one aloft…. I will cut off all of the horns of the wicked; the horns of the righteous one will be raised aloft" (Psa 75.4–10).

Formerly, the Lord's **right hand** had saved Israel from her enemies (Exod 15.6, 12; Psa 44.3; 138.7). But now, the Lord had **turned** His **right hand** (2.4) **away… from the face of the enemy,** so that the Israelites were no longer delivered (Psa 74.10–11).

"The LORD your God is a fire that eats up" (Deut 4.24 ≡ Heb 12.29). Formerly, He had been a fire "eating up" Israel's enemies and destroying them (Deut 9.3). But now, He had turned that **fire** against Israel herself, eating up every part of the land **round about,** even to the foundations of Zion (4.11)—just as His prophets had warned (Jer 17.27; 21.14; Zep 1.18). And if we today, after receiving the knowledge of the truth, reject the sacrifice of His Son, we too will face "a certain fearful expectation of judgment, and the zeal of a fire that is going to eat up the adversaries" (Heb 10.27).

> **All of the horn of Israel.** The exact wording deserves attention. As comparison with Jer 48.25 shows, it does not mean "every horn of Israel" (NKJV) or "all the horns of Israel" (*al de hoornen van Israël*, Renkema 162/226), but "all that had been Israel's

horn" (*alles was Israels Horn war,* Keil 577/384; Gerlach 54), i.e., "all the strength of Israel" (NASB).

His right hand. The next verse (2.4) and Psa 74.11 show that the right hand is the LORD's, not Israel's.

2.4 He has trodden His bow like an enemy;
　　　His right hand *is* set up like an oppressor;
and He has killed
　　　all *those that were* desirable to *the* eye;
in *the* tent of *the* daughter of Zion,
　　　He has poured out like fire His fury.

Formerly, the Lord had directed **His right hand** against Israel's enemies and oppressors (v 3). Often the Scriptures depict Him shooting arrows at those enemies from **His bow** (Deut 32.23; Psa 64.7; 18.13–14). But now everything was turned around. The Lord was setting **His right hand** against Israel, and using **His bow** against Israel (see the comments on 3.12–13)—as if He Himself had become Israel's **enemy** and **oppressor.**

When Israel had hearkened to the Lord's voice, he had been "an enemy to your enemies" (Exod 23.22); but now, when He brought about the Babylonian conquest of Jerusalem, He was acting **like an enemy** to His own people (see also v 5). Yet even so, His compassions had not ended (3.22): "If He causes grief, then he will have compassion, in accordance with the abundance of His lovingkindnesses" (3.31–33, 25). "If we are faithless, He remains faithful, for He cannot deny Himself" (2 Tim 2.13).

Enmity always arises on our side, never on His. "He first loved us" (1 Jn 4.19; Eph 2.1–5). But whenever we set our mind on the flesh, and want to be friends of the world, we make ourselves enemies of God (Rom 8.7; Jas 4.4). He has done everything that is needed to reconcile His enemies to Himself (Col 1.20–22; Rom 5.10; 2 Cor 5.19). Yet if we persist in rejecting His reconciliation, He will ultimately punish those who remain His enemies (Luke 19.14, 27).

So, because Jerusalem persisted in rejecting the Lord, He **killed all** those who looked **desirable to the eye** (see the comments on 1.7, 10–11). He **poured out** His **fury,** like a **fire,** in her **tent.** "The tent of upright ones flourishes," but "the house of wicked ones is destroyed" (Prov 14.11; Psa

52.5; 69.24–25; cf. Psa 91.10). In the same way, the "zeal of [His] fire" is "going to eat up [His] adversaries" on the last day (Heb 10.27).

> **He has trodden** [*drk*] **His bow.** That is, He has "stretched" it (*enteso*, VRV 1602–1960) and "bent" it (KJV)—placing His foot on the lower part of the bow, to keep it in position while the arrow is attached (HALOT 1.231, §2). He is also described as treading *(drk)* a "winepress" (see 1.15) and the earth's high places (Amos 4.13; Mic 1.3): there is nothing in heaven or on earth that cannot be placed under His feet (Exod 24.10; Psa 18.9; Nah 1.3; cf. 1 Cor 15.27).
>
> **Right hand** *(ymn)* usually takes feminine verb-forms, but here it takes a masculine form, **set up** *(nṣb)*—which often happens when (as here) the verb precedes the noun (GKC §145*o;* JM §148*k*). In fact, in the first half of Exod 15.6 **right hand** takes a masculine verb-form even though the verb follows the noun. In the present passage some translators have construed **set up** as an active (Pi'el) form, resulting in the sense "He has set His right hand" (NASB), but this verb is not likely to have ever had any Pi'el form (none is found anywhere else in the Scriptures).
>
> **And He has killed.** The line is remarkably short. Some tidy-minded critics have suggested that a word or two has been accidentally lost from it; yet its unexpected abruptness would suit the unexpectedness and abruptness of the killing ("suddenly my tents are destroyed, my curtains in a moment," Jer 4.20; 15.8). Compare the destruction of Sodom, which happened "as if in a blink" (Lam 4.6), and the "sudden destruction" of the wicked on the last day (1 Thes 5.2–3).
>
> **Desirable to the eye.** ESV has "to our eyes," and NKJV "to His eye," but the Hebrew does not limit the statement to any specific observer, and therefore emphasizes the all-encompassing scale of the disaster. No one was spared; **all** those in whom anything **desirable** might be seen (by anyone) suffered (cf. 1.7, 10).
>
> **The tent of the daughter of Zion,** in this context, is the whole city (as in Isa 33.20; 54.2).

2.5 *The* Lord has become like an enemy;
He has swallowed up Israel;

He has swallowed up all of her citadels;
He has destroyed his inaccessible places;
and He has multiplied in *the* daughter of Judah
lamenting and lamentation.

The Lord is a friend to those who keep His commands (John 15.14; Jas 2.21–24), but He behaves **like an enemy** to those who persist in rejecting Him (see the comments on v 4). So He had **swallowed up** and **destroyed** even the places in **Israel** that had been best protected (the **citadels**) and most **inaccessible** (see the comments on v 2).

As a result, **lamenting and lamentation** had been **multiplied** in Judah. Those who reject God will have "many pains" and "multiplied griefs" (Psa 32.10; 16.4), whereas those who serve Him faithfully will have "hundred-fold" blessings, even in the present life (Mark 10.30).

> **Her** citadels are the daughter of Zion's (v 4); **his** inaccessible places are Israel's (v 5).

> **Citadels.** Often translated "palaces" (KJV), but this should not be misunderstood as "homes of the rich" or "homes of rulers"; rather, a **citadel** *('rmwn)* is a securely protected place (parallel to "a town of strength," Prov 18.19; Isa 25.2; cf. BDB 74).

> **Lamenting and lamentation** *(t'nyh w'nyh).* Two forms of one Hebrew word, emphasizing the repeatedness of the **multiplied** grief. (NASB's translation "mourning and moaning" misses this point.) The effect has been imitated by the LXX *(tapeinoumenēn kai tetapeinōmenēn)* and by some of the standard German versions *(Weh und Wehgeschrei*, ELB; *Traurigkeit und Trauer*, NZB).

2.6 And He has wronged His tabernacle, as *in* a garden;
He has destroyed His appointed *assembly;*
the LORD has made to be forgotten in Zion
appointed *assembly* and sabbath;
and He has despised in *the* indignation of His anger
king and priest.

The Lord **has wronged** *(ḥms)* **His tabernacle.** Jerusalem had been "full of wrong [*ḥms*]" (Ezek 7.23; 8.17). Her people had **wronged** "the stranger, the orphan, and the widow" (Jer 22.3); her priests had **wronged** God's Law (Ezek 22.26). Therefore she was repaid in accordance with her deeds: the Lord brought on her the Babylonians, who did wrong *(ḥms)* to her in many ways (Jer 51.35; Hab 1.9). If we do evil, we shall be punished by being repaid with evil (Psa 28.4). That truth should not be softened, but neither should it be twisted blasphemously. God is never evil; He is entirely good, and all His deeds are good (Psa 119.68; 145.9); yet the worst evil deeds of wicked conquerors unwittingly carry out His plans (Isa 10.5–7). Indeed, even those who once gathered together, in opposition to His Law, to do the most evil deed ever committed on the face of the earth, were simply performing "whatever Your hand and Your will had decided beforehand to come about" (Acts 4.27–28). From that standpoint, therefore, it may truly be said, "If there is an evil in a city, then hasn't the Lord done it?" (Amos 3.6)—not because He Himself is guilty of any evil, but simply because He has chosen to include it in His own plan, which is a good one. Joseph's brothers "planned evil against" him, but "God planned it for good" (Gen 50.20).

When Jerusalem was conquered by the Babylonians, the **tabernacle**—the place of **appointed assembly**—was **destroyed** by fire (Jer 52.13), just as earlier prophets had foretold (Psa 74.7; Isa 64.11; see also the comments on v 7). After that, the Lord's appointed times of worship under the old covenant (including the **sabbath**) were neglected, **forgotten** (see the comments on 1.4, "none are coming to the appointed assembly").

The Lord deals with us as we deal with Him (Psa 18.25–26; 1 Sam 2.30). The people of Israel had despised Him and His word (Isa 1.4; 5.24). Even those who were most honored among them—the king and the priests—had despised Him; therefore He **despised** them **in the indignation of His anger** (Ezek 22.26–31). The Babylonian conquerors carried out His indignation by capturing Jerusalem's king (see the comments on 4.20) and dishonoring her priests (4.16). "Who shall stand before the face of His indignation? And who shall set himself up in the burning of His anger?" (Nah 1.6; Jer 10.10).

> **He has wronged** *(ḥms)*. The word is nearly always—if not always—applied to acts of "extreme wickedness," and except in this passage, "God is never the agent involved in such behavior" (NIDOTTE 2.177–80, especially §§2–3). Many English translations have tried to soften it here ("broken down," RSV;

"laid waste," NIV; "stripped," JPS). The rendering "done vio-lence" (NKJV) is not quite accurate. *ḥms* is not applied to all forms of violence (e.g., "natural catastrophes"), but only to "sin-ful violence" (TDOT 1.297); and it is also applied to sinful deeds that do not necessarily involve violence (false witness, Exod 23.1; Deut 19.16; enticement to sin, Prov 16.29).

His tabernacle *(śk)*. This particular Hebrew form does not ap-pear anywhere else, but it corresponds to **His appointed as-sembly** in the next line, so it is apparently a variant spelling of *sk*, "tabernacle" or "booth" (a term for the Lord's temple in Jerusalem, Psa 76.2; cf. *skwt*, the temporary dwellings in which the Israelites lived each year during the Feast of Tabernacles, Lev 23.34, 42–43). Various other Hebrew words can likewise be spelled either with *s* or with *ś* (see also 3.8; further examples are given in Fuerst 2.962, §2; GT 575): such variations were probably matters of individual or regional preference (like, e.g., preference for -*ize* or -*ise* in our own language).

As [in] a garden *(kgn,* also found in Deut 11.10). The Lord's glo-rious tabernacle *(śk)* in Jerusalem has been torn down as if it were nothing more than a booth in a garden: "The daughter of Zion is left like a booth [*skh*] in a vineyard" (Isa 1.8). In itself, Hebrew *k-* (**as**) could compare the **tabernacle** either directly to a **garden,** or else to something **in** a **garden;** the context here shows that the latter is meant (in such cases, English requires an additional preposition, **in,** but Hebrew does not: JM §133*h;* BDB 455).

Appointed assembly *(mw'd).* The term encompasses both the times appointed by God ("the day of an appointed assembly," v 7) and the place appointed by Him ("the tent of appointed as-sembly," Exod 27.21). In this verse, the first instance is talking primarily about the place (which can be **destroyed**), and the second primarily about the time (which is parallel to **sabbath**).

2.7 *The* Lord has cast away His sacrificial altar;
　　　He has repudiated His holy place;
He has delivered into *the* hand of *the* enemy
　　　the walls of her citadels;
they have given forth a sound in *the* house of *the* LORD,
　　　like *the* day of an appointed *assembly.*

The Lord told the people of Jerusalem that they had "defiled My holy place with all your detestable things, and with all your abominations" (Ezek 5.11). Therefore He **repudiated** that **holy place** and rejected (**cast away**) its **sacrificial altar,** just as His prophets had foretold (Jer 7.4–14; Ezek 24.21; 7.22; 1 Kgs 9.6–9; see also the comments on v 6). As the prophets had also foretold (Ezek 7.24), even the **walls** of Jerusalem's **citadels** were handed over totally to the enemy's power (**delivered into** the enemy's **hand**).

In the days when the Lord had been worshiped faithfully, there had been a great **sound** inside the temple (the **house of the Lord**) on every day of **appointed assembly:** "a voice of shouting and thanksgiving, a tumult that is celebrating" (Psa 42.4; 26.7; 47.1; 98.4–6; 118.15). But now, the **sound in the house of the Lord** was produced by its destroyers—who had no authority even to enter the place (see the comments on 1.10). They "roared in the midst of Your appointed assembly"; they were "like one who was lifting up axes in a thicket of trees; and all its carvings they were hammering down with choppers and hammers" (Psa 74.4–6).

> **Delivered** [*hsgyr*] **into the hand.** The Qal form of *sgr* means "shut" (like a besieged city, Josh 6.1), and the Hiphʿil form *hsgyr* may also carry something of that connotation ("shut up into s[ome]o[ne]'s hand," NIDOTTE 3.225, §2): when David was "shut [*nsgr*]" in "a city of gates and bars," its people could "deliver [*hysgrw*]" him into King Saul's hand (1 Sam 23.7, 11–12). When the Babylonians attacked Jerusalem, her inhabitants were "walled up" with no escape from their **hand** (3.7, 9).
>
> **Citadels.** See the comments on v 5.
>
> **They have given forth** [*ntnw*] **a sound.** The plural may be used either because **enemy** (ʾwyb) is treated as a collective (GKC §§145*b, d*) or else because the subject is treated impersonally (GKC §144*f;* "a clamor was raised," RSV). The meaning is not affected.

2.8 *The* Lord has planned to destroy
    the wall of *the* daughter of Zion;
He has stretched out a measuring-line;
    He has not turned His hand back from swallowing up;

and He has caused rampart and wall to mourn;
>   together they have languished.

2.9 Her gates have been embedded in *the* ground;
>   He has destroyed and crushed her bars;
her king and her leaders *are* among *the* nations;
>   there is no Law;
also her prophets have not found
>   *any* vision from *the* LORD.

The destruction in Jerusalem (**Zion**) was not accidental or haphazard; it was totally **planned** by the LORD, as if he had marked out the condemned areas with a **measuring-line** (2 Kgs 21.13)—just as He also did when other nations were destroyed (Isa 34.11). (When He later rebuilt the city, that too was totally planned, marked out with a measuring-line: Zec 1.16.) All of the city's defenses—**rampart and wall, gates** and **bars**—failed **together;** when the attack came, they were **destroyed** and **crushed** (Neh 1.3). The broken defenses were left in a state of mourning (Jer 14.2; cf. Isa 3.26). What had once been strong was now made utterly weak (Lam 1.14; Isa 40.30; Luke 1.51–52).

The Lord allowed the enemy to break through Jerusalem's **gates** because the people had misused those gates for purposes forbidden by His old covenant Law (Jer 17.19–27). If we misuse His blessings, He will take them away from us (Hos 2.8–10; Matt 25.24–29).

The **gates** of the city had been the place where the elders (v 10) had sat, delivering judgment in accordance with God's word (see the comments on 5.14). But now, not only the place of judgment, but also the judges themselves and the standard of judgment were taken away. The city's **king** and **leaders** were carried into captivity **among the nations** (2 Kgs 24.14; Ezek 17.20). More terribly still, the people were deprived of God's **Law** (Ezek 7.26; cf. 2 Chr 15.3), and Jerusalem's **prophets** were no longer able to obtain **any vision from the LORD** (Psa 74.9; cf. Mic 3.4–7). The same dreadful punishment had already been inflicted on the northern tribes of Israel: "They will wander from sea to sea, and from the north even to the sunrise they will roam about to seek the word of the LORD; and they will not find it" (Amos 8.11–12). Other people in those days still had written copies of God's **Law** (Dan 9.2) and living **prophets** (Jer 1.1–3; Ezek 33.21; Dan 1.21); but the people of Jerusalem were no longer allowed access to them

(Ezek 20.1–3). They were eating the fruit of their own way: because God had called to them and they would not listen, they would now call to Him and He would not listen (Mic 3.4–7; Prov 1.24–31; cf. 1 Sam 28.6).

2.10 *The* elders of *the* daughter of Zion
   are sitting down to *the* ground, they are still;
they have cast up dust on their head;
   they have girded themselves with sackcloth;
they have bowed down their head to *the* ground—
   the virgins of Jerusalem.

Instead of sitting at the city gates speaking judgment with authority (see v 9), Jerusalem's **elders** were now **sitting** on the **ground** in humiliation (cf. Job 2.13; Isa 47.1; Ezek 26.16), wearing **sackcloth** (cf. Gen 37.34; Isa 22.12; Neh 9.1), and with **dust** on their heads (cf. Josh 7.6; Job 2.12; Rev 18.19).

Not only the **elders,** but also the young are afflicted: the "young children and sucklings" (v 11) and the **virgins of Jerusalem,** who are mourning in humiliation like their elders (see on 1.4): **they have bowed down their head to the ground.** This expression does not appear anywhere else in the Scriptures, but it is presumably equivalent to falling on one's face (cf. also 3.29): Ruth "fell on her face, and bowed down to the ground" in humility before Boaz (Ruth 2.10), as even the Son of God did in prayer to His Father (Matt 26.39 ≡ Mark 14.35).

> **They are still** (*ydmw;* see the comments on 3.26). They are as inactive as a stone (Hab 2.19; Exod 15.16). Elders would normally give counsel to the people, but now they had none to give (Ezek 7.26). The rendering "sigh" (NEB) is impossible in v 18.

2.11 With tears, my eyes have come to an end;
   my inner parts have been churning over;
my liver has been poured out down to *the* ground,
   because of *the* crushing of *the* daughter of my people,
in *the* fainting of young children and sucklings
   in *the* wide places of *the* town.

2.12 To their mothers they are saying,
    "Where *is* grain and wine?"
as they *are* fainting away, like *one* who is pierced,
    in *the* wide places of *the* city,
as their soul *is* pouring itself out
    to *the* bosom of their mothers.

Deeply—not only with his **eyes** (see on 1.16) but also with his **inner parts**—the prophet grieves over the sufferings of Jerusalem's people. In their **crushing** (Jer 14.17), he too is crushed (Jer 8.21)—just as God Himself is (Isa 63.9).

    Young children and sucklings are **fainting away... in the wide places of the city,** as if they had been **pierced** in battle (like the city's fighting men, Jer 14.18; Ezek 6.4, 7). In their hunger (v 19) they are pleading desperately **to their mothers**—pouring out **their soul** to them—for food and drink (4.4), **grain and wine.** If we sin, and suffer because of it, our **young children and sucklings** may also suffer. God does not hold them responsible for our sins (Ezek 18.20), but they may still suffer the consequences (Exod 34.7)—as the young children in the wilderness suffered (Num 14.33) even though they had no knowledge of evil (Deut 1.39).

> The **liver** (Exod 29.13) and **inner parts** (encompassing a diversity of internal organs: Gen 15.4; 25.23; Jnh 1.17) indicate that the prophet's concern extends throughout the depths of his being (as in 1.20; Jer 4.19; Psa 40.8). Whoever "may see his brother having a need, and may shut up his inner parts from him—how does the love of God abide in him?" (1 Jn 3.17).
>
> **Crushing** *(šbr).* The term is applied to the crushing of bones by a lion (Isa 38.13) and the shattering of a pot that cannot be mended (Jer 19.11).
>
> **The daughter of my people** (Isa 22.4; Jer 4.11; cf. Ezek 13.17). See the comments on the comparable term "daughter of Zion" (1.6).
>
> **The wide places.** The *plazas* (VRV 1602–1960)—the "open spaces" (NAB) or "broadways" (Rotherham) inside the city (see the notes on 4.18).
>
> **Their soul is pouring itself out.** Such renderings as "they gave up the ghost" (Geneva) and "their lives ebb away" (NIV) are

inconsistent with Scripture usage. This expression always re-
fers to intense pleading (1 Sam 1.15; Psa 42.4; cf. Lam 2.19;
Psa 102.0; 62.8; 142.2), never to death. The self-referential
(Hithpaʿel) verb-form *hštpk* is discussed in the notes to 4.2.

2.13 How will I support you†? to what will I liken you†,
    O daughter of Jerusalem?
to what will I compare you† and I will comfort you†,
    virgin daughter of Zion?
for great as *the* sea *is* your crushing;
    who will heal you†?

In his concern for the sufferings of Jerusalem, the prophet seeks to **support** and **comfort** her. But **how** could he do this? **Who** could **heal** a suffering that is so great—**great as the sea?** Jerusalem's **crushing** is beyond
cure; no one on earth has the power to heal it (Jer 30.12–15; see also the
comments on v 14). Among everything that has happened to the human
race, **what** can be likened or compared to this city, suffering so greatly?
(See the comments on 1.12.)

Only the Lord can provide **comfort** for the suffering caused by human
sin (Isa 40.1; 49.13; Psa 23.4); only He can **heal** it (Psa 103.3; 147.3; Jer
17.14). He has done both through the death of His Son (comfort, Isa 61.2
≡ Luke 4.19; healing, Isa 53.5 ≡ 1 Pet 2.24). If troubles are **great as the
sea,** He is even greater (Psa 93.4; 89.9; 65.7).

> **Support.** In other passages Hebrew *ʿwd* can mean "admonish"
> (NASB) or "testify unto" (ASV), but neither of those senses
> would suit the present context, where it apparently corresponds
> to **comfort** (just as **liken** corresponds to **compare**) and there-
> fore should mean something like "console" (NKJV), as it does
> in Psa 146.9; 147.6; 20.8 (NIDOTTE 3.339, §12; TLOT
> 2.839). It has sometimes been argued that *ʿwd* is here used in
> the sense "repeat," so that the meaning is "What duplicate of
> you will I find?" (cf. NAB; Albrektson 108), but there is no
> clear instance of this elsewhere (the closest is Jer 49.19, "Who
> is like Me, and who *yʿydny*?"—but that is usually regarded as a
> form of *yʿd*, "appoint").

2.14 Your[†] prophets have seen for you[†]
    worthlessness and whitewash,
and they have not uncovered *what is* over your[†] iniquity
    to restore your[†] restoration,
and they have seen for you[†]
    worthless uplifted oracles and misleading things.

Jerusalem's **prophets** have been no help in this time of trouble. "They have healed the crushing of My people in a slight way, saying 'Peace, peace,' when there is no peace" (Jer 6.14). When they proclaim what they **have seen,** their **uplifted oracles** have been **worthless, misleading,** and **whitewash.** "Her prophets have smeared whitewash, seeing worthlessness, and divining falsehood for them, saying 'Thus said the Lord GOD,' when the LORD has not spoken" (Ezek 22.28). In addition, "the prophets prophesied by Baal, and walked after things that did not profit" (Jer 2.8).

Instead, these prophets should have **uncovered** the **iniquity** of Jerusalem (Jer 23.22; Isa 58.1; Ezek 13.22). "Do not share in the unfruitful works of darkness, but rather even expose [*elegchete*] them" (Eph 5.11), as a great prophet—even at the cost of his own life—exposed the iniquity of Herod the tetrarch (Luke 3.19). In the days of the Lamentations, the people could be restored only if they acknowledged their **iniquity** (Lev 26.40–42; 1 Kgs 8.47–49; Neh 1.6–8); and we today can be restored only if we acknowledge our own iniquity (1 Jn 1.9; Psa 32.1–5 ≡ Rom 4.7–8). If we give people the impression that they are at peace when there is no peace, we are not doing them any good; on the contrary, we are greatly harming both them and ourselves (cf. Ezek 3.18).

> **Whitewash.** Hebrew *tpl* can be applied either to something insipid (something that cannot be eaten without salt, Job 6.6) or to something smeared over a wall (Ezek 13.10–16; cf. TWOT 2.978). These have often been regarded as two unrelated words, but there may well be a connection between them (cf. HALOT 4:1775–76): even though both of the supposedly different words are very rare, both are used, in similar contexts, to describe the false prophets at the time of the Babylonian captivity (Jer 23.13; Ezek 13.10–16; 22.28).
>
> **Uncovered what is over** [*glw 'l*] **your iniquity.** Just as people's skirts may be uncovered (*glh*, Pi'el; Nah 3.5; Isa 47.2; 22.8) in

order that their nakedness might be uncovered (Isa 47.3), so here and in Lam 4.22 what is **over** *('l)* the **iniquity** needs to be uncovered, in order that the iniquity itself might be uncovered (Job 20.27). *Glh 'l* is thus equivalent to *het doek wegtrekken over* ("pull aside the veil [that is] over," Renkema 205/285), and emphasizes the existence of an obstacle that any true prophet would have removed: everything that hides or veils an evil must be stripped away by the light of God's word (John 3.20; Heb 4.12–13). BDB (163, §3) suggests "made known concerning," which is grammatically possible but fails to explain why *'l* is used at all; if that were the meaning, why not simply say "made known your iniquity" with a direct object (cf. Job 20.27)?

To restore your restoration *(lhšyb šbytk)*. The second word has often been regarded as a form of *šbh* ("take captive"), but in Biblical expressions of this kind, both the verb and the noun are forms of the same word (GKC §§117*p*–*r*; JM §§125*q*–*t*; IBHS §§10.2.1f–g)—which in this case must be *šwb* ("return" or "restore"). This is confirmed by the fact that the expression is applied to the restoration of Job (Job 42.10), who certainly had not been taken captive. The sense therefore is not "to ward off your captivity" (NIV) or "to bring back your captives" (NKJV) but **to restore your restoration** or "to return your returning" (NIDOTTE 4.58–59, §9; TDOT 2.896; HALOT 4.1385–86). The rendering "restore your fortunes" (ESV) is potentially misleading, since it imports a concept from pagan mythology. In the Scriptures, changes of condition are not matters of fortune, but are planned and determined by God (see the comments on vv 17, 8).

Uplifted oracles. *Mś'wt*, an *m*-prefixed form of *nś'* ("lift up"); applied to prophetic utterances of all kinds, false (as in this verse) or true (Zec 9.1; 12.1; Mal 1.1; Nah 1.1; Hab 1.1). The meaning may be either that the utterance is lifted up with the voice by the speaker ("Hear this word, which I am lifting up [*nś'*]," Amos 5.1; HALOT 2.639–40; BDB 672) or that it is lifted up as a burden by the hearers (TLOT 2.773–74, §4(b); TWOT 2.602)—although not all *mś'wt* appear to be primarily burdensome (e.g., Zec 12.1). Ezek 12.10 and (possibly) Jer 23.33–36 apparently play on the two senses "oracle" and "burden" (GT 512, §4).

Misleading things. *Mdwḥym,* an *m*-prefixed form of *ndḥ* ("lead away"). When the people of Israel were "led away" by false **prophets** (Jer 23.2; Deut 13.5), the LORD "led them away" into **captivity** (Jer 23.3; 24.9), and therefore some versions translate *mdwḥym* in the present passage as "causes of banishment" (KJV): the false prophets' utterances not only led the people away from the Lord, but also caused them to be led away into captivity.

2.15 They have clapped their palms against you†,
      all *those* who pass over *the* road;
they have hissed and have shaken their heads
      against *the* daughter of Jerusalem:
"*Is* this the city of which they were saying,
      '*The* whole of beauty, *the* gladness of all *the* earth?'"

As previous prophets had foretold, passersby (**all those who pass over the road**) now **clapped their palms, hissed,** and shook their **heads** in scorn against Jerusalem (1 Kgs 9.8–9; Jer 19.8). Was this really **the city** that used to be called **The whole of beauty, the gladness of all the earth** (Psa 48.1–2; 50.2; Isa 64.11)? Our Lord Himself endured similar signs of scorn when He suffered for our sins (Psa 22.7–8; Matt 27.39). We are not to pour scorn on those who are suffering, but to comfort and help them (Job 16.4–5)—just as the Lord does with us, even when our sufferings are well deserved (Psa 107.17–20; Ezek 16.5–6).

2.16 They have opened their mouth against you†,
      all of your† enemies;
they have hissed and they have gnashed *their* teeth;
      they have said: "We have swallowed *her* up;
surely this *is* the day that we have awaited;
      we have found *it*, we have seen *it*."

All of Jerusalem's **enemies** now **opened their mouth** against her (3.46), **hissed** (v 15), **gnashed their teeth,** and rejoiced (v 17) in the long-**awaited** day of their triumph over her. Wicked people often delight in the downfall of those who profess to be the people of God (Wis 2.12–20; Matt

27.39–43). But the Lord does not delight in the downfall of anyone—not even the wicked (Ezek 18.32; John 3.16). Those who gnash their teeth against the righteous (Psa 37.12; Acts 7.54) will one day gnash their teeth over their own sufferings (Psa 112.10; Matt 22.13).

> **We have swallowed her up.** The ax is boasting over its wielder (Isa 10.15). In fact it is the LORD who has done the swallowing (see vv. 2, 5).

2.17 *The* LORD has done what He planned;
>He has carried out His saying,
which He commanded from days of beforehand;
>He has demolished, and has not spared,
and He has made *the* enemy joyful over you[†];
>He has raised aloft *the* horn of your[†] oppressors.

The Babylonian conquest of Jerusalem was no accidental or chance occurrence. It had been appointed by the LORD long ago (**commanded from days of beforehand**), and now He had **carried out** what He had **planned.** It had been foretold repeatedly by His prophets for almost a thousand years, ever since the time of Moses (Lev 26.27–39; Deut 28.47–68; Psa 74.1–9; 79.1–7; Isa 64.10–11; Jer 7.13–34; Ezek 7.2–27). The fulfillment of these prophecies was complete and total: He **demolished** everything that He had said, and did not spare any of it (see the comments on 2.2). What He has planned invariably comes to pass in every detail (Isa 55.10–11; 14.24–27; 46.9–11; Psa 33.9–11; Prov 19.21; Dan 4.35). And His new covenant prophets have issued warnings that all those who oppose Him in the present age will face a similar but even greater destruction (1 Thes 5.2–11; 2 Pet 3.7–13). The destruction of ancient Jerusalem is therefore an example for us today to heed (cf. Zec 1.4–6; 1 Cor 10.6, 11–12).

When Jerusalem was conquered, the **horn** (power) of her **oppressors** was **raised aloft** (see the comments on 2.3), and they were **joyful** over her (see the comments on vv 15–16 and 1.21). This too was no accident: **the LORD** was the one who raised them aloft and gave them reason to be joyful (Psa 75.4–7).

2.18 Their heart has cried out to *the* Lord,
  the wall of *the* daughter of Zion.
Make tears run down[†] tears like a wadi,
  daytime and night;
give[†] yourself[†] no slackening;
  do not let *the* daughter of your[†] eye be still[†].

2.19 Stand[†], shout[†] in *the* night,
  at *the* head of *the* watches;
pour out[†] your[†] heart like waters,
  in front of *the* Lord's face;
lift up[†] your[†] palms to Him
  because of *the* soul of your[†] young children,
the *ones* who are fainting with hunger
  at *the* head of all of *the* streets:

Jerusalem's prophets have misled her (v 14); her passersby have mocked at her (v 15); her enemies have triumphed over her (vv 16–17). But in this time of distress, a **heart** has been crying out **to the Lord** for help. At first it is described simply as **their heart,** but later it is identified itself more fully, as the **soul of** Zion's **young children**—those who are guiltless of the city's sin, yet are suffering the consequences of it, **fainting with hunger** in the **streets** (see the comments on vv 11–12). They are appealing **to the Lord** because He, and He alone, is the **wall of the daughter of Zion** (just as He told the city later, "I will be for her a wall of fire round about," Zec 2.5; cf. Isa 26.1; 60.18). All of her other, earthly walls have been delivered over to the enemy (v 7) and destroyed (v 8). But "the name of the LORD is a tower of strength; the righteous one runs into it, and is secure" (Prov 18.10; Psa 18.2; 27.1; 28.8; 61.3; 91.2).

 The prophet continues his address to Jerusalem (vv 13–17), urging her to come before the **Lord's face** and pray (**lift up your palms to Him**) on behalf of these **young children.** She is to **pour out** her **heart** in this plea (see on v 12), with **tears** that are abundant (**like a wadi**), never at rest (never **still:** see on 3.26), and persistent (**daytime and night**), without respite (with **no slackening;** Psa 77.2). "All the day and all the night they shall not be silent; you who put the LORD in mind, let there be no rest for you, and give Him no rest, until He establishes and makes Jerusalem a praise in the earth" (Isa 62.6–7). Persistent prayer can achieve great things (Luke 18.1–8; Jas 5.16).

We today, similarly, are to entreat the Lord constantly and from the heart for all people (1 Tim 2.1; Rom 10.1; cf. 1 Sam 12.23), who are **fainting** with spiritual **hunger** and must perish unless they receive from Him the only food that can bring life—His Son (John 6.53–54; cf. Psa 63.1; Amos 8.11–13).

> **Their heart has cried out to the Lord.** NIV assumes that the subject is the nation generally ("The heart of the people cries out…"), but nothing in the context supports this; the only plural subjects in the vicinity are Jerusalem's **oppressors** (v 17) and her **young children** (v 19). Her enemies would not cry out from the **heart** to the Lord, so the subject is evidently the **young children** (especially as **heart** in v 18 matches **soul** in v 19). In English we are accustomed to put the subject at the start of a statement, but in Hebrew it is commonly left unidentified until later: "They have clapped their palms against you, all those who pass over the road" (v 15); "They have opened their mouth against you, all of your enemies" (v 16). One unusual feature of vv 18–19 is that the subject is held in suspense so long before it is identified (there is an even longer delay in 3.1–18; see the notes on 3.1). Another unusual feature is that v 19 has four, not three, parts. Both of these features give vv 18–19 an exceptionally extended, long drawn character, appropriate in a passage stressing persistence **daytime and night** with **no slackening.**

> **The wall of the daughter of Zion.** This could also be construed as a vocative spoken by the children's heart **to the Lord:** "O wall of the daughter of Zion!" But the following lines cannot continue the vocative, because they are not spoken **to the Lord** (see the next paragraph); and it is difficult to see what sense an isolated exclamation "O wall of the daughter of Zion!" would have (Mackay [111–12] compares 2 Kgs 2.12, but that passage raises very different issues from the present one). Alternatively, the phrase could describe the place where the children are crying out (GKC §§118*d*, *g*): "at the wall of the daughter of Zion" (REB), "upon the walls of the daughter of Sion" (DRCV)—although if that had been the meaning, "in the streets…" would have been expected (cf. vv 11–12, 19; Isa 33.7; 42.2; Prov 1.20).

> **Make tears run down… give yourself no slackening… do not let… stand, shout… pour out your heart… lift up your**

palms. All this is addressed to Jerusalem, not to the Lord; therefore, it cannot be the plea that the children's **heart has cried out** (which is addressed **to the Lord,** not to Jerusalem). In fact the prophet is simply continuing the address to Jerusalem that began in v 13. His remarkable series of seven successive imperatives (unique in the Hebrew Scriptures) provides a practical illustration of the very thing that he is urging her to do—to be persistent in entreaty.

A wadi *(nḥl)* is a valley that fills with running water in times of rain (Psa 104.10; Prov 18.4; cf. Psa 78.20; 1 Kgs 17.7: Jer 47.2; Amos 5.24).

Slackening. Renderings such as "rest" (KJV), "respite" (ASV), and "relief" (NASB) may not convey the full force of the term. Forms of Hebrew *pwg* always describe a negative, unpleasant state (BDB 806); thus the sense here is approximately "Do not let yourself wilt," "Do not let yourself weaken" (cf. Psa 77.2).

The daughter of your eye. The most highly treasured part of the eye (Psa 17.8), usually understood to mean the pupil of the eye (an idiom still used in Spanish: *las niñas de tus ojos,* VRV 1602–1960). "Apple" (KJV) is an early English equivalent of "pupil."

The head of the watches. The **head** of a time period is its beginning (the "head of the months" is "the first month of the year," Exod 12.2). The night was divided into a number of **watches,** each of which had its **head** (e.g., "the head of the middle watch," Jdg 7.19). There should be **no slackening** in Jerusalem's entreaties: she should utter her pleas in each part of the night—and very early (at the **head**) in each part of it ("I have desired You at night... I will seek You at dawn," Isa 26.9; "before the watches," Psa 119.147–148; "in the middle of the night," 119.62; cf. Psa 63.6; 134.1; 22.2; 77.2; Luke 6.12; Mark 1.35; Acts 16.25).

2.20 "See†, Lᴏʀᴅ, and look†;
    with whom have You† dealt severely like this?
Should women eat their fruit,
    the young children of *their* nurture?

Should *there* be killed in *the* Lord's holy place
      priest and prophet?

The rest of the chapter gives the prayer that Jerusalem is being instructed in vv 18–19 to make. The speaker in vv 20–22 is therefore Jerusalem herself (**my virgins and my young men,** v 21, are Jerusalem's virgins and young men; **those who terrify me,** v 22, are those who terrify Jerusalem).

The prayer begins with an appeal to the LORD to **see** how **severely** He had **dealt** with His people. Those who had said, "Sword and famine will not be in this land," had been destroyed by sword and famine (Jer 14.13–15). During the famine (v 19), "hands of compassionate women cooked their children… as food" (4.10), just as Moses and Jeremiah had prophesied (Deut 28.56–57; Jer 19.9). And when the enemy entered the city, **priest and prophet** were **killed in the Lord's holy place** (which they had defiled with their sins: 2 Chr 36.14; Jer 23.11). **Should** such things be allowed to happen? In every age, as long as the world and its evil are permitted to continue, the righteous ask: "How long, God, will the oppressor reproach?" (Psa 74.10; 94.3; Zec 1.12; Rev 6.10).

> **Nurture** *(ṭphym)*. "Tender care" (ESV); *crías* (VRV 1602–1909). The corresponding verb appears in v 22, where the context shows that it refers to child care or upbringing (NIDOTTE 2.382, §2). There is also a term *ṭph* meaning "handbreadth" (Ezek 40.5), and this has given rise to such renderings as "children of a span long" (KJV); but that sense would not fit in v 22.

2.21 They have lain down to *the* ground *in the* streets,
      youth and old *man;*
my virgins and my young men
      have fallen by *the* sword;
You[†] have killed in *the* day of Your[†] anger;
      You[†] have slaughtered; You[†] have not spared.

The Lord has **not spared** any part of Jerusalem's population from the slaughter. Young and old (**youth and old man**), male and female (**virgins and young men**) have alike **fallen by the sword** and been **killed** (2 Chr 36.17; Jer 16.1–4). That is what He had warned them: "Because you have defiled My holy place with all your detestable things, and with all your abominations… then My eye will not spare, and I will not pity" (Ezek 5.11). The **sword** may have been in the hand of a Babylonian soldier, but ultimately the one who **killed** and **slaughtered** was the LORD (cf. Isa 10.5; Rom 13.4; Psa 44.3), and there is no standing before His **anger** (see the comments on v 22).

2.22 You† have been calling, like *the* day of an appointed *assembly,*
            those who terrify me from round about,
and there was not, in *the* day of *the* LORD's anger,
            one who was delivered or a remnant;
those whom I nurtured and brought up,
            my enemy has made an end of them."

Those who terrify Jerusalem were summoned (**called,** 1.15) by the LORD, and came against the city **from** the regions **round about** it—just as worshipers would come to Jerusalem from the regions round about, on the **day of an appointed assembly** (see the comments on 1.4). They were like "invited guests" (Quarles).

Everyone in the city was afflicted—no **remnant** of the population was **delivered** (Jer 11.11; cf. Amos 9.1–4). So Jerusalem's **enemy made an end** of her children (those whom she had **nurtured and brought up**). No one on earth can stand before **the LORD's anger** (Nah 1.6; Psa 76.7; Jer 10.10; Rev 6.17). And if we today reject His word, we "will certainly not escape" any more than the people of Jerusalem did (1 Thes 5.3; Heb 12.25).

> **You have been calling** *(tqr').* The word stands out sharply, not only because it is the word that completes the acrostic, but also because it is the sole Yiqtol verb-form jutting out among a long succession of Qatal forms. These Qatal forms describe actions that happened prior to the text's reference point (Joosten 193–223): **have lain down… have fallen… have killed… have slaughtered… have spared… was… nurtured… brought up… made an end.** Yiqtol forms can be broader and more diverse in meaning. When a passage is dealing with past or present events (as this one does), they generally describe actions "that come about repeatedly or habitually" (Joosten 276–77, 285–87; IBHS §§31.2–3): the Lord "has been clouding" Jerusalem (v 1), children "are saying" to their mothers (v 12), people "were

saying" about Jerusalem (v 15). Thus the Yiqtol form here is indicating that the LORD has **been calling** Jerusalem's adversaries against her not on one occasion only, but repeatedly (and it leaves open the possibility that He is still doing so: "Thou call'st" [Donne], *Tu convoques* [S21]). Moses had warned the Israelites that if they persistently disobeyed God, "all of these curses will come on you and pursue you and reach you, until you are destroyed" (Deut 28.45). So the LORD's anger against Jerusalem continued and did not turn back (Jer 4.8) until the full punishment had been accomplished (Lam 4.22; Isa 40.2; Jer 31.28). The use of Yiqtol here was not forced by the acrostic; it would have been easy to complete the alphabetic scheme with a Qatal verb (e.g., *tmkt*, "You have upheld...").

Rotherham construed the opening section of this verse not as a statement, but as a question: "Wilt thou proclaim... my terrors round about?" This is quite possible (cf. Joosten 278–79; JM §113*d*), especially as Yiqtol verb-forms are used twice in that way a few clauses earlier: "Should women eat [Yiqtol] their fruit...? Should they be killed [Yiqtol]...?" (v 20). In Hebrew there is no definite boundary between statement and question, and especially between question and exclamation (JM §§161*a*– *c*, 162*a*); the Yiqtol clauses in both v 20 and v 22 not only state what has been happening, but also raise the question whether it should be allowed to continue.

Those who terrify me [*mgwry*] **from round about.** The expression "terror from round about" occurs repeatedly in the Scriptures (Jer 6.25; 20.3, 10; 46.5; 49.29; Psa 31.13). The Jeremiah passages show that *mgwr* is a form of *gwr*, "be terrified" (Psa 22.23)—not to be confused with the similarly spelled words that mean "sojourn" (Lam 4.15) and "attack" (Isa 54.15). Here (as in Jer 20.4) it describes people who cause terror (*ceux qui me terrorisent*, S21).

Brought up. Hebrew *rbyty*, "made great" (as the LORD had made Jerusalem herself "great," *rb*, 1.1).

LAMENTATIONS 3

Summary

In the first two chapters, Jerusalem's sufferings are mainly described in the third person ("How she has sat alone, the city," 1.1), supplemented by passages where Jerusalem herself speaks ("See, LORD, my affliction," 1.9).

Chapter 3 is markedly different. There are no third person descriptions of affliction, and no passages spoken by Jerusalem herself. The whole chapter is apparently spoken in the first person by a male sufferer (a "man," *gbr*, v 1).

> First person singular word-forms (corresponding to English "I," "me," and "my") appear in every verse of vv 1–21, 24, 48–49, 51–63; first person plural word-forms (corresponding to English "we," "us," and "our") appear in every verse of vv 40–43, 45–47. The difference from the first two chapters is marked in the most prominent possible way at the outset. The very first word in the acrostic is a first person singular pronoun, *'ny* ("I"), and the very next word identifies this person as male, *gbr* (a "man").

In the opening verses (1–20) the sufferer describes his afflictions in detail. Then (vv 21–39) he fixes his hope in the LORD, recalling the LORD's unfailing compassion and His goodness to those who seek Him. He speaks on behalf of the whole nation (vv 40–54), confessing that "we have transgressed, and we have rebelled," and exhorting them all to return to the LORD. Finally (vv 55–66) he appeals to the LORD to hear his cry, knowing that the LORD has come near in the day when He is called upon, and that He will repay the enemies in accordance with their deeds.

The sufferer's afflictions are described in many different ways. He has been deprived of light (vv 2, 6); his flesh has been worn out and his bones

103

have been crushed (v 4); he has been walled up, so that he cannot go out (vv 5, 7); he has been chained (v 7); his paths have been made crooked (vv 9, 11); he has been assailed by a bear and a lion (v 10); he has been shot with arrows (vv 12–13); he has been mocked by his own people (v 14); his teeth have been crushed in the gravel (v 16); he has been hunted by his enemies like a bird (v 52); he has been put in a well-hole (vv 53, 55); he has been stoned (v 53); waters have flowed over his head (v 54); he has been plotted against (vv 60–62).

In the Scriptures, many of these expressions can describe either earthly or spiritual sufferings. Daniel faced earthly lions (Dan 6.16–23); Christ on the cross faced spiritual lions (Psa 22.13, 21). Jonah was submerged by earthly waters (Jnh 2.3, 5); Christ on the cross was submerged by spiritual waters (Psa 69.1–2).

The sufferer's afflictions have come from the LORD (vv 1, 3). At least some of them have not been caused by his sins, but have happened "for no reason" (v 52), like the sufferings of Christ (Psa 69.4 ≡ John 15.25) and the young David (1 Sam 19.5). Nevertheless he knows that it is good for him to suffer these things (v 27). Speaking on behalf of the nation, he humbly acknowledges that "we have transgressed, and we have rebelled," and need to "search our ways" and "return to the LORD" in order to be forgiven (vv 40–42). Compare Daniel's prayer for the nation whose sins he personally had not committed, but in whose sufferings he shared: "We have sinned, and done iniquity, and done wickedness, and rebelled, even turning aside from Your commandments..." (Dan 9.4–19).

Who is this sufferer? There have been two main answers: (1) the prophet himself, the writer of the chapter (this was the universal view in ancient times: see, e.g., Theodoret 792–93/187–88); (2) a personification of the people of Jerusalem (this has become the common view in the last two centuries: see, e.g., Ewald 328/103). Few things in the chapter enable us to discriminate between these options, but those few favor the first answer. The speaker distinguishes himself from the people as a whole ("my people," vv 14, 48, 51); and he "speaks *to* the people, not *as* the people" (Parry 95) in vv 40–41. Moreover, the very fact that he moves from singular ("I," vv 1–24) to plural ("we," vv 40–47) indicates that he is one individual among others—but also indicates that he "is not speaking merely of himself" (Kaiser 84–85); he is one individual, but he is not the only one in the situation he is describing.

Whichever of those two options is correct, at any rate "it is not every individual Jew who speaks here" (Laetsch 388). Nevertheless, the speaker's own sufferings are presented as representative of the sufferings of the people in general: he is appealing to the LORD "because of" their sufferings, not merely his own (vv 48–51). Many of his statements could have been said by any or all of those who survived the Babylonian destruction. Indeed, many of them could also have been said by sufferers in other ages, such as Job or David—and above all by the One who suffered for all human sins committed in all ages.

3.1 I *am* the man *who* has seen affliction
    by *the* rod of His fury;
3.2 He has led me and made *me* walk
    in darkness and not light;
3.3 surely against me He is turning, He is turning back
    His hand all of the day.

The Scriptures describe the Lord as using His **rod** when He administers **affliction** to those who "commit iniquity" (2 Sam 7.14) and "do not keep My commandments" (Psa 89.31–32). It is a "rod of uprightness" (Psa 45.6), because, however painful it may be, everything that the Lord does to us is upright (Deut 32.4; Psa 119.128). When He does afflict us, He does so in compassion (see the comments on vv 32–33) and faithfulness (Psa 119.75). His **rod** destroys those who refuse to serve Him, breaking them like a potter's vessel (Psa 2.9–12), but it corrects His children and gives them wisdom (cf. Prov 29.15; 23.13–14; 1 Cor 11.32). "Before I was afflicted, I was unaware; but now I have kept Your saying" (Psa 119.67). Therefore "it is good for me that I have been afflicted, in order that I learn Your decrees" (Psa 119.71; Heb 12.11).

"The pathway of righteous ones is like a shining light," because the Lord gives **light** to their path, but "the way of wicked ones is like deep darkness" (Prov 4.18–19; 2.13; Psa 36.9; 1 Jn 1.5–7; see the comments on v 6). If we sin against the Lord, He will blind our eyes and make us walk in that **darkness** (Zep 1.17; Isa 59.7–12; Deut 28.28–29; Rom 11.7–10). If we reject the light of His word, He will remove it from us (2.9; Amos 8.11–12). He urges us to glorify Him, believe on His light, and walk in His light, so that the darkness may not come upon us (Jer 13.16; John 12.35–36).

The Lord is watching over "all the sons of humanity," **all of the day** and "in every place" (Psa 33.13–15; Prov 15.3; 2 Chr 16.9; Heb 4.13). When we are in His favor, His constant care is a great blessing to us (Isa 27.3; Psa 121.4; Deut 11.12). But if we sin against Him, He will turn **His hand** against us constantly (**all of the day**); and then how shall we stand (Amos 7.5; Psa 39.13)?

The following verses contain an exceptional number of rare words and unusual grammatical constructions (see the comments on vv 8, 11, 16, 17). The destruction of Jerusalem was an unprecedented situation (see the comments on 1.12), and is appropriately described in unprecedented language.

> **The man** (*gbr*, "mighty man," a form of the common Hebrew word for "might": BDB 149–50). The feminine forms *(gbyrh, gbrt)* are applied only to women in positions of authority (Gen 16.9; 1 Kgs 11.19; 15.13; Psa 123.2; Isa 47.5); the masculine form is applied to adult men (Exod 12.37) capable of war, of governing a household, and of other responsibilities (Joel 2.8; Jdg 5.30; Psa 127.5; Mic 2.2; 1 Chr 26.12). The form used in v 1 is unambiguously masculine, and is always applied to males as distinct from females (Prov 30.19; Deut 22.5); the generic rendering "I am one who…," adopted by the majority of recent English versions (e.g., NRSV), is therefore inaccurate. Now the former "mighty man" has become "like a mighty one to whom there is no might" (Psa 88.4). The enemy is the one who has become mighty [*gbr*] now (1.16).

> **His fury.** Just as the speaker (**I**) is identified only indirectly, so the possessor of the fury (**His**) is identified only indirectly; His name—LORD—is first mentioned only in v 18. The implication is that He is so well known that He does not need to be named (Adeney 184).

> **He is turning back His hand.** Elsewhere the expression is always used of steering a chariot (1 Kgs 22.34; 2 Kgs 9.23). Like a warrior in a chariot, the Lord is hunting down the **man** who is His target (v 12); wherever the latter may go, the Lord **is turning** His course **against** Him (Amos 9.1–4; Psa 139.7–12; cf. Job 7.17–19).

3.4 He has made my flesh and my skin wear out;
   He has crushed my bones;
3.5 He has built against me and surrounded *me*
   with poison and weariness;
3.6 In dark places He has made me dwell,
   like *those* who have been dead *from* lasting time.

The Lord's affliction is not slight or superficial. It penetrates every part of one's being, from the **skin** right through to the **bones.** "There is no soundness in my flesh because of Your indignation; there is no peace in my bones because of my sin" (Psa 38.3; 32.3; 102.3–5). The sufferer is besieged (**built against,** 2 Kgs 25.1; Ezek 4.1–2) and **surrounded**—walled up, with no possible escape (v 7). And the siege walls surrounding him are not mere brick and soil; they are far worse—**poison** (Jer 8.14; 9.15; 23.15) and **weariness** (Neh 9.32), like the weariness of those who are traveling through a wilderness (Num 20.14; Exod 18.8). He is walking in darkness (see the comments on v 2) and dwelling **in dark places,** like those who are **dead** (Psa 88.3–6; 143.3). "A person who goes astray from the way of understanding will rest in the assembly of the departed spirits" (Prov 21.16).

> **He has crushed my bones.** The picture is developed further in Jer 50.17: "Israel is a scattered sheep; the lions have driven him away... and this last one who has crushed his bones is Nebuchadrezzar king of Babylon" (cf. Isa 38.13).
>
> **Poison** *(r'š).* The word is elsewhere applied to the poison of snakes (Deut 32.33; Job 20.16) and the poison of poisonous plants (Deut 29.18; 32.32).
>
> **Lasting time** (*'wlm,* corresponding to Greek *aiōn,* Psa 110.4 ≡ Heb 5.6). The term is applied to remote periods of indefinite length ("ages," HCSB; "long ago," NKJV)—e.g., since the time of Abraham's father (Josh 24.2); since the time of Moses (Isa 63.11); since the time of David and his early descendants (Amos 9.11).

3.7 He has walled me up, and I will not go out;
   He has made my bronze *chain* heavy;

3.8 even when I cry out and cry for help,
  He has shut out my entreaty;
3.9 He has walled up my roads with hewn stone;
  my paths He has made crooked.

The sufferer is hemmed in, unable to move (v 5). He is **walled up,** so that he cannot **go out;** he is chained with a **heavy** chain, like a prisoner (Jdg 16.21; 2 Chr 33.11; 36.6; 2 Kgs 25.7); the roads around him are **walled up** with **stone,** and do not lead in the right direction (they are **crooked;** cf. v 11). "A person's heart plans his way, but the LORD establishes his steps" (Prov 16.9). We can make no progress unless He allows it (John 3.27); when Israel disobeyed Him, He told her: "I will hedge up your way with thorns, and I will wall up a wall, and she will not find her paths" (Hos 2.6). God makes straight paths for the righteous (Prov 3.6; 11.5); but if we turn aside from those paths and walk in crooked ways (Jer 3.21), He will give us over to our own counsel (Psa 81.11–12; 109.17), forcing us to walk in the very kinds of paths that we have desired—crooked ones (cf. Psa 18.26; Lev 26.23–24). In that situation, He will **shut out** our **entreaty,** and will not hear us **even when** we **cry for help.** "Your sins have hidden His face from you, so that He does not hear" (Isa 59.1–2; 1.15; Prov 1.24–28; 28.9; 15.29; Psa 66.18). That is how He treated the sinners in Jerusalem in Jeremiah's time: no matter how they cried out to Him, and no matter how many sacrifices they offered, He refused to hear them (Jer 14.12; Ezek 8.17–18). Because He had called to them and they had not listened, they would call to Him and He would not listen (Zec 7.13). "They will cry out to the LORD, and He will not answer them; and He will hide His face from them at that time, because their deeds were evil" (Mic 3.4). See also the comments on v 44.

> **Bronze chain** *(nḥšty).* The Hebrew word was pointed by the Masoretic scribes as a singular, but could also be construed as a dual (as in Jer 39.7), "my bronze [chain]s," describing a pair of chains (for the hands or feet).

> **He has shut out** *(śtm).* This form is unknown elsewhere; the context suggests that it is probably a variant spelling of *stm,* a term applied to the sealing of a scroll (Dan 12.4, 9) and the blocking of a well (Gen 26.15, 18). Another word beginning with *ś-* instead of the more common *s-* appears at 2.6 (see the comments there).

Hewn stone was building material of high quality, which would fit together more closely than unhewn stone and would be more secure (cf. Isa 9.10).

3.10 A bear lying in wait He *is* to me,
a lion in hiding places;
3.11 my roads He has turned aside, and He has made me limp;
He has made me desolate;
3.12 He has trodden His bow, and He has set me up
as a target for *the* arrow.

3.13 He has sent into my kidneys
the sons of His quiver;
3.14 I have become laughter for all of my people,
their music all of the day;
3.15 He has filled me with bitternesses;
He has sated me *with* wormwood.

Just as the Lord's abundant blessings can be described in manifold ways, so can His chastenings. He acts like a **bear** or **lion** (Hos 13.7–8; 5.14), blocking the way (cf. Prov 26.13) so that the sufferer's path is **turned aside** from the straight, smooth roads, forcing him to **limp** on crooked, uneven ground (cf. v 9; Isa 40.4; Heb 12.13; Jer 18.15). He stretches **His bow** ("treads" it: see on 2.4) and shoots His **arrows** (the **sons of His quiver**), which penetrate all the way into the sufferer's innermost parts (**kidneys,** Jer 17.10; cf. Heb 4.12). He fills the sufferer "to the full" (Payne Smith 594), not with food, but with **bitter** substances such as **wormwood** (Jer 9.15). The **people** around the sufferer laugh at him (see the comments on 2.15) and make up songs about him (cf. v 63; Psa 69.12; Job 30.9).

> **My roads He has turned aside** *(swrr)*. Generally construed as a unique Polel form (GKC §72*m*; JM §59*a*) of *swr*, which, especially in relation to **roads**, most often means "turn aside" (out of the straight way: Deut 2.27; 1 Sam 6.12; BDB 693, §1; HALOT 2.748, §1a). The rendering "He has strewn my paths with thorns" (Stone) follows Rashi's proposal that the word is an otherwise unknown verb corresponding to *syrh*, "thorn" (Hos 2.6; cf. Fuerst 2.974, who suggests that *swrrym*, "obstinate ones" [Jer 6.28], is "derived from the sting of thorns").

He has made me limp *(pšḥny)*. The original Hebrew text was unpointed. The medieval Masoretic scribes pointed this word as *pšḥny* because they were familiar with an Aramaic verb *pšḥ* meaning "tear in pieces," which would suit the mention of a **lion** in the previous verse. But there is no evidence that *pšḥ* existed in Hebrew, and the next clause (**He has made me desolate**) hardly sounds like the result of being torn in pieces. On the other hand, there is certainly a Biblical Hebrew word *psḥ* meaning "limp" (2 Sam 4.4; 1 Kgs 18.21; BDB 820; HALOT 3.947), and Lamentations tends to use *š* in words that are more commonly spelled with *s* (see on 2.6; 3.8). This yields the meaning **He has made me limp,** which would be a plausible result either of being **turned aside** from the **roads** or of having the **roads** strewn with thorns.

My people *('my)*. A few Masoretic manuscripts (supported by Syr) have the expected form *'mym*, "the peoples." A somewhat similar situation occurs at Psa 144.2, where most Masoretic manuscripts read *'my*, "my people," but some have *'mym*, "the peoples." In that case, the context shows that the latter reading must be correct.

3.16 And He has crushed my teeth in *the* gravel;
  He has made me suffer in *the* ashes;
3.17 and my soul has been cast out from peace;
  I have forgotten goodness;
3.18 and I said, "My enduringness has been destroyed,
  and my hope from *the* LORD."

The LORD has deprived the city of food (1.11; 4.4; cf. 5.4); her inhabitants are now searching for anything edible on the **gravel** of the ground (cf. Prov 20.17) and among the **ashes** in the garbage (Psa 102.9–10). Our King forces His enemies to lick the dust (Psa 72.9), where they sit in humiliation and grief (Jer 6.26).

Those who hate **peace** (Psa 120.6) will be deprived of **peace** (Isa 57.20–21). So, in His judgment on Jerusalem, "I have taken away My peace from this people, says the LORD" (Jer 16.5); it has been replaced by war (Jer 12.12; Ezek 7.25), and the former time of **goodness** has been **forgotten** (cf. Gen 41.30; Jer 8.15).

The sufferer even voices the thought that he no longer has any enduring **hope** (Ezek 37.11)—although when he reflects on the LORD's lovingkindness and faithfulness, he continues to maintain his hope (see the comments on vv 21, 24, 26). "The hope of wicked ones is destroyed" (Prov 10.28; 11.7), whereas "a needy one will not be forgotten to enduring time [*nṣḥ*]; the hope of afflicted ones will not be destroyed to continuing time" (Psa 9.18). Even if they perish, the righteous are not like those "who have no hope" (1 Thes 4.13–18); they have a **hope** that will endure forever and never disappoint (Rom 5.5; Heb 6.18–19; Prov 23.18; 24.14).

> **He has crushed.** A causative (Hiph ʿil) form of *grs*, "crush" (Psa 119.20). **He has crushed my teeth in the gravel** could mean either "He has made my teeth grind on gravel" (ESV) or "He has broken my teeth with gravel" (NASB). Evildoers seek to tear the righteous with their teeth (Psa 124.6; 57.4); the LORD prevents this by breaking their teeth (Psa 58.6; 3.7).
>
> **He has made me suffer.** A Hiph ʿil form of *kpš*, a word that occurs nowhere else in the Scriptures. "He has fed me" (NJB) derives from the LXX rendering *epsōmisen*, which may be merely a guess based on the mention of **teeth** in the previous clause, although the idea is certainly found in Scripture (Psa 102.9). "He hath covered me" (KJV) derives from the Syriac rendering *plny* ("He has sprinkled me"), which is probably also a guess (cf. the sprinkling of **ashes** in Exod 9.8, 10). "He has trampled me" (NIV) and "He has made me cower" (NASB) treat *kpš* as a spelling variant of *kbš*, "subjugate" (1 Chr 22.18)—but that would ordinarily be Qal, not Hiph ʿil (BDB 461; HALOT 2.460; even in Jer 34.11, the Qal is generally regarded as the correct reading). At any rate the passage clearly describes some form of suffering; therefore, we have rendered it simply **He has made me suffer.**
>
> **My soul has been cast out** [*wtznḥ*] **from peace.** The Hebrew could be construed either as an active (Qal) form ("Thou hast removed my soul," KJV) or as a passive (Niph ʿal or Hoph ʿal) form (**my soul has been cast out**). The Masoretic scribes chose the former option, but nearly all modern translators prefer the latter, since God is nowhere else addressed directly in this passage. On any view, the wording is unusual; nowhere else is the Qal followed by *m-* (**from**), and no passive forms of *znḥ* are found elsewhere in the Scriptures.

And I said *(w'mr).* This introduces a provisional statement, which is quoted so that it can be considered, in order to see whether it is correct. (Compare Psa 31.22: "I said in my haste, 'I have been axed down from before Your eyes'; yet surely You have heard the voice of my appeals for favor"; Job 29.18; Psa 139.11.) The Masoretic scribes construed it as a Wayyiqṭol form, *waʾōmar,* marking a past utterance, **And I said** (as in Gen 24.39, etc.). Some translators have construed it as a timeless Wᵉqaṭal form, *wᵉʾōmar* ("So I say," NASB), as in Ezek 13.15; but the Wayyiqṭol form of this verb is much more common, and is supported by the fact that the statement is withdrawn in v 21.

Enduringness. Elsewhere Hebrew *nṣḥ* never refers to the past, but to what will endure in the future (TDOT 9.531). The same must surely be true here, since it corresponds to **hope** in the next clause. Therefore, the meaning is not that the sufferer has lost his previous "strength" (KJV), but that he is deprived of his "lastingness" (NIDOTTE 3.139)—his "future" (HCSB), his promised security (*fiducia,* ND), his "lasting" hope (NJB). Compare 5.20 ("to enduring time"), where the same word is used. Here (and often elsewhere) the LXX renders it *nikos* ("victory"), as the Holy Spirit does in 1 Cor 15.54 ≡ Isa 25.8.

3.19 *I am* mindful of my affliction and my straying,
　　　 wormwood and poison;
3.20 being mindful, my soul is mindful of it
　　　 and is sinking down over me.
3.21 This I am bringing back to my heart;
　　　 therefore I am hoping:

3.22 *the* lovingkindnesses of *the* Lᴏʀᴅ—for they have not been finished,
　　　 for His compassions have not ended;
3.23 *they are* new at *each of the* mornings;
　　　 great *is* Your† faithfulness;
3.24 "My portion *is the* Lᴏʀᴅ," my soul has said;
　　　 therefore I am hoping for Him.

The sufferer brings to mind his troubles (as in Psa 42.3–4), and is brought low by the thought (his soul **is sinking down,** an expression used also in Psa 44.25). David's sufferings had similar effects: "The enemy has pursued my soul… he has made me dwell in dark places, like those who have been dead from lasting time. My spirit is fainting away within me; in the midst of me, my heart is desolate; I have been mindful of the days of old" (Psa 143.3–5).

Such humiliation is deeply painful, but it is not necessarily a bad thing (Heb 12.11). It can turn sinners back to the Lord (like Manasseh in the days of his distress, 2 Chr 33.12–13), and it can keep faithful souls steadfast in the Lord (like Paul with his thorn in the flesh, 2 Cor 12.7–10). "The LORD is near to those who are broken of heart, and He saves those who are crushed in spirit" (Psa 34.18; 51.17). So, when this sufferer is **mindful of** his troubles, he is also bringing to mind (**bringing back to his heart**) **this** truth: the existence of the LORD's **lovingkindnesses** and **compassions,** which **have not been finished** *(tmm)* and **have not ended** *(klh).* Calling that truth to his mind, the sufferer continues **hoping** (waiting with expectation; Psa 130.5–8; 33.18–22; Rom 8.25).

The LORD's **lovingkindnesses** and **compassions** are abundant, multitudinous, and constantly being manifested (Isa 63.7; Psa 145.8–9; 40.11; 103.8). "Morning by morning He gives His justice" (Zep 3.5). Just as He is constantly ready to bestow corrections and punishments **at each of the mornings** (Psa 73.14; cf. Psa 101.8), so He is constantly ready to save and help His people **at each of the mornings** (Isa 33.2). Therefore we can pray to Him: "Fill us in the morning with Your lovingkindness" (Psa 90.14; 143.8). But we cannot presume on His lovingkindness. If we persist in sin, He will ultimately destroy us too (Ezra 9.13–15; Luke 13.1–9). Only if we turn away from sin and purify ourselves can we truly fix our **hope** on **Him** (Zep 3.12–13; 1 Jn 3.3; Col 1.22–23).

A person's **portion** *(ḥlq)* is the amount that he inherits—the amount that is allotted to him (Josh 18.5–7; Isa 57.6). The wicked receive "fire and brimstone" as their portion (Psa 11.6), but those who serve the LORD and keep His words receive the finest possible portion; they are allotted **the LORD** Himself as their **portion** (Jer 10.16; Psa 119.57). That is the **portion** that this sufferer has chosen—as Jesus Himself did (Psa 16.5). Those who have chosen that portion have an unshakeable **hope,** regardless of what may happen to them in the flesh (Psa 73.26–28), for they are continually with Him (Psa 73.23–24). "I have been confident in the lovingkindness of God to lasting time and continuing time" (Psa 52.8).

[I am] mindful [*zkr*]... [my soul] is mindful [*tzkwr*]. The verbs could be construed as imperative and second person singular, "Be mindful... You are mindful" (addressed to the LORD, as in 5.1), but are probably infinitive construct and third person feminine singular, describing the sufferer himself and his soul as **mindful,** in view of the surrounding verbs in vv 17–21: **my soul has been cast out... I have forgotten... I said... my soul is sinking down... I am bringing back... I am hoping.**

My soul **is sinking down** (*tšyh*, a Hiph'il form, K; *tšwh*, a Qal form, Q). Both readings are forms of *šwh* (as in Psa 44.25)—a variant of *šhh*, which appears in the analogous passages Psa 42.5–6, 11; 43.5 ("my soul is sunk down over me"). As always, the Masoretic manuscripts give the pointing only of their marginal reading (Q); the form in their text (K) could therefore be read with either *š* or *ś,* and could in theory be a form of *śyh* ("murmur," "ponder," as in Psa 77.3). But the spellings in Psa 42 and 43 have no such ambiguity.

My soul is sinking down **over me** *('ly)*. The usual rendering is "within me" (ASV), but that is most unlikely to be the meaning of the Hebrew (Renkema 274/381), and the sense **over me** is confirmed by the analogous passage in Psa 42.4–7: "I will pour out my soul over me ['*ly*].... My soul is sunk down over me ['*ly*].... All Your breakers and Your rolling waves have passed over me ['*ly*]." Waves pass **over,** not within, someone; similarly, to pour out something *'l* someone is to pour it **over** them, not within them (Deut 12.16, 27; 1 Kgs 18.28; Ezek 36.18; in Acts 2.17–18 ≡ Joel 2.28–29 the Holy Spirit adopts the Greek rendering *epi,* "over" or "upon"). Thus the picture here is of the sufferer's soul **sinking down** like a heavy burden (Nägelsbach 38/113) "upon," on top of, him (Wordsworth 146).

My straying. See the comments on 1.7. In both verses, it is paired with **affliction.**

Wormwood and poison. The previous uses of these terms (see on vv 15, 5) suggest that they describe the pain of the **affliction** and **straying** ("I remember my affliction and my wandering, the bitterness and the gall," NIV) rather than the pain of being **mindful** ("The thought of my affliction and my homelessness is wormwood and gall," NRSV).

This I am bringing back [*'šyb*] **to my heart.** In other words, "I call this to mind" (HCSB). The meaning is shown by the use of same expression in 1 Kgs 8.47; Isa 44.19; 46.8.

This *(z't)* refers to what follows, not to what precedes. (The same is true in most similar passages, e.g., Ezek 20.27: "In this also your fathers blasphemed Me: in dealing treacherously with Me.") The sufferer has hope because of **this:** because of the LORD's **lovingkindnesses** (not because the sufferer is **mindful of** his **affliction**).

My heart. In modern English we regard the "heart" as feeling and the "mind" as remembering, but in the Scriptures there is no difference between the two. Like the mind, the **heart** is the part of oneself that thinks (Isa 10.7) and remembers (Isa 65.17).

Therefore I am hoping [*'wḥyl,* v 21]... **Therefore I am hoping** [*'wḥyl,* v 24]. Most English versions treat v 21 as a statement about the present and v 24 as a statement about the future ("therefore I have hope... therefore I will wait," NIV), but the Hebrew uses the same Yiqṭol form in both clauses. In themselves Yiqṭol forms can describe either present or future actions, especially if they are continuing or repeated (JM §§113*b–d;* Joosten 266–67, 276–80). In this context, the action is clearly present (the sufferer has already made this resolution), and he intends to continue it in the future.

They have not been finished. The textual situation is exceptionally complex. The significant points are as follows.

- In Hebrew, all but one of the known Masoretic manuscripts have *l' tmnw,* which looks like a first person plural form equivalent to *l' tmwnw* ("we have not been finished," as in Num 17.13; Jer 44.18), although it might be a third person plural form equivalent to *l' tmmw* ("they have not been finished"; exactly the same uncertainty exists in Psa 64.6, and a substitution of *-mn-* for *-mm-* might be compared with, e.g., the apparent substitution of *-zn-* for *-zz-* in *m'znyh,* Isa 23.11; cf. Böttcher 1, §300b; GKC §20*o*). The medieval Judaic commentators Rashi and Ibn Ezra already recognized both of those possibilities. The other Masoretic manuscript (Kennicott 109) has the undoubted third person plural form *l' tmw* ("they have not been finished"), but its testimony is not significant, as it has a relatively large number of transcriptional errors elsewhere.

- In Greek, most of the Antiochene manuscripts (22 etc.) have *ouk exelipomen* ("we have not ceased to exist"), but some (including 62) have *ouk exelipon me* ("they have not forsaken me"). The Hexaplaric manuscript 88 has *ouk exelipen me* ("He has not forsaken me"); *-en* is a common copyist's error for *-on* in ancient Greek manuscripts. Probably because of an accidental oversight, the whole of vv. 22–24 was omitted by the major uncials (Vaticanus, Alexandrinus, and Venetus; the page of Sinaiticus containing this section of Lamentations has not been found).
- The Aramaic Targum and the Syriac Peshitta both have "they have not been finished," which could be a rendering either of *l' tmnw* or of *l' tmw*.
- The Latin Vulgate has "we are not consumed," which is certainly a rendering of *l' tmnw*.

In summary, the textual evidence is overwhelmingly in favor of *l' tmnw*, and the context suggests that it is a third person plural ("they have not been finished") matching the undoubted third person plural *l' klw* ("they have not ended") in the next clause.

3.25 *The* LORD *is* good to *those* who are waiting for Him,
    to *the* soul *that* is seeking Him;
3.26 *it is* good that *he is* hoping and *in* stillness
    for *the* salvation of *the* LORD;
3.27 *it is* good for a man that he bears
    a yoke in His youth.

Everything that the LORD has done is **good** (1 Tim 4.4; Gen 1.31; cf. Deut 32.4), and every good thing comes from Him (Jas 1.17). He is good to all people (Psa 145.9; Acts 14.17; Matt 5.44–45), but above all He is **good to those who are waiting for Him** and **seeking Him** (those who are upright and pure in heart, Psa 73.1; those who fear Him, Psa 31.19; those who call on Him, Psa 86.5). "Those who are seeking the LORD do not lack any good thing" (Psa 34.9–10). He never holds back good from them (Psa 84.11; Matt 7.11); they receive it all the days of their life (Psa 23.6); all things work together for good to them (Rom 8.28). Therefore **those who are waiting for Him** will never be put to shame (Isa 49.23; Psa 25.3), and those who are **seeking Him** with all their heart will certainly find Him (Deut 4.29; Jer 29.13; cf. John 6.37).

Even affliction, although it is a burden to **bear** (a **yoke,** 1.14), is **good** for us: "it is good for me that I have been afflicted, in order that I learn Your decrees" (Psa 119.71, 67; Heb 12.6–11). Right from the outset, in our **youth,** we are likely to go astray unless the LORD afflicts us with His rod (Prov 22.15; cf. Prov 23.13–14), as He did in their youth to Joseph (Psa 105.17–18), David (Psa 59.1–4; 57.4), and Daniel (Dan 1.1–8).Yet in spite of those afflictions, His **yoke** is easy, and His burden is light (Matt 11.30). "Therefore I am well pleased with weaknesses, with harmful things, with distresses, with persecutions, with constraints, for Christ's sake; for when I am weak, then I am strong" (2 Cor 12.10).

> **Stillness** (*dwmm;* see the comments on 2.10) is the condition of being at rest (*en repos,* Ostervald; терпеливо ожидает, RST), like a stone (Exod 15.16) or the sun after Joshua commanded it to stop (Josh 10.12–13). It is the opposite of being disturbed or fretful (Psa 37.7–8; cf. Lam 2.18).

3.28 He will sit alone, and he will be still,
    for He has laid *it* on him;
3.29 he will set his mouth in *the* dust;
    perhaps there will be hope;
3.30 he will give his cheek to *the one* who smites;
    he will be filled with reproach.

When a yoke of affliction is imposed on him (v 27), a faithful servant of the LORD **will sit alone** (cf. Jer 15.17) and **be still** (v 26), knowing that the LORD **has laid** this yoke **on him.** He will **set his mouth in the dust**—that is, he will humbly submit to degradation in the presence of his King (see the similar expressions in Psa 72.9; Mic 7.17; and cf. Lam 2.10). Instead of resisting his tormentors, he will turn **his cheek to the one who smites** him (Matt 5.39), and he will accept his **reproach** (v 61) in all its fullness (Psa 69.7). "If, when you do good and suffer, you will endure, this finds favor with God" (1 Pet 2.20; Jas 1.12). To do that is to follow in the steps of the One who said, when facing the heaviest yoke ever imposed on any human being, "Not My will, but Yours be done" (Luke 22.42; 1 Pet 2.21–23).

> **He will sit alone, and he will be still... he will set... he will give... he will be filled.** All these Yiqtol verb-forms could also be construed as expressing obligation (jussives; GKC §48*b*; IBHS §31.5): "let him sit alone and keep silence... let him put... let him give... let him be filled" (ASV). In a situation of this kind there is no definite boundary between those two options, because in such a situation what will be is generally the same as what should be.

> **He has laid [*ntl*] *it* on him.** The LORD also laid [*ntl*] on David the choice of three things (famine, enemies, pestilence) when he had sinned (2 Sam 24.12). David bore this patiently, because he knew that he had sinned (2 Sam 24.10).

3.31 For *the* LORD will not cast out
　　　to lasting time;
3.32 for if He causes grief, then He will have compassion,
　　　in accordance with *the* abundance of His lovingkindnesses,
3.33 for He does not afflict from His heart
　　　and grieve *the* sons of man.

The afflicted people of Jerusalem could accept the yoke that was imposed on them (vv 27–30) **for** the reason that **the LORD** would **not cast** them **out** permanently. That was what He had promised them through His prophets: "In an overflow of anger I have hidden My face from you for a moment, but with lasting lovingkindness I will have compassion on you" (Isa 54.8; Jer 12.15; 31.20; 33.25–26). Yes, there are circumstances when He does cast people out permanently—"many" people (Luke 13.24–25; cf. 2 Chr 28.9; Deut 29.20). Even the ten northern tribes of Israel had been cast out permanently; but Judah herself would not be: "I will no longer proceed to have compassion on the house of Israel... but I will have compassion on the house of Judah, and I will save them by the LORD their God" (Hos 1.6–7). To this day, whenever someone of Jewish ancestry turns to the Lord, it is proof that "God has not cast out His people whom He foreknew" (see Rom 11.1–2).

No people (**sons of man**) can hope to escape sorrow and suffering in this life. At times the LORD will indeed **afflict** and **grieve** them (cf. v 38).

But He will always **have compassion** on them again, if they return to Him (v 40). "Let the wicked one leave his way, and the man of iniquity his thoughts; and let him return to the LORD, and He will have compassion on him" (Isa 55.7; Prov 28.13; Deut 30.1–3). He does this because of the **abundance of His lovingkindnesses** (Isa 63.7; Psa 106.44–46). That is the very basis on which we can appeal to Him for forgiveness: "Show favor to me, God, in accordance with Your lovingkindness; in accordance with the abundance of Your compassions, wipe out my transgressions" (Psa 51.1; 69.13; Neh 13.22).

> **From His heart** *(mlbw)*. Most English versions interpret this phrase as a statement that the LORD does not do these things "willingly" (KJV) or does not "enjoy" doing them (HCSB). However, nowhere else does such a phrase have any such meaning. Elsewhere in the Scriptures, to do something **from** one's **heart** is generally to do it on one's own initiative (Num 16.28; 24.13; Ezek 13.2, 17; Neh 6.8). This supports Rashi's explanation: the LORD is imposing this affliction because of people's sins (v 39), not because of anything that originated within Himself *(mrṣwnw)*. We cannot blame His heart or His will for our problems (cf. Jas 1.13–14; Prov 19.3). "Because of their way of transgression, and because of their sins, foolish people afflict themselves" *(ytʿnw*, a self-referential [Hithpaʿel] form; Psa 107.17). "The LORD's hand is not shortened so that it cannot save, and His ear is not heavy so that it cannot hear; but your iniquities have been separating between you and your God, and your sins have made Him hide His face from you, so that He does not hear" (Isa 59.1–2). So, when Jerusalem was suffering terribly at the hands of the Babylonians, the cause was her own sin: "Your iniquities have turned these things away, and your sins have kept good back from you" (Jer 5.25). "Have you not done this to yourself, by your forsaking the LORD your God?" (Jer 2.17).

3.34 To crush beneath his feet
    all of *those* of *the* land *who are* in bondage,
3.35 to turn away a man's justice
    before *the* face of *the* High One,

3.36 to deal crookedly with a person in his contention—
has not *the* Lord seen *these things?*

3.37 Who *is* this *who* has said *it,* and it has come to be?
has not *the* Lord commanded *it?*

3.38 from *the* mouth of *the* High One, does there not come out
both the evil *thing*s and the good?

3.39 why does a living person lament,
a man, on account of his sin?

The design of this passage is extraordinary, indeed unique. It begins in a most unusual way, by listing a series of injustices (**To crush beneath his feet... to turn away a man's justice... to deal crookedly with a person,** vv 34–36a) without any preamble that would explain why these acts are being mentioned. While these injustices are being presented in isolation, the reader may wonder whether they are simply examples of human iniquity in general, or whether they are specific iniquities committed either by the people of Jerusalem or by their conquerors. In fact both Jerusalem and her conquerors had done such deeds. The Israelites had **crushed** their poorer brethren (Isa 3.15), turned away **justice** (Isa 10.1–2), and rejected their victims' contentions (Isa 1.23). Generation after generation, the Lord had sent prophets urging the nation to repent of its sins; but the people refused to listen, and finally the Lord raised up the Babylonians to punish them (Jer 51.20–23; Zec 1.2, 6). However, the Babylonians went beyond what was just and right; they themselves did what was unjust (Jer 51.24; Zec 1.15), much as the Israelites had done. They **crushed** the people underfoot (Jer 51.34). They did not treat the people with **justice** (Hab 1.7). They **dealt crookedly** with the people (v 59) and rejected their contentions (Jer 50.34). The LORD told Babylon: "I was angry with My people... and gave them into your hand. You showed them no mercy; you laid your yoke very heavily on the old" (Isa 47.6).

Only after these injustices have been presented, in vv 36b–39, are we told why they have been named: to consider whether such **evil things** have come from the **Lord** (the **High One,** Psa 97.9; Isa 14.14). Presumably, then, the **evil things** under consideration are those done by the conquerors. Nowhere else do the Lamentations ask whether the Lord has rightly allowed *Jerusalem* to do **evil things.** Every section of the book—including this section (cf. vv 31–33)—asks whether the Lord is rightly allowing her *conquerors* to do **evil things.**

Yet in other respects vv 36b–39 are ambiguously worded, so that they can be read in apparently opposite ways. The above translation prints the whole of vv 36b–39 as a series of questions. But in the Hebrew, only vv 37a and 39a are unambiguously marked as questions. All the other clauses could be read either as questions or as statements. This markedly alters the sense of the passage; and yet, remarkably, it makes good sense both ways.

1. Reading the whole of vv 34–39 as questions (cf. Parry 106–15), the passage asks: **Has not the Lord seen** the unjust deeds done to Jerusalem? Indeed He has: "You have seen, Lord, the crooked dealing done to me… You have seen all of their vengeance… You have heard their reproach" (vv 59–61). In fact, "the Lord sees all the sons of Man" and "understands all their works" (Psa 33.13–15) "in every place" (Prov 15.3). Every sin that is committed is done in His presence, **before** His **face** (Hos 7.2). If evil was allowed to happen in Jerusalem, **the Lord** must have **seen** it. If evil had **come to be** in Jerusalem, **the Lord** must have **commanded** it; it must have **come out** from His **mouth** (Eccl 7.14; Job 2.10). Even when Satan unjustly inflicted evil things on Job, they happened only because the Lord's command permitted this (Job 1.12; 2.6). "If there is an evil in a city, then hasn't the Lord done it?" (Amos 3.6; Isa 45.7; see also the comments on 2.6). So when a **man**, a **living person**, suffers **on account of his sin, why** should he **lament**? His sufferings have been authorized by the Lord. Even at worst, they are only what he deserves (1 Pet 2.20); and often they are less than he deserves (as was the case with the Babylonian destruction of Jerusalem, terrible though it was: Ezra 9.13). Therefore his attitude should be: "I will bear the indignation of the Lord, because I have sinned against Him" (Mic 7.9).

2. Reading only vv 37a and 39a as questions (cf. Renkema 294–305/411–26), the passage declares: "The Lord has not seen these things! Who is this who has said it, and it has come to be? The Lord has not commanded it! From the mouth of the High One, there does not come out evil, but good! Why does a living person lament? Let a man lament on account of his own sin." This may sound practically the opposite of the previous option, yet it too is fully consistent with Scripture. The Scriptures describe the Lord as seeing all things—but they also describe Him as refusing to see wickedness

(4.16; Hab 1.13; Psa 34.15–16; cf. 2 Kgs 3.14). The Scriptures describe even Satan as accomplishing his evil deeds only by the Lord's permissive command—but they also describe sinners as doing evils that the Lord never **commanded** (Jer 7.31; 32.35). In that sense, only **good,** and not **evil,** ever comes out **from the mouth of the High One** (Psa 5.4; 119.68; 145.9; Jas 1.17). **Why** then should a **living person lament?** Not because of anything that God has done, but rather because of his own **sin** (Jas 1.13–15).

3. Many English versions construe the passage in ways that lie somewhere between the previous two options. They read some of the ambiguous clauses as questions, but others as statements. The commonest of these variations are discussed in the small print paragraphs below.

Wherever the Spirit of God has tied a knot in the text of Scripture, making the sense difficult to unravel, we may be sure that He has some good reason for doing so. In the first place, this knot acts "to slow the reading process down and to require our closer attention" (Dobbs-Allsopp 121). But it has other effects too. The Lord could have issued a straightforward explanatory statement or command here ("You shall not lament about injustices, because…"). But He did not. First He merely listed the injustices, without previously explaining why He was listing them—so that the reader is forced to puzzle over the list for himself. And even when He did explain why He was listing them, He did not simply tell the reader what to conclude. He gave the explanation (at least partly) in the form of ambiguously worded questions (**Why does a living person lament…?**)—so that the reader is still forced to supply the answers himself. (Compare the Lord's stunning barrage of questions to Job in Job chapters 38–41, which forced Job to draw the conclusions himself.) But whatever avenue we may explore while reading this passage, the final answer is the same. If we say that the Lord has **seen** and **commanded** the **evil things** that have happened to Jerusalem—then the conclusion will be that the sufferer has no reason to **lament.** Yet if we say that the Lord has **not seen** and **not commanded** these **evil things**—then the conclusion will again be that the sufferer has no reason to **lament.** The road traveled along the way may be different, but it does not alter the destination.

> **To crush beneath his feet… to turn away a man's justice… to deal crookedly with a person.** Such a series of clauses would

ordinarily be preceded by a verb (as in, e.g., Jer 44.3; JM §124*o*). Therefore a few translations construe these clauses with the verbs that precede them (in v 33): "He does not torment capriciously, nor afflict man, to crush under His feet all the prisoners of the earth, to deny a man justice in the presence of the Most High, to wrong a man in his conflict; the Lord does not approve" of these things (Stone). However, the statement "He does not do X in the presence of the Most High" would be grammatically awkward ("… in His presence" would be expected); and what would be the point of saying it at all? Could the Lord ever do anything other than in His own presence?

Beneath his feet. Beneath the crusher's feet. All of our Lord's enemies must be placed beneath His feet (1 Cor 15.25), but in the present passage the **feet** are probably the evildoer's feet (cf. Isa 51.23; Jer 51.34), because the corresponding clauses in the next two verses describe acts of injustice by evildoers (**to turn away a man's justice… to deal crookedly with a person in his contention**).

In bondage. A form of the same word is used to describe the chaining of King Zedekiah by the Babylonians (Jer 39.7; 40.1).

Deal crookedly with (*'wt;* another form of the word appears in v 59). "Make crooked" (NASB mg), the opposite of making straight (Ecc 1.15; 7.13); in Spanish, *trastornar* (VRV 1602–1960). "The Almighty will not deal crookedly with justice" (Job 34.12), but "the way of the wicked He makes crooked" (Psa 146.9).

Contention *(ryb).* A disputed "cause" (KJV) or "conflict" (Stone) involving a question of "justice" (NJB), either between nations or between individuals (e.g., between Israel and Ammon in the days of Jephthah, Jdg 12.2; between Saul and David, 1 Sam 24.15; between Abram's and Lot's herdsmen, Gen 13.7–8). Not necessarily a "lawsuit" (NASB): see NIDOTTE 3.1105–06. In the present context the reference would be mainly to the conflict between Jerusalem and her enemies (vv 52–53). The Lord had promised her, "I will contend with the one who contends with you" (Isa 49.25; Jer 50.34; 51.36).

Has not the Lord seen these things? who is this who has said it, and it has come to be? has not the Lord commanded it?

As noted above, the first and last clauses could also be read as statements: "The Lord has not seen these things! Who is this who has said it, and it has come to be? The Lord has not commanded it!" However, many English versions take a third approach. They construe the first clause as a statement but the last clause as a question: "The Lord does not approve [of the evils described in vv 34–36]. Who is he who speaks and it comes to pass, when the Lord has not commanded it?" (NKJV). Nevertheless, the Hebrew wording of the two clauses is identical except for the verb itself (**seen** in v 36, **commanded** in v 37), and they occupy identical positions in immediately adjacent verses; so it is scarcely credible that they would have different functions.

Who is this who has said it, and it has come to be? has not the Lord commanded it? In the Hebrew, the verse closely echoes Psa 33.9: "He Himself has said it, and it is; He Himself has commanded it, and it stands."

Evil *(r')* can refer either to wickedness (as in Jer 1.16, etc.) or to "adversity" (HCSB; as in Lam 1.21, etc.). Here the reference is to the adversity caused by the acts of wickedness mentioned in vv 34–36: **to crush beneath his feet… to turn away a man's justice… to deal crookedly with a person.**

The evil things are plural *(hr'wt)*, whereas **the good** is singular *(htwb)*. Overall, the good done by the Lord is far more abundant than any amount of evil (cf. Rom 5.17, 20–21), but the people of Jerusalem are currently experiencing far more evil than good ("I have forgotten goodness," v 17).

A living person. "Whoever is joined to the living, there is hope" (Ecc 9.4); he may still be reconciled to the Lord (v 40). "As long as God spares a man's life why does he murmur? The chastisement is really for his good; only let him use it aright, and he will be thankful for it in the end" (Payne Smith 596).

Lament *(yt'wnn)*. A Hithpo'lel form of *'nn* (related to *'nh*; cf. HALOT 1.72). Related forms, "lamenting and lamentation [*t'nyh w'nyh*]," occur in 2.5. The Hithpo'lel itself appears elsewhere in Num 11.1 ("The people were lamenting of evil in the ears of the LORD") and Sir 10.25 (a wise person "will not lament").

A man [*gbr*]**, on account of his sin.** The LBLA construes *gbr* as an adjective, "mighty" (as in Gen 10.8–9), and renders the line *¡[Sea] valiente frente a sus pecados!* ("[Let him be] mighty against his sins!"). But if that had been the meaning, the jussive *ygbr* would have been expected.

His sin *(ḥṭ'w).* The Masoretic text (K), supported by LXX, has the singular form *ḥṭ'w* (**his sin**); the Masoretic margin (Q), supported by Syr and Vg, has the plural form *ḥṭ'yw* ("his sins"). Moreover, Hebrew *ḥṭ'* can refer either to sin itself or to the punishment for sin (see the comments on 4.6). Thus v 39 could mean either "Why does a living person lament on account of the punishment for his sin?" (accepting the singular form) or "Why does a living person lament? [Let] him [lament] on account of his sin(s)" (accepting either the singular or the plural).

3.40 Let us search our ways, and let us search *them* out,
　　　　and let us return to *the* LORD;
3.41 let us lift up our heart to *our* hands
　　　　to God in *the* heavens;
3.42 *as for* us—we have transgressed, and we have rebelled;
　　　　as for You†—You† have not forgiven.

The sufferer here recognizes that the people of Jerusalem **have transgressed** and **rebelled** against God, and that God has **not** yet **forgiven** their sins. They need to **search** their **ways** and **return to the** LORD (see on 5.21), praying to Him (lifting up their **hands** to Him, Psa 141.2; 1 Tim 2.8) and obeying Him from the heart (lifting up their **heart** to Him).

All of us have an obligation to **search our ways,** to see whether we are in the LORD; and if we are not, to **return** to Him. "Test yourselves, if you are in the faith; examine yourselves" (2 Cor 13.5; 1 Cor 11.28). "Come near to God, and He will come near to you; cleanse your hands, you sinful ones, and purify your hearts, you two-souled ones" (Jas 4.8). "Let the wicked one leave his way, and the man of iniquity his thoughts; and let him return to the LORD, and He will have compassion on him; and to our God, and He will multiply to forgive" (Isa 55.7).

Recognizing that one has sinned is not enough to obtain forgiveness. It also requires action—action with the **hands** and action with the **heart.**

Under the new covenant, those who are already God's people, and who sin against Him, are required to pray (**lift up… our hands to God**) in order to be forgiven: "Repent therefore of this wickedness of yours, and pray to God, if indeed the thought of your heart may be forgiven you" (Acts 8.22). So it was for Israel under the old covenant: "You will call upon Me, and go and pray to Me, and I will hear you; and you will seek Me and find Me, when you search for Me with all your heart" (Jer 29.12–13).

As that last passage shows, the Lord must be sought "with all your heart." It is not enough solely to **lift up… our hands to** Him in prayer; we must **lift up our heart** as well (cf. Psa 25.1; 86.4; 143.8). We are to love Him with all our heart (Mark 12.30 ≡ Deut 6.5), and to be "obedient from the heart" to His teaching (Rom 6.17). Those who "honor Me with their lips, but their heart is far away from Me" cannot please Him (Matt 15.8 ≡ Isa 29.13; Psa 78.36–37).

> **Let us lift up our heart to [**'*l*]** our hands to [**'*l*]** God.** When the hands are raised **to** God, the heart should be raised **to** them also (Keil 601/420). "Let us lift up our heart as well as our hands to God" (NRSV) is a less plausible rendering, since it treats two immediately successive instances of the preposition '*l* in two different ways.

3.43 You[†] have covered *us* with anger, and You[†] have pursued us;
    You[†] have killed; You[†] have not spared;
3.44 You[†] have covered Yourself[†] with a cloud,
    from *the* passing over of entreaty;
3.45 You[†] have set us *as* offscouring and refuse
    in *the* midst of the peoples.

So far, the Lord has not forgiven the people of Judah (v 42). On the contrary, He has **covered** them with His **anger,** just as He had warned many centuries earlier: "They will forsake Me and break My covenant…. And My anger will burn against them, and I will forsake them and hide My face from them… and many evils and afflictions will find them" (Deut 31.16–17). He has **pursued** them (Jer 29.18) by sending "pursuers" against them (see the comments on 1.3). He has **killed** them by the hand of those pursuers (see the comments on 2.21), and has **not spared** them (see the comments on 2.2).

Their sins have hidden His face from them, so that He will no longer hear their **entreaty** (see the comments on v 8; Isa 59.1–2; Ezek 39.23–24). "The prayer of the humble one pierces the clouds" (Sir 35 [32].21), whereas these people find their **entreaty** blocked by a **cloud,** so that it cannot pass over to the Lord—just as He had told His prophets: "They will cry out in My ear with a great voice, and I will not hear them" (Ezek 8.18). "Do not make an entreaty for this people, and do not lift up an outcry or entreaty for them; for I will not hear in the time when they call to Me" (Jer 11.14; 14.11–12). They are merely discarded rubbish, **offscouring** (*shy,* like dirt scraped off a wall, Ezek 26.4) and **refuse** (*m'ws,* material that is "rejected," 5.22). They had rejected the word of the Lord (Jer 6.19; 8.9; Ezek 5.6), and therefore He had rejected them (Jer 7.29; cf. Hos 4.6). "They will call them 'rejected silver,' for the Lord has rejected them" (Jer 6.30). "One who turns aside his ear from hearing the Law, even his entreaty is an abomination" (Prov 28.9) and will not be heard by the Lord (Prov 15.29).

> **You have covered… You have pursued us; You have killed; You have not spared.** The suffix -*ny* (**us**) applies to all four verbs, as often in Hebrew (cf., in this chapter, vv 2, 5, 66: "You will pursue [them] in anger, and You will destroy them"; JM §125*x*). Some English versions treat the first verb as self-referential ("Thou hast covered Thyself with anger," NASB), but in Hebrew that would require the addition of *lk* ("Yourself"), as in the next verse (v 44).

3.46 They have opened their mouth against us,
    all of our enemies;
3.47 dread and *the* pit have come to us,
    devastation and crushing;
3.48 *with* streams of waters my eye has run down,
    because of *the* crushing of *the* daughter of my people.

3.49 My eye has poured out and does not cease,
    far from *any* slackening,
3.50 until *the* Lord looks down and sees
    from *the* heavens;
3.51 my eye has dealt severely with my soul,
    because of all of *the* daughters of my city.

Not only were the people of Judah mocked by the invading **enemies** (who **opened their mouth against** them, 2.16), but they also suffered **devastation** (like a city that is left uninhabited, Isa 6.11) and **crushing** (like bones crushed by a lion, Isa 38.13; see the comments on 2.11). They faced **dread and the pit**—elsewhere listed as two of the major punishments for a sinful nation ("The one who flees from the sound of the dread will fall in the pit," Isa 24.17–18; Jer 48.43–44). Those who dread the LORD and heed His word (Psa 119.120) have no reason to dread anything on earth (Prov 3.24–25; 1.33; Psa 91.5). When He led Israel from Egypt to the promised land, "they did not dread" (Psa 78.53); instead, the dread of them fell on all the surrounding nations (Deut 2.25; 11.25). But now the situation was reversed. Those who had "no dread of God" (Psa 36.1) were subjected to a **dread** and destruction from which He did not defend them (Prov 1.26–27). So it will be on the last day (2 Thes 1.8–9; 2 Pet 3.7).

Because of those terrible punishments, the sufferer weeps **streams of waters** without ceasing (1.2, 16; 2.11, 18; Jer 9.1; 13.17). His weeping is so intense that it **has dealt severely with** his **soul** (cf. Psa 6.6)—a powerfully negative expression (see the comments on 1.12), which is not easy to translate in English ("hath wasted my soul," DRCV; "torment my soul," NAB). In the same way our Lord Himself wept, foreseeing the later destruction of Jerusalem by the Romans (Luke 19.41–44). In the same way Paul wept over "the enemies of the cross of Christ, whose end is destruction" (Php 3.18–19; Rom 9.1–3). Which one of us has never suffered the pain of witnessing beloved friends, relatives, or neighbors on the path to destruction? "With streams of waters my eyes have run down, because they have not kept Your Law" (Psa 119.136).

The sufferer would continue to weep **until** the LORD **looks down** from heaven to restore His people (Psa 80.14–15; Deut 26.15; cf. 1 Kgs 8.35–39; Dan 9.16–19). "The LORD has looked down from the heavens… to hear the groaning of the one in bondage, to free the sons of death" (Psa 102.19–20).

> **Far from any slackening** (see the notes on 2.18). The Hebrew uses, in effect, a double negative (*m-* plus *'yn*) to convey emphasis: *m'yn hpgwt*, "*away from* there *not* being a slackening" (cf. Isa 5.9; 6.11; GKC §152*y*).
>
> **Because of the crushing of the daughter of my people** [v 48]… **because of all of the daughters of my city** [v 51]. The two lines

stand in corresponding positions at the end of successive stanzas; therefore, both presumably refer to the sufferings of the city's young women (a prominent concern in this book: 1.4, 18; 2.20, 21; 5.11). The term **daughters** is sometimes applied to the villages surrounding a city (Num 21.25; Jer 49.2), but that is not likely here; throughout Lamentations the focus of attention is fixed firmly on Jerusalem herself (no other city of Judah is even named).

3.52 They have hunted me like a bird,
    my enemies, for no reason;
3.53 they have consumed my life in *the* well-hole,
    and they have cast stone against me;
3.54 waters have flowed over my head;
    I have said, "I have been cut off."

3.55 I have called on Your† name, LORD,
    from a well-hole of *the* lowest places;
3.56 my voice You† have heard; do not hide† Your ear
    to my breathing, to my cry for help;
3.57 You† have come near in *the* day *when* I have been calling on You†;
    You† have said, "You† shall not fear."

Again (as in vv 1–18) the sufferer's hardships are described in a vivid diversity of ways (see the comments on vv 10–15). He has been **hunted** (as a **bird** is hunted, Psa 124.6–7) by enemies **for no reason,** like Jesus ("Those who hate me for no reason have abounded," Psa 69.4 ≡ John 15.25), David (1 Sam 19.5), and other righteous people, generation after generation (Prov 1.10–13). He has been put into a **well-hole of the lowest places** (Psa 88.4), like Joseph (twice: Gen 37.24; 40.15; 41.14) and Jeremiah (twice: Jer 37.15–16; 38.6–13). **Waters have flowed over** him, as they did over Jesus (Psa 69.1–2, 14–15) and Jonah (Jnh 2.3–6). His life has been **consumed, cut off**—also terms that are applied to the sufferings of Jesus (Psa 69.4 ≡ John 15.25; Psa 119.139 ≡ John 2.17; Isa 53.8 ≡ Acts 8.33). Whatever afflictions, distresses, persecutions, or punishments we may be required to undergo in this life, we will never experience anything that our Master has not undergone as well (Heb 4.15; 2.14–18).

Jerusalem was being punished for a very clear reason—"because of the abundance of her transgressions" (see the comments on 1.5)—but her punishment also caused suffering **for no reason** to people who had not been guilty of those transgressions, either because they had consistently opposed the nation's evil, like Jeremiah, or because they were too young to know anything of it, like the babies in the city (see the comments on 1.5; 2.11–12). Yet even when we suffer **for no reason,** we are simply walking in the path that our Master also trod (1 Pet 2.19–24; 3.18).

In the time of his distress (in the **well-hole**), the sufferer has **called on** the LORD for **help.** Even while he is pleading with the LORD to hear (**do not hide Your ear**), he knows that he is indeed heard (**my voice You have heard**). No **lowest places** are so low, or so dark, that the LORD cannot **come near** and answer a prayer offered in accordance with His will (Psa 130.1–2; 139.11–12; 138.6–8; Jnh 2.2). "The LORD is near to all those who call on Him, to all who call on Him in faithfulness" (Psa 145.18; 34.18). We today have the same promise: "Come near to God, and He will come near to you" (Jas 4.8). "This is the confidence that we have before Him, that if we may ask anything in accordance with His will, He hears us; and if we know that He hears us in whatever we may ask, we know that we have the asked things that we asked from Him" (1 Jn 5.14–15).

The LORD has said to the sufferer, **"You shall not fear."** That is what He told Jeremiah when He first called him to be a prophet: "Do not be fearful of their faces, for I am with you to deliver you" (Jer 1.8). That was what He told all His faithful people under the old covenant (Isa 35.4; 41.10–14; 43.1–2, 5; Isa 51.7–8; 54.4). And it is what He tells all His faithful people under the new covenant: "He Himself has said, 'I will not leave you at all, nor will I forsake you at all'—so that we ourselves boldly say, 'The Lord is my helper; I will not fear; what will Man do to me?'" (Heb 13.5–6; Luke 12.4–5; Rev 2.10).

> Most of the actions in vv 52–63 are reported in Qaṭal verb-forms, which usually describe actions that happened prior to the text's reference point (Joosten 193–223): **They have hunted me… they have consumed my life… they have cast stone against me.** Three times, however, the text moves between a Qaṭal form and a form that apparently asks the LORD for a future action on the same subject: **My voice You have heard** [Qaṭal]; **do not hide Your ear** [Yiqṭol with jussive meaning; v 56].… **You have contended, LORD, for the contentions** [Qaṭal]… **judge my judgment** [imperative; vv 58–59].… **You**

have seen all of their vengeance [Qaṭal]**... look on their sitting** [imperative; vv 60, 63]. This has been explained in several ways:

1. The sufferer mentions past (Qaṭal) actions as a foundation for his prayer for future actions ("as You have heard my voice in the past, so do not hide Your ear from me now"). Compare: "Pardon [imperative] the sin of this people... as You have forgiven [Qaṭal] the sin of this people from Egypt even till now" (Num 14.19).

2. The sufferer describes future actions in Qaṭal forms because he knows they have already been determined in the will of God. Compare: "Babylon has fallen [Qaṭal].... Call [imperative] against her the kingdoms" (Jer 51.8, 27; cf. Rev 18.2, 21; Lam 4.22). See Joosten 207–08; Rogland, *Alleged Non-Past Uses of Qatal in Classical Hebrew*, §3.4.5.

3. The Qaṭal forms express prayers for future action, just as the imperatives and jussives do: "Hear my voice—do not close Your ears" (Hillers 112). However, it is doubtful whether Qaṭal forms can express prayers or wishes unless there is some preliminary marker, e.g., "If only [*lw*] we had died [Qaṭal]" (Num 14.2). See JM §112*k;* Joosten 211–12.

4. The jussive in v 56 does not express a future prayer, but merely quotes the content of the past (Qaṭal) prayer: "You have heard my voice: 'Do not close Your ear'" (NKJV). However, this explanation would not account for the imperatives in vv 59 and 63.

For no reason could be construed either with **hunted** (they have hunted me for no reason; cf. Psa 119.161) or with **enemies** (they are my enemies for no reason; cf. Psa 69.4).

Consumed. The Hebrew word *(ṣmt)* is translated into Greek as *kataphagetai*, "consume" (John 2.17 ≡ Psa 119.139); its basic idea may possibly be "silencing in a more or less permanent way" (NIDOTTE 3.819), although there is no definite evidence of that in the Scriptures. It does not imply death (Jesus did not die when he was "consumed" by zeal, Psa 119.139 ≡ John 2.17, and the sufferer here did not die when his life was **consumed** in the well-hole; cf. vv 55–57).

They have cast stone against me. The expression *ydh 'bn b-*, "cast stone against," can only describe the punishment of stoning, as in "All Israel cast stone against [*b-*] him" (1 Kgs 12.18). In these passages, as in Lev 20.2, 27, the singular form **stone** *('bn)* indicates the number of substances used (one substance, **stone**), not the number of items of that substance. Therefore the rendering "threw a stone at me" (Green) understates the severity of the act. "Placed a stone on me" (NASB) would require the preposition *'l* (as in Gen 29.2–3; Josh 7.26; 10.27; 2 Sam 18.17; Dan 6.17) or *'l* (Josh 10.18).

My voice you have heard. The Lord does not hear the entreaties of those who are in their sins (v 44), but He does hear those who repent of their sins and seek His forgiveness (2 Chr 7.14).

Do not hide Your ear to [*l-*] **my breathing** [*rwḥty*]**, to** [*l-*] **my cry for help.** Three main ways of rendering this clause have been suggested:

1. The two *l*-phrases are grammatically parallel, and therefore would be expected to have comparable meanings. This suggests that *rwḥh* is a form of *rwḥ*, "breath" (4.20; Gen 7.22; Exod 15.8; etc.), and means something like **breathing** (KJV) or "sighing" (NKJV).

2. Elsewhere *rwḥh* occurs elsewhere only in Exod 8.15, where it must mean "relief," "respite." If that is the meaning in the present passage, then the two *l*-phrases cannot be parallel, and the sense must be "for [*l-*] my relief [i.e., in order to relieve me], do not hide Your ear to [*l-*] my cry for help" (cf. NIV). However, the Hebrew word order is against this. Nowhere else in the Hebrew Scriptures does a statement of purpose ("for my relief") separate such an action ("do not hide Your ear") from its object ("to my cry for help").

3. Occasionally *rwḥh* has been rendered "[prayer for] relief" (NASB), in order to preserve the parallel with **cry for help.** However, there is no evidence elsewhere that *rwḥh* can have any such meaning.

3.58 You[†] have contended, LORD, for *the* contentions of my soul;
You[†] have redeemed my life;

3.59 You† have seen, Lord, *the* crooked dealing *done* to me;
     judge† my judgment;
3.60 You† have seen all of their vengeance,
     all of their plans for me.

3.61 You† have heard their reproach, Lord,
     all of their plans against me;
3.62 *the* lips of *those* who stand against me, and their murmuring,
     are against me all of the day;
3.63 look† on their sitting and their standing;
     I *am* their music.

The sufferer appeals to what the Lord has **seen** and **heard**: the **plans** of those who **stand against** him, their **reproach,** their **vengeance,** and their **crooked dealing.** Whether evildoers are **sitting** or **standing,** they are doing evil (Mic 2.1; Isa 59.7–8), in contrast to the righteous (Deut 11.18–19)—but the Lord has **seen** it all (Psa 139.1–4).

When Jerusalem was destroyed, her people became "a reproach to those who dwell near us, a mockery and a scorn to those round about us" (Psa 79.4; Jer 51.51; Ezek 5.14–15; 22.4; Dan 9.16; Neh 1.3; 4.4). In that time of distress, their enemies took **vengeance** on them (Ezek 25.12, 15), dealt crookedly with them (v 36), and mocked them with **music** (cf. v 14). The sufferer asks the Lord to **look on** these things and deliver him, contending for his **contentions** (see the comments on v 36) and judging his **judgment.**

"Judge me, God; contend for my contention from a nation that is not lovingkind; deliver me from a man of deceit and injustice" (Psa 43.1). The righteous do not **contend** for their own **contentions.** Often their oppressors are stronger than they themselves are. But even if the righteous had the power to take vengeance on their oppressors, they would not; they would wait for the Lord to **contend** and **judge** for them (1 Sam 25.39; 24.15; Psa 35.1–3; 43.1; 119.154; cf. Rom 12.19). And however strong their oppressors may be, the Lord is even stronger (Prov 23.10–11; 22.22–23; cf. Luke 11.21–22; 1 Cor 1.25).

The sufferer already knows that the Lord has **seen** his sufferings (Psa 10.14), **contended** with his oppressors, and **redeemed** his **life** from the threat of death (Psa 103.4). The prophets had promised that the Lord would do those things when Jerusalem was destroyed by the Babylonians:

"Their Redeemer is strong; the LORD of Hosts is His name. Contending, He will contend for their contention... and He will agitate those who dwell in Babylon" (Jer 51.35–36; 50.33–34).

> **Redeemed** *(g'l)*. To redeem is to buy back something that has fallen into someone else's possession (Lev 25.25–27, 47–52). When the Israelites fell into slavery in Egypt, the LORD "redeemed them from the hand of the enemy" (Psa 106.10; Exod 6.6). He has the power to redeem a **life** even from death (Psa 103.4; Hos 13.14 ≡ 1 Cor 15.54–57); so, when the **life** of this sufferer seemed to be "cut off" and "brought... to an end" (vv 53–54), He **redeemed** it.
>
> **Crooked dealing** *('wth)* is the opposite of straightness (see the comments on v 36); "the bending of the law against me" (HALOT 2.802).
>
> **Judge my judgment.** "Shall not the Judge of all the earth do judgment?" (Gen 18.25)—unlike evildoers, who "do not judge the judgment of the needy" (Jer 5.28).
>
> **Their plans** *(mḥšbtm,* an *m*-prefixed form of *ḥšb*). The LORD "planned [*ḥšb*] to destroy the wall of the daughter of Zion" (2.8)—but those whom He raised up to carry out that plan had other **plans** of their own, which were not pleasing to Him (cf. Gen 50.20); see the comments on 2.6.
>
> **Their plans for me** [*ly,* v 60]... **their plans against me** [*'ly,* v 61]. The first preposition is neutral ("in regard to me"), and could in itself describe either a positive act (e.g., "one who comforts for me [*ly*]," 1.21) or a negative one (as here). The second preposition has more strongly negative connotations ("over against me"): "He has built against me [*'ly*]" (v 5); "He has called against me [*'ly*] an appointed assembly, to crush my young men" (1.15).
>
> **Reproach** *(ḥrph;* see the comments on 5.1). Jesus Himself suffered reproach (Psa 22.6–7; 69.7–10, 19–20 ≡ Rom 15.3), and so do all those who walk in His steps—whether before His first coming (Heb 11.26; Jer 15.15; 20.8) or after it (Heb 13.13; Matt 5.11; 1 Pet 4.14). Those who reproach the LORD's people are reproaching Him (Prov 17.5; 1 Sam 17.10, 45).
>
> **Murmuring** *(hgywn).* Or "growling"; the sound of a dove (Isa 38.14; 59.11) or a lion (Isa 31.4). "Their heart murmurs de-

struction, and their lips speak trouble" (Prov 24.2; Isa 59.3, 13). Sometimes translated "thoughts" (ESV), but it is usually, as here, an act done with the mouth, tongue, or **lips** (HALOT 1.237; TDOT 3.322–23, §II*e;* TWOT 1.468).

3.64 You† will give back to them for *their* dealing, LORD,
    in accordance with *the* work of their hands;
3.65 You† will give to them shielding of heart;
    Your† sworn oath *will be* against them;
3.66 You† will pursue *them* in anger, and You† will destroy them
    from beneath *the* heavens of *the* LORD.

The evildoer will reap as he has sown (Prov 22.8; Gal 6.7–8): "he has loved cursing, and it will come to him" (Psa 109.17–20). The **LORD** would **pursue** Jerusalem's enemies **in anger** and **destroy** them (4.21–22); those who had cast Jerusalem down would themselves be cast down (Zec 1.15, 18–21).

"God's anger is revealed from heaven against all irreverence and un-righteousness of people" (Rom 1.18), and "He destroys all the wicked ones" (Psa 145.20). He "will give back to each one **in accordance with** his **works**," so that "every soul of Man doing evil," and "not obeying the truth but obeying unrighteousness," will receive "anger and indignation, affliction and distress" (Rom 2.6–8; Matt 16.27; 2 Cor 5.10; Rev 22.12; Jer 17.10). "The **dealing** of his **hands** will be done to him" (Isa 3.11).

> **You will give back to them… You will give to them… You will pursue them… You will destroy them.** All four Yiqtol verb-forms could also be construed as entreaties (jussives; GKC §48*b;* IBHS §31.5): "Render unto them… give them… persecute and destroy them" (KJV). There is little practical difference in meaning, because what the LORD **will** do is the same as what we should entreat Him to do if we are praying in accordance with His will (1 Jn 5.14). Jesus Himself tells us that God's chosen people entreat Him day and night for vengeance *(ekdikēsin),* and that He will indeed do it (Luke 18.7–8). "It is a righteous thing for God to give back affliction to those who afflict you… at the revealing of the Lord Jesus from heaven with His mighty angels in a fire of flame, giving vengeance

[*ekdikēsin*] to those who do not know God and to those who do not obey the gospel of our Lord Jesus" (2 Thes 1.6–8). Everyone who prays for His will to be done (Matt 6.10) is, in effect, praying for this, since it is part of His will.

Shielding of heart. A unique expression (with *mgnh*, a form of *mgn*, "shield," as in 2 Chr 17.17; 32.5; Jer 46.9; like the scales of Leviathan, Job 41.15). Like a hardening (Exod 4.21; Deut 2.30; Rom 9.18) or a veil (2 Cor 3.15), a shield prevents the heart from being pierced (cf. Eph 6.16). To make people's hearts hardened, veiled, and shielded against His word is one of the terrible punishments imposed by the LORD on those who disobey Him, so that they are unable to turn to Him and be healed (John 12.40; cf. Josh 11.20).

Your sworn oath (with *t'lh*, a *t*-prefixed form of *'lh*, "swear an oath," as in 1 Kgs 8.31). Just as the LORD has sworn solemnly to bless His faithful servants (Gen 22.16–18; Psa 89.35–37), so He has sworn solemnly to destroy His enemies (Exod 17.16; Psa 95.11; 1 Sam 3.14; Isa 14.24–27; Jer 49.13).

LAMENTATIONS 4

Summary
Verses 1–20 mourn over the afflictions of Jerusalem. Those who used to be prosperous are now starving and desolate, wandering in her streets and far off among the nations. The LORD has poured out His fury on her because of the sins of her priests and prophets. Her people have watched for help in vain; they have been hunted down by their pursuers.

Each of the other four Lamentations ends with a prayer directly addressed to the LORD (1.20–22; 2.20–22; 3.55–66; 5.19–22), but in this chapter the pattern is varied. It ends, not with a prayer addressed to the LORD, but with a prophecy foretelling the future, addressed to Israel's closest neighbor, Edom (vv 21–22). Jerusalem will not continue to be exiled, whereas Edom, whose sins are exposed, will drink the cup of the LORD's anger herself.

4.1 How *the* gold is darkened,
>   the good gold is changed;
> stones of holiness pour themselves out
>   at *the* head of all of *the* streets.

4.2 The precious sons of Zion,
>   those who were weighed against gold,
> how they have been accounted as jugs of earthenware,
>   *the* work of *the* hands of a potter.

When Jerusalem's inhabitants (**sons**) served the LORD faithfully, they were holy and **precious** in His sight (Jer 2.3; Psa 116.15)—like the Son whom Jerusalem rejected (Isa 28.16 ≡ 1 Pet 2.6; Acts 3.14), and those who follow faithfully in His steps today (1 Pet 2.5, 9). But when they disobeyed Him and suffered at the hands of the Babylonians, they were tarnished (**darkened, changed** in appearance: see vv 7–8) and were reduced in value to mere **earthenware** vessels (vessels "for dishonor," contrasted with **gold**, and destined to be destroyed, 2 Tim 2.20; Rom 9.21–22; Jer 19.11). **All of** the city's **streets** were strewn with the sufferers and the dead (see the notes on 2.21, 19).

> **Gold.** The passage uses three different words: *rhb* (v 1a), *ktm* (v 1b), *pz* (v 2). The three are used interchangeably in the Scriptures, and all refer to the same substance (*zhb* of Ophir, 1 Kgs 9.28; *ktm* of Ophir, Isa 13.12; *ktm pz*, Song 5.11; *zhb* and *pz*, Psa 19.10; *zhb* and *ktm*, Job 31.24). Payne Smith (599) suggests that *pz* refers specifically to solid gold—in which case, v 2 would contrast not only gold with earthenware, but also the solidity of the former with the hollowness of the latter.

> **Holiness** (*qdš*, as in Jer 2.3, etc.). The rendering "holy place" (Smith) is also possible (as in Exod 26.33, etc.). In that case, v 1 would refer to the "stones of the temple" (HCSB), torn away when the temple was destroyed (as in Luke 21.5–6). However, the description of them strewn **at the head of all of the streets** fits slain humans (2.21) rather than precious materials (which were zealously seized by the conquerors: 1.10; Jer 52.17–23; 2 Chr 36.18); and the precious things in the next verse (v 2) are unambiguously the **sons of Zion.**

> **Pour themselves out.** As in 2.12 and Job 30.16, the Hebrew has a Hithpaʻel verb-form, *tštpknh*. A Hithpaʻel is generally self-referential (**pour themselves out**); it can be simply passive ("are poured out," KJV), but with this verb, the ordinary Niphʻal form would be expected in that case (as in 2.11). Those who disobey God harm themselves (Jer 44.7; 25.7; 26.19; Hab 2.10). "One who sins against me [Wisdom] is wronging his own soul; all those who hate me have loved death" (Prov 8.36).

> **Sons.** Hebrew *bn* is masculine (contrasted with "daughters," Gen 5.4; Jer 3.24), but its plural form often includes both male and female: "the sons of Israel" included "every man and woman" (Exod 35.29).

Who were weighed [*msl'ym*] **against gold.** Jerusalem's inhabitants were so **precious** that they would have counterbalanced
the most precious materials (cf. Job 28.15–19). **Weighed** is
written here with ', but with *h* in Job 28.16, 19 (a difference
of dialect?). Other examples of the interchange of ' and *h* are
listed in GT 1.

4.3 Even tan-animals have drawn out *the* breast;
　　　they have suckled their young *ones*;
the daughter of my people *has become* cruel,
　　　like yaen-birds in *the* wilderness.

4.4 *The* tongue of *the* suckling has stuck
　　　to the palate for thirst;
young children have asked for bread;
　　　there is no *one* dividing *it* for them.

The **animals** and **birds** here can no longer be identified precisely, but this
does not interfere with the sense of the passage. The people of Jerusalem
have become **cruel,** and no longer provide their **young children** with food
(see the comments on 2.11–12), in the way that **even** many animals do
(cf. Prov 6.6–8)—just as the people have failed to know their Master, and
their appointed duties, in the way that many animals do (Isa 1.3; Jer 8.7).

Tan-animals (*tnyn,* K; *tnym,* Q). Nearly all translators have
tried to guess the identity of these animals, but their guesses
have varied considerably. Indeed the three major editions of
the Spanish VRV offer three different translations: *serpientes*
(VRV 1602 ≡ "serpents," Brenton); *monstruos marinos* (VRV
1909 ≡ "sea monsters," KJV; cf. "whales," REB); *chacales* (VRV
1960 ≡ "jackals," ASV). Renkema (358–59/499–501) rightly
objects that renderings like "jackals" are more precise than the
evidence warrants; he adopts a more general translation, *wilde
dieren* ("wild beasts"). Nevertheless Hebrew *tn* and apparently
related word-forms are not applied to all wild animals, but
only to three specific kinds: animals that live in dry and uninhabited regions and make a sound like lamentation (singular
tn, Isa 35.7; 43.20; Jer 9.11; 49.33; Mal 1.3; Mic 1.8); large
sea or river animals (*tnyn,* Gen 1.21; Psa 74.13; *tnym,* Ezek

29.3; 32.2); and venomous snakes (*tnyn*, Deut 32.33; Exod 7.9–10; Psa 91.13). The derivations of these word-forms are unknown (HALOT 4.1759, 1764). In the present passage, the Masoretic marginal reading (Q) has the usual Hebrew plural ending -*ym;* the reading in the text itself (K) has the dialect (and Aramaic) plural ending -*yn* (GKC §87*e;* JM §90*c*), like *šwmmyn* ("gates") in 1.4.

The daughter of my people. Like "daughter of Zion" (see the notes on 1.6), "daughter of Judah" (1.15), and "daughter of Jerusalem" (2.13), this term usually applies to the people generally (see, especially, vv 6–7; Jer 8.11, 21–9.1; 14.17); it need not be limited to the women.

Cruel (*'kzr*). The term is applied to the poison of snakes in Deut 32.33 (where the word *tnyn* also occurs). Therefore, the meaning need not be that **yaen-birds** are **cruel** to their own young; they might be predatory birds, which are **cruel** to those whom they attack. (The words traditionally translated "ostrich" and "cruel" in Job 39.13–16 are unrelated to anything in the present passage.)

Like yaen-birds translates the Masoretic marginal reading (*ky'nym*, Q), which is supported by the association with **tan-animals** (see the following paragraph). The reading in the text itself (K) is *ky 'nym*, "for [they are] afflicted [one]s" (masculine), referring to **my people** (also masculine).

Yaen-birds (*y'nym*, Q). The masculine form is found only here. A feminine form, *bt y'nh*, describes a bird (Lev 11.16) that dwells in uninhabited regions (Isa 13.21; Jer 50.39) and makes a sound like mourning (Mic 1.9); this is repeatedly associated with **tan-animals** (Job 30.29; Isa 34.13; 43.20; Jer 50.39; Mic 1.8), so it is presumably the same as the creature in the present passage. The traditional rendering "ostriches" (KJV) derives from LXX *strouthion*, although *strouthion* could refer to a small bird (Muraoka 640) and in any case the LXX translators cannot be trusted in ornithological matters (they identified another bird of dry country as *pelekan*, "pelican"). Ostriches do not dwell in ruins (as yaen-birds do, Isa 13.21), and therefore HALOT 2.421 suggests "a kind of owl" (cf. *chats-huants*, Martin), but this too goes beyond what can be established from Scripture.

4.5 The *ones* who were eating delightful things
      have been made desolate in *the* streets;
the *ones* who were nursed on scarlet
      have embraced *the* dirt.

God gives **delightful things** (*m'dnym,* an *m*-prefixed form of *'dn,* "delight") to those who seek refuge in Him (Psa 36.8). When the Israelites first entered the promised land, they received great blessings from Him "and delighted [*wyt'dnw*] in Your great goodness" (Neh 9.25). But now, as a result of Israel's departure from the LORD, the king of Babylon had "filled his belly with [those] delightful things" (Jer 51.34). The people who had been living prosperously in Jerusalem, **eating delightful things** and being reared **on scarlet** cloth (a mark of honor: cf. Exod 26.1; Nah 2.3), were left **desolate in the streets,** clinging to the **dirt.** "The LORD makes poor, and makes rich; He brings low, and also lifts up; He raises the poor one from the dust, and lifts up the needy one from the dirt" (1 Sam 2.7–8; Psa 113.7–9). Indeed "everyone who raises himself high shall be made lowly, and the one who makes himself lowly shall be raised high" (Luke 14.11).

> **Have been made desolate.** Hebrew *nšmw,* a Niph'al form of *šmm.* Its Niph'al forms can describe either an emotional reaction (e.g., in Jer 4.9; "be appalled," BDB 1031, §2) or a change of condition (e.g., in Jer 12.11; "be desolated," BDB 1031, §1). The context here shows that the latter is meant. The rendering "perish" (ESV) is probably too strong (as TDOT 15.241, §III.1b, points out, in Ezek 4.17 it is the context, not the use of *šmm,* that indicates that the people are dying). Qal forms of *šmm* are used in 1.4, 13, 16; 3.11; 5.18.

> **Dirt** (*'šptwt,* places comparable to "dust" and inhabited only by the lowly: 1 Sam 2.8; Psa 113.7). Related word-forms are applied to setting Christ in the dust of death (Psa 22.15) and setting a pot on a fire (2 Kgs 4.38; Ezek 24.3). Renderings such as "dunghills" (KJV) and "ash pits" (NASB) are, in different ways, more specific than the Scripture information warrants (cf. BDB 1046).

4.6 And *the* iniquity of *the* daughter of my people
      has been greater than *the* sin of Sodom,

which was overturned as if *in* a blink,

    and no hands turned against her.

In disobeying the LORD, Jerusalem (the **daughter of my people**) had committed worse evils than **Sodom:** "Sodom your sister did not do, she and her daughters, as you have done, you and your daughters…. Because of your sins that you did more abominably than they did, they are more righteous than you" (Ezek 16.48, 52). "Ask now among the nations; who has heard things like these?" (Jer 18.13). "Has a nation changed its gods, and they are not gods? But My people have changed their glory for that which does not profit" (Jer 2.10–11).

As a result, in many respects, Jerusalem suffered worse punishment than Sodom (Dan 9.12). True, Sodom was completely destroyed, whereas a remnant of Jerusalem was left (Isa 1.9). But Sodom **was overturned** instantly, **as if in a blink,** whereas many of Jerusalem's inhabitants underwent even greater sufferings, since they died slowly of hunger (see v 9) or were carried away into captivity. "Do not weep for the dead, and do not mourn for him; but weep, weeping, for the one who goes away, for he will not return again or see the land of his birth" (Jer 22.10). And even after this life, the sinners of Sodom will suffer less than those of Jerusalem. "That slave who knew his Lord's will, and did not get ready, nor did he do in accordance with His will, shall be beaten with many blows; but the one who did not know it, and who did deeds that were worthy of blows, shall be beaten with few" (Luke 12.47–48). So "it will be more tolerable for the land of Sodom in the day of judgment," than for those who knew the Lord and rejected Him (Matt 11.24; Luke 10.12)—even though the men and women who were in Sodom, when it was destroyed, were unrepentant sinners (cf. Gen 18.32).

By the same principle, those who know the Lord's new covenant message today, and yet turn away from it, will suffer an even more severe punishment than the people in Jerusalem who knew and turned away from His old covenant message. "Anyone who has set aside the Law of Moses dies without mercy on the basis of two or three witnesses. Of how much worse punishment do you think he will be counted worthy, the one who has trodden down the Son of God, and has considered unclean the blood of the covenant by which he was made holy, and has insulted the Spirit of grace?" (Heb 10.28–29; 12.25; 2.1–3).

Iniquity… sin. Hebrew *'wn* (**iniquity**) can refer either to iniquity itself (as in 2.14; 4.13; BDB 730–31, §1) or to the punishment for iniquity (as in v 22; BDB 731, §3). Similarly, Hebrew *ḥṭ'* (**sin**) can refer either to sin itself (as in 1.8; 4.13; 5.7; BDB 307–08, §1) or to the punishment for sin (BDB 307–08, §3). In the present verse, some translations emphasize mainly the greatness of the sin, others the greatness of the punishment. In practice the two cannot be separated. The Lord always judges righteously (Psa 96.13; Acts 17.31; 1 Pet 2.23; Jer 11.20), and punishes each sinner in accordance with his sins (Rom 2.5–6; Jer 17.10).

No hands turned [*ḥlw*] **against** [*b-*] **her.** This clause has been translated in various different ways.

1. *ḥlw* is usually construed as a form of *ḥwl* ("turn" or "writhe"). This has led to several different renderings:

   1a. When Sodom was destroyed, no human hands turned **against** her ("without a hand laid on" her, HCSB ≡ *sin que manos actuaran contra ella*, LBLA; cf. Dan 2.34, 45). *ḥwl b-* appears to have a similar meaning in Hos 11.6 ("the sword will turn against their cities"). Sodom's punishment came directly from the Lord (cf. 2 Sam 24.14), and was not aggravated by the unrighteous deeds of human conquerors, as Jerusalem's punishment was (Zec 1.15; see the comments on 3.34–36).

   1b. When Sodom was destroyed, "no hands writhed [with pain] in [*b-*] her" (cf. Isa 26.17–18; Joel 2.6). Her destruction was instant (**as if in a blink**); none of the people in Sodom lingered in a state of suffering, as those in Jerusalem did (v 9).

   1c. When Sodom was destroyed, "no hands were wrung for her" (ESV). However, in that respect Jerusalem was better off than Sodom: some people did sympathize with her in her sufferings (Jer 8.21; 9.1). Moreover, the ESV rendering would require the preposition *l-*, not *b-*; and there is no evidence that Hebrew *ḥwl* could refer to wringing of the hands in sympathy, as distinct from writhing in pain (Keil 611/435).

   1d. Sodom was destroyed "without a hand turned to help her" (NIV). However, this faces some of the same problems as the ESV rendering: it would require *l-*, not *b-*, and it does not suit the context here (Salters 299).

    2. Sometimes *ḥlw* is construed as a form of *ḥlh* ("become weak").

       2a. When Sodom was destroyed, "no hands were wearied against her." "No human hands were wearied by destroying her, but she was suddenly consumed by the hand of God" (Wordsworth 148). This meaning (which is similar to 1a) seems to have been the intent of the KJV rendering ("no hands stayed on her"). However, it would require a Niphʻal form of *ḥlh* (as in Jer 12.13), not a Qal form.

       2b. When Sodom was destroyed, no hands "weakened in her." Her inhabitants perished instantly (**as if in a blink**), without "lingering and wasting away with disease or want" (Blayney 403). The resultant meaning is similar to 1b.

4.7 Her outstanding ones were cleaner than snow;
      they were clearer than milk;
in strength, they were redder than corals;
      their cut *was* like lapis lazuli.

4.8 Their form became darker than blackness;
      they were not recognized in *the* streets;
their skin shriveled on their bone;
      it was dried up, it became like wood.

In the past, while they were **in** a condition of **strength,** Jerusalem's **outstanding** people were healthy and flourishing, like the ideal Bridegroom in the Song of Songs ("my love is clear and red," with features comparable to milk and lapis lazuli, Song 5.10, 12, 14). They could be measured against precious substances (cf. v 2), such as **corals** (Job 28.18; Prov 31.10) and **lapis lazuli** (Job 28.16; Ezek 28.13). They looked pure—**clean** (*zkk*, Job 9.30; 15.14; Isa 1.16) and **clear** (*ṣḥḥ*, Isa 32.4). But outward appearance is no guide to inner reality. "There was no man as beautiful as Absalom in all of Israel; from the sole of his foot even to the crown of his head there was no blemish in him" (2 Sam 14.25; cf. Matt 23.25–28; Acts 23.3). Outwardly Jerusalem's people appeared beautiful, but inwardly their sins were very great (v 6).

Now "the good gold is changed" (v 1), to such an extent that the people are no longer recognizable. Their apparent purity—cleanness and clearness—has gone. Their **skin** has **dried up** (*ybš*, like people and places deprived of the LORD's blessings, Isa 40.24; Jer 23.10). It looks like **wood** (the opposite of a precious substance; 2 Tim 2.20).

> **Outstanding ones** *(nzyryh)*. Hebrew *nzyr*, "set apart," "outstanding," includes not only those set apart under the Law of Moses by a special vow (Nazirites, Num 6.2–21), but also those set apart in other respects (such as "princes," ESV, and/or "dignitaries," HCSB): Joseph was "outstanding [*nzr*] among his brothers" (Gen 49.26; Deut 33.16).

> **Strength** (*ṣm*, as in Deut 8.17; Job 30.21) has an adverbial function, indicating the state or condition **in** which **they were red**—like "she has gone down [in] marvels" (i.e., "marvelously") in 1.9 (many other examples are listed in GKC §118*q*; IBHS §10.2.2d). Its placement before the verb (as in Lev 6.16; Psa 75.2) may give it "a certain emphasis" (GKC §118*n*; JM §126*a*). The medieval Masoretic scribes pointed the word to mean "bone," but bones (consistently distinguished from skin and flesh: v 8; Ezek 37.7–8; Mic 3.2–3; etc.) could hardly be described as **red**. The Masoretic error is understandable, because *ṣm* meaning "bone" does appear in the very next verse (v 8). The rendering "body" (KJV) cannot be supported from the usage of *ṣm* elsewhere.

> **Their cut** *(gzrtm)*. Another form of Hebrew *gzr* appears in 3.54 ("I have been cut off"). Elsewhere the word is applied to the cutting down of trees (2 Kgs 6.4); the cutting apart of an animal sacrifice (Gen 15.17); the cutting apart of the Red Sea (Psa 136.13); the cutting apart of the child disputed by the two women (1 Kgs 3.25–26); the cutting off of a person at death (Psa 88.5; Isa 53.8); and an area "cut off" from the rest of the temple (Ezek 41.12–15). In the present passage, it is usually explained as the "form" (ESV), the "cut" of the body; if so, Spanish *talle* (VRV 1960) and French *taille* (VDF) would be more exact translations than anything possible in English. The cutting of a jewel might also involve "polishing" (KJV; cf. BDB 160). Blayney (404) suggests "veining," because the veins "divide or intersect... on the surface of the body" and look blue

(like **lapis lazuli**). "Hair" (NRSV; cf. Hillers 140–41) is not likely to have been described in Hebrew by any form of *gzr.*

Lapis lazuli *(spyr).* This, and not "sapphire" in the modern sense, was the common blue gemstone of the ancient Middle East (HDB 4.620, §5). Moreover, *spyr* could be engraved (Exod 28.18, 21); no method available in ancient times would have been capable of engraving a substance as hard as sapphire.

Were cleaner… were clearer… were redder… became darker… were not recognized… shriveled… was dried up… became. All the verbs in these verses are Qaṭal forms; neither they, nor anything else in the wording, mark any shift in time, tense, or verbal aspect between v 7 and v 8. Nor are there any markers of contrast—any terms like *'kn* ("yet surely," Psa 31.22; 66.19) or *ky 'm* ("but rather," Psa 1.2, 4), or even a simple *w-* ("and," "but," Psa 32.10; 55.13). (A striking lack of contrast markers is seen elsewhere in these Lamentations, e.g., "Tan-animals have drawn out the breast… the daughter of my people has become cruel," v 3; "young children have asked for bread; there is no one dividing it," v 4.) The two opposite conditions are directly juxtaposed and presented with exactly equal force and immediacy.

4.9 Those pierced by *the* sword *were* better
　　　than those pierced by hunger,
those who flowed away, stabbed,
　　　away from *the* fruits of *the* countryside.

It is a blessing to die rapidly (see the comments on v 6), rather than to linger on and witness the sufferings to come (Ecc 4.1–2; 2 Kgs 22.20; cf. Est 8.6; Gen 21.16). Therefore, those who perished suddenly **by the sword** were "better off" (HCSB) than those who perished more slowly **by hunger.**

Those who [š-] flowed away, stabbed. Š- nearly always refers back to the leading subject of the sentence, regardless of any subsequent terms in it: "He sent signs and wonders… among Pharaoh and all His servants, who [š-] smote many nations" (Psa 135.9–10); "He has given their land for an inheritance…

to Israel His servant… who [*š*-] has been mindful of us in our lowliness" (Psa 136.21–23). This would suggest that **those who flowed away, stabbed,** are **those pierced by the sword** (not **those pierced by hunger**). Further, elsewhere all forms of *dqr* (**stabbed**) invariably refer to those pierced by a **sword** or some similar sharp implement, never to those perishing in any other way (Num 25.8; Jdg 9.54; 1 Sam 31.4; 1 Chr 10.4; Prov 12.18; Isa 13.15; Jer 37.10; 51.4; Zec 12.10; 13.3).

Flowed away. Elsewhere the term "flow" *(zwb)* always refers to the flowing of liquids (e.g., blood, Lev 15.19, 25; water, Psa 78.20; 105.41; milk and honey, Jer 11.5; 32.22). It is used here to evoke the flowing of blood when the victim is **stabbed.** (Mackay [188] mistakenly says that **flowed away** "envisages a much slower fate" than **stabbed.** On the contrary, it would be the exact result of being stabbed.) "The life of all flesh is its blood" (Lev 17.14), and therefore when the blood flows away, the life flows away.

Away from [*m*-] the fruits of the countryside. In this context, *m*- could mean either "separate from" (as in "their houses are in peace, away from [*m*-] fear," Job 21.9) or "deprived of" (as in "my flesh has dwindled away from [*m*-] oil," i.e., deprived of oil; Psa 109.24).

Two views of the phrase have been presented.

1. According to one view, the phrase continues the reference to **those pierced by the sword** (Hornblower 158–59). At the very moment when they were **stabbed** and **flowed away,** they became once and for all separate from (or deprived of) the **fruits of the countryside.** They therefore did not have to suffer continuing pangs of hunger, as the others did.

2. According to another view, this phrase refers to **those pierced by hunger** (Gordis 190–91). Just as a reader would naturally link the word **stabbed** with the word **sword,** so a reader would naturally link the expression **away from the fruits of the countryside** with the word **hunger.** If so, the comparison in the first half of the verse would be repeated in the second: "Those pierced by the sword [were] better than those pierced by hunger; those who flowed away, stabbed, [were better than those] deprived of the fruits of

the countryside." (Similar syntax is seen in Prov 3.14: "Her merchandise [is] better than the merchandise of silver, and her produce [is better than that of] gold.")

4.10 Hands of compassionate women
    cooked their children;
they became food for them
    in *the* crushing of *the* daughter of my people.

Moses had warned the Israelites that, if they persisted in disobeying the LORD, "the tender and delicate woman among you, who did not venture to set the sole of her foot on the ground because of her delicateness and tenderness—her eye will be evil... against her sons whom she bears; and she will eat them in the lack of everything, in secret, in the siege and affliction with which your enemy will afflict you" (Deut 28.56–57). The northern kingdom of Israel had already suffered this (2 Kgs 6.26–29), and now the kingdom of Judah, in the time of her affliction (**crushing,** 2.11), suffered it too (see 2.20). "The kindness of a human being is done sparingly" (Eighteen Psalms 5.15), so that human mothers may forget their own children (Isa 49.15); but the LORD's "compassions have not ended" (3.22; Eighteen Psalms 5.14, 16). In every place, and at every time, "like a father who has compassion on sons, the LORD has had compassion on those who fear Him" (Psa 103.13).

4.11 *The* LORD made an end of His fury,
    He poured out *the* fierceness of His anger,
and He set alight a fire in Zion,
    and it ate up her foundations.

Although He is eternally compassionate (see the comments on v 3.32), the LORD is also eternally "a consuming fire" (Heb 12.29)—and now He had "poured out like fire His fury" against the daughter of Zion (see the comments on 2.4). The **fire** was so thorough that it consumed even Zion's **foundations** (cf. Jer 21.14; Deut 32.22); and it did not stop until the LORD's **fury** was at an **end.** "The one who is far away will die by the plague, and the one who is near will fall by the sword, and the one who remains, and is kept back, will die by the hunger—and so I will **make an end of** My **fury** upon them" (Ezek 6.12; 5.12–13; 13.14–15). "When the destroying wind passes, then there is no longer a wicked one; but a righteous one is a foundation to lasting time" (Prov 10.25). The LORD had promised to set in Zion, for those who believe, a **foundation** that could never be destroyed (Isa 28.16 ≡ 1 Pet 2.6–7).

> **Made an end of His fury.** Translations such as "gave full vent to His wrath" (ESV) miss the point, as Salters (310–11) observes. The meaning is not that the LORD unleashed His fury without any restraint, or to its fullest possible extent (on the contrary, He "held back" His punishment "to less than our iniquities," Ezra 9.13). It is simply that He completed (*cumplió*, VRV 1602–1960) the task that He had set Himself. "The LORD has done what He planned" (2.17).

4.12 *The* kings of *the* earth did not believe,
and all of *those* dwelling in *the* world,
that an oppressor and an enemy would come
in *the* gates of Jerusalem.

In the past, the surrounding nations had regarded **Jerusalem** as "the whole of beauty, the gladness of all the earth" (2.15). "All the earth" sought to hear the wisdom of Solomon (1 Kgs 10.23–24). "All the kingdoms of the lands that were round about Judah" were awed by the LORD's protection of Jehoshaphat (2 Chr 17.10). In the time of Hezekiah, no one else, "among all the gods of the lands, delivered their land" out of the hand of the Assyrians (2 Kgs 18.33–35; 19.17); not even Egypt escaped (Isa 20.4)—and yet **Jerusalem** remained uncaptured (2 Kgs 19.32–35). But "the things impossible with people are possible with God" (Luke 18.27; 1.37; Job 42.2).

4.13 *It was* because of *the* sins of her prophets,
the iniquities of her priests,
those who have shed in her midst
the blood of *the* righteous *ones*.

Jerusalem's punishment (vv 11–12) happened **because of** *(m–)* the **sins** and **iniquities** done **in her midst**, especially by her **prophets** and **priests** (Jer 23.11). Jerusalem's **prophets** had committed adultery (Jer 23.14), prophesied falsely (Jer 5.31), and proclaimed "worthless uplifted oracles and misleading things" (see the comments on 2.14)—both by prophesying in the name of Baal (Jer 2.8), and by issuing in the name of the LORD messages that He had not given them (Jer 14.13–14; 23.16–17; Ezek 22.28). Her **priests** had also dealt falsely (Jer 6.13), departing from the Law that they had been appointed to hold (Jer 2.8), and profaning the holy things that the LORD had appointed (Ezek 22.26; Zep 3.4). Both the **priests** and the **prophets** had been covetous (Jer 6.13) and had **shed... the blood of the righteous ones** in Jerusalem (Ezek 22.25), as they had tried to do even to Jeremiah himself (Jer 26.8–9).

Under the old covenant, both **prophets** and **priests** were appointed by God to teach the people of Israel (2 Kgs 17.13; Dan 9.10; Heb 1.1; Mal 2.7; Deut 24.8). Those who teach His word are judged more severely than other people (Jas 3.1), because they are required to teach their hearers "all the counsel of God" (Acts 20.26–27); if they neglect part of it, they will be held responsible not only for their own personal sins, but also for the sins of those hearers whom they have misled (Ezek 3.17–18; 33.7–8).

4.14 They have wandered *as* blind *ones* in *the* streets;
    they have been desecrated with blood,
without *people* being able
    to touch their garments.

4.15 "Turn aside^{pl}! Unclean!" they called to them;
    "Turn aside^{pl}! Turn aside^{pl}! Do not touch^{pl}!"
When they flew away, they also wandered;
    they said among the nations, "They will not continue to sojourn *here*."

4.16 *The* face of *the* LORD has dispersed them;
    He will not continue to look to them;
they have not uplifted *the* face of priests;
    they have not shown favor to elders.

When Jerusalem was invaded (v 12), the sinners were **dispersed** by the LORD. They **wandered** through the **streets** like **blind** people. When they

flew away to distant places, they still **wandered** (just as an earlier generation of sinners wandered in the wilderness, Num 32.13). Even "among the nations" they could not find rest (see the comments on 1.3); they were not allowed **to sojourn** anywhere in peace. All this had been foretold long before, in the time of Moses: "You will grope at noon as a blind person gropes in the darkness…. And the LORD will scatter you among the peoples, from the end of the earth even as far as the end of the earth…. And among these nations you will have no respite, and there will be no resting place for the sole of your foot" (Deut 28.29, 64–65).

When He first called the Israelites out of Egypt, the LORD had told them that, if they obeyed Him, they would be "a holy nation" (Exod 19.5–6; Lev 20.26; Deut 7.6). But the people had disobeyed Him. As a result, they were **desecrated.** Although they boasted of their holiness and ordered other people to avoid them (Isa 65.5), they became the opposite of holy—**unclean** (Lev 10.10; Ezek 22.26)—and had to be avoided by other people.

Under the old covenant Law, a woman who had a discharge of **blood** became **unclean** (Lev 12.2; 15.25). If other people touched anything that had come into contact with her, they would also become unclean (Lev 15.19–27). Under the same Law, a person who had the disease of leprosy also became **unclean** (Lev 13.2–3). He had to live in a separate place, and call out a warning to the people around him: "Unclean! unclean!" (Lev 13.45–46). Uncleanness had to be avoided (Lev 13.45–46); otherwise, it would contaminate all those around it (Hag 2.13).

Diseases like leprosy and discharges of blood were not sins; they were simply earthly uncleannesses, under the terms of the Law of Moses. Nevertheless, as with the other earthly regulations of the old covenant Law, they provided an instructive earthly image (a "shadow") of a spiritual pattern that remains eternally valid (cf. Heb 8.5; 10.1; 9.24; Col 2.17). Spiritual uncleanness (sin) likewise contaminates anyone who comes into contact with it, and has to be avoided. That is why the Lord commands us today: "Come out from the midst of them and be separate, says the Lord, and do not touch an unclean thing, and I Myself will welcome you…. Let us cleanse ourselves from all defilement of flesh and spirit, making our holiness complete in the fear of God" (2 Cor 6.17–7.1).

During the time that led up to the Babylonian destruction, Jerusalem had been filled with bloodshed (2 Kgs 21.16; Jer 2.34; 22.17). The inhabitants of Jerusalem were **desecrated** by that bloodshed (Isa 59.3; cf. Isa 1.15) and became **unclean** (Ezek 36.17–18). This was one of the main reasons why the city had to be punished by the hand of the Babylonians (2 Kgs 24.3–4). And when that happened, their punishment caused the neighboring peoples to spurn them because they were **unclean** like a leper. They became "a byword **among the nations,**" just as the LORD had warned them would happen if they disobeyed Him: "I will cut off Israel from the face of the land that I have given them; and this house—which I have made holy for My name—I will cast out from My face, and Israel will be a proverb and a byword among the nations. And this house, which is so high—everyone who passes by it will be devastated and will hiss, and they will say, 'Why did the LORD do this to this land and this house?' And they will say: 'Because they forsook the LORD… therefore He brought on them all this evil'" (1 Kgs 9.6–9; Deut 29.22–28; Ezek 39.23).

Yet there was something even worse. Not only had the **nations** turned away from them, but so had the LORD Himself. He would **not continue to look at them.** "The Lord's eyes are on righteous ones, and his ears are toward their request; but the Lord's face is over against those that are doing evil things" (1 Pet 3.12 ≡ Psa 34.15–16; 5.3–6). That was what He did to the people of Jerusalem at the time of the Babylonian captivity: "I have set My face against this city for evil not for good, says the LORD; into the hand of the king of Babylon it will be given, and he will burn it with fire" (Jer 21.10; 33.5; Lev 26.17; Ezek 15.7).

> **They have wandered.** These wanderers are described as **blind** and **unclean,** so they are not the righteous people mentioned in v 13, but must be either the priests and prophets (also mentioned in v 13) or the nation in general. It would be hard to distinguish between those options, and there is little practical difference between them; the afflictions of the priests and prophets were the same as the afflictions of the rest of the people.

> **They have wandered.** Hebrew *nw'* describes motion to and fro: the swaying of trees in a wind (Isa 7.2), the movement of Hannah's lips as she prayed voicelessly (1 Sam 1.13), the traveling of drought-stricken people to a source of water (Amos 4.8), the wandering of the Israelites in the wilderness (Num 32.13), the departure of Israel from God (contrasted with restraining [*hśk*] one's feet, Jer 14.10). Often the motion

described is more or less unsteady (*esaleuthēsan*, LXX ≡ "staggered," Brenton; "stumbled," HCSB in v 14).

They have wandered as blind ones. Earlier prophets had warned the nation that this would happen: "They will walk like blind ones, because they have sinned against the LORD" (Zep 1.17; Deut 28.29). "By what things someone sins, by these he is punished" (Wis 11.16). The sinners in the nation had "loved to wander" from the LORD (Jer 14.10)—and therefore He punished them by making them wander (cf. Psa 109.10; 59.11). They had been blind to His pathway (Isa 56.10; 59.10)—and therefore He punished them by making them blind (Deut 28.28; Isa 6.10 ≡ John 12.40). In doing this, He deprived them of what they had deprived themselves of ("they have shut their eyes," Matt 13.15 ≡ "He has blinded their eyes," John 12.40). "Whoever does not have, even what he thinks himself to have will be taken away from him" (Luke 8.18).

Without [*bl'*] **people being able** (BDB 520, §4a; GKC §120*g*). The rendering "so that men are not able" (KJV) is impossible; *b-* is an extremely common preposition, and nowhere else does it express a result ("so that").

Touch their garments. Hebrew *ng' b-* can mean either to touch something ("touch the inheritance," Jer 12.14) or to touch "with" something ("touches with his skirt," Hag 2.12). In the latter case, the meaning here would be "[that which] they are not allowed [BDB 407, §1d], they [the Israelites] touch with their garments" (Albrektson 187). However, the similar expression **Do not touch** in the next verse almost certainly refers not to the Israelites touching unclean things with their garments, but to other people touching the **unclean** Israelites.

They have been desecrated. The same Hebrew term *(g'l)* is applied to people unqualified for the priesthood (Neh 7.64; 13.29), to offerings presented by those who dishonor the LORD (Mal 1.7), and to the danger of being defiled by unclean food or wine (Dan 1.8).

"Turn aside! Unclean!" Some translations regard this as what "people cried at them" (ESV); others regard this as what "they cried of themselves" (NASB). The latter view may be supported by the fact that **"Unclean!"** is singular—which is not how a group of unclean people would most naturally be addressed by others, but is precisely what each of the unclean people in the group would be saying of himself (as in Lev 13.45).

When [*ky*] they flew away, they also wandered. "When they went abroad… they travelled with step as uncertain as at home" (Streane 387).

They flew away *(nṣw)*. Diverse renderings of this word have been suggested.

1. "They flew away" (*ils s'en sont envolés*, Martin), a form of the same word as *nwṣh*, "plumage" (Ezek 17.3, 7). They journeyed very far away, as a bird can ("Who will give me wings like a dove? I will fly off ['*wph*]… to be far away," Psa 55.6–7). Some, for instance, **flew away** of their own choice "as far as Tahpanhes" in the land of Egypt (Jer 43.4–7). Others **flew away** against their will into captivity in Babylon (as if they had been flung out of a sling, Jer 10.18). They were scattered "among all the peoples from the end of the earth even as far as the end of the earth" (Deut 28.64).

2. "They were ruined" (House 432, 445), a form of *nṣh*, "ruin" (as in Jer 4.7). This is feasible, although it does not match **they wandered** as closely as the previous option does.

3. "They quarreled" (DRCV), a form of *nṣh*, "fight" (as in Exod 2.13).

4. "They fled away" (KJV). However, this rendering "cannot be defended on the basis of other OT evidence" (Provan 119).

5. "They are loathsome" (Stone; *eran contaminados*, VRV 1602), accepting Rashi's suggestion that the term is a form of *yṣ'* ("go out") and means "filth." However, this too has no Scripture support (Rashi cites Lev 1.16, but the subject there is a bird's body parts, so even there the sense "plumage" would fit perfectly).

They said among the nations, "They will not continue to sojourn here." The passage could also be punctuated: "They said, 'Among the nations they will not continue to sojourn'" (Gordis 192–93). The Israelites had sought to "live among the nations" (v 20; 1.3), but they were rejected by the **nations** (2.15–17) and became "a reproach, a parable among the nations" (Joel

2.17, 19; Jer 22.8–9; Deut 29.24–28). Yet this would change in the future: "When the LORD restores the restoration of Zion... then they say among the nations, 'The LORD has done great deeds with them'" (Psa 126.1–2; cf. Psa 79.10).

The face of the LORD. Hebrew *pnym*, the word here translated **face,** does not in itself mean "anger" (KJV), but of course the dispersion of the Israelites was indeed a result of His anger. "We have been ended in Your anger.... You have placed our iniquities before You, our hidden sins in the light of Your face" (Psa 90.7–8). "Because of the anger of the LORD, this came about in Jerusalem, until He cast them out from His face" (2 Kgs 24.20).

Has dispersed them [*ḥlqm*]. Hebrew *ḥlq* here describes the dispersion of a people (as in Gen 49.7, where it is equivalent to *pwṣ*, "scatter"). In principle it could also be construed as a noun ("The face of the LORD [is] their portion," as in 3.24), but that would be less suited to the present context. There is no evidence in the Hebrew Scriptures that it could mean "destroyed them" (NJB).

Uplifted the face (in German, *das Angesicht... erhoben,* NZB). A common Scripture expression indicating favor (Prov 18.5; Psa 82.2) and/or acceptance (Job 42.8–9; Mal 1.8–9).

They have not uplifted the face of priests; they have not shown favor to elders. Most likely the subject here (**They**) is the foreign **nations** (those mentioned in the previous verse, v 15). This is certainly so in the comparable passage Deut 28.49–50: "The LORD will raise up against you a nation from far away... who will not uplift the face of the old" (so also Bar 4.15). Sometimes the subject in the present passage is viewed as a nonspecific plural, meaning simply "no honor was shown to the priests, no favor to the elders" (ESV). But in Hebrew, that would be very unusual (JM §155*c*; possible examples are listed in GKC §144*g*); and nothing in the context here suggests it. Alternatively, the subject could be the same as in v 14 (**They have wandered**), in which case it would be describing the Israelites' disrespect for their own leaders (Isa 3.5). The nation's **priests** and **elders** were to be treated with honor (Lev 19.32; Deut 17.12; Sir 7.29; Acts 23.5), just as elders and teachers in the Lord are to be treated with honor today (1 Thes 5.12–13; Heb 13.17; 1 Pet 5.5).

4.17 Our eyes have still been coming to an end
   for our help—a futile thing;
in our watching, we have watched
   for a nation *that* will not save.

Those who love the Lord with all their heart, mind, soul, and strength (Mark 12.30) will expend the last drop of their resources seeking help from Him: "My eyes have come to an end for Your salvation" (Psa 119.123; 69.3). But these Israelites were seeking just as wholeheartedly a form of **help** that was **futile:** they were looking for help from a **nation that will not save.** Anything other than the true God "is a false hope for salvation" (Psa 33.16–17; 146.3–5; Acts 4.12).

> **Have… been coming to an end.** Hebrew *tklnyh*, a Yiqtol form of *klh*, also used in 2.11 ("With tears, my eyes have come to an end"), 22; 3.22; 4.11. Yiqtol forms indicate nothing about the time of the action, which could theoretically be either past ("failed," KJV) or still present ("fail," ASV), or even future ("shall… fail," Rotherham).

> **Still** (*'wd*, as in Jer 2.9) indicates that the act is or was a continuing one ("all the while," HCSB). Its suffix (GKC §100*o*) is a third person feminine plural *(-ynh)* in the Dead Sea Scroll 5QLam[b] and the text (K) of most Masoretic manuscripts, but a first person plural *(-ynw)* in the text of some Masoretic manuscripts and the margin (Q) of the others. The third person feminine plural would match the noun **eyes** and the verb **have… been coming to an end,** whereas the first person plural would match the pronoun suffix **our;** but the variant does not affect the sense of the verse.

> **A futile thing** (*hbl*, as in Jer 2.5) could describe either the help itself ("looking for our vain help," ASV) or the search for it ("looking in vain for help," NIV). The former option would more closely match the second half of the verse (**a nation that will not save**). But both options are true.

> **In our watching** construes Hebrew *bṣpytnw* as an infinitive absolute. Alternatively, it could be a noun ("in our watchtower," Rotherham).

4.18 They have hunted our steps
  from walking in our wide places;
our end has come near, our days have been filled up,
  for our end has come.

4.19 Our pursuers have been swifter
  than *the* vultures of *the* heavens;
on the mountains they have hotly pursued us;
  in *the* wilderness they have lain in wait for us.

In times of peace, a city's **wide places** (its *plazas,* BTX) would be thronged with people (Zec 8.4–5). That was where public announcements were made (Prov 1.20; Est 6.9, 11), and where the whole population gathered for meetings (Neh 8.1–3). But now the inhabitants were **hunted, hotly pursued,** and ambushed (**lain in wait** for) by **pursuers,** preventing them **from walking** in the public places at all.

The LORD's prophets had recently warned that an **end** was coming because of Israel's sins: "An end, the end has come on the four corners of the land; now the end is upon you" (Ezek 7.2–3). The foreign invaders would pounce on the sinful nation swiftly, "like a vulture hurrying to eat" (Hab 1.8; Jer 4.13; Deut 28.49). Now those prophecies had been fulfilled; the **end** had not only **come near,** but had actually **come.** In making an end of His fury (v 11), the LORD had made an **end** of the people. Wherever they were—even in places where people might ordinarily hide from **pursuers,** such as the **mountains** or the **wilderness** (1 Sam 14.22; 23.15, 19, 24–26; Rev 12.6)—they did not escape (Amos 9.2–4). No one can "outflee [*ekpheuxē*] the judgment of God" (Rom 2.3; Ezek 17.15, 18; 1 Thes 5.3).

Indeed, the Scriptures remind us that all people on earth have an **end**—that is, a time when their **days have been filled up** (Psa 139.16; 2 Sam 7.12). "Make known to me, LORD, my end, and the measure of my days, what it is; let me know how ceasing I am" (Psa 39.4–5). Tomorrow will not always be like today (Isa 56.12; Psa 10.6; Luke 12.19–20). "You do not know what a day will give birth to" (Prov 27.1; Jas 4.13–16).

> **They have hunted** (*ṣdw*). This could be a form of either *ṣwd* ("hunt," as if hunting a bird or a food animal, Ezek 13.18, 20; Gen 27.3, 5) or *ṣdh* ("lie in wait" in order to kill someone, Exod 21.13; Num 35.20, 22; 1 Sam 24.11). Either way, the idea is that the nation had been harassed by **pursuers** intent on killing them.

> **Vultures.** Hebrew *nšrym*, the largest birds of prey in the Middle
> East, where the griffon vulture often reaches speeds of 50 me-
> tres per second (over 110 miles per hour) when plummeting to
> its prey (Xirouchakis and Andreou, "Foraging Behaviour and
> Flight Characteristics of Griffon Vultures," 41). Not "eagles"
> (KJV), nor a "comprehensive term" including both eagles and
> vultures (BDB 676–77), because Mic 1.16 shows that baldness
> was characteristic of *nšrym* (not merely that a proportion of
> *nšrym* were bald).

4.20 *The* breath of our nostrils, *the* Lord's anointed one,
>   has been captured in their pits,
of whom we said, "In his shadow
>   we will live among *the* nations."

The **Lord's anointed one** was the king (the successor of Saul and David:
1 Sam 24.6, 10; 2 Chr 6.42). The people of Judah had regarded their king
as their very lifebreath, the **breath** of their **nostrils,** without which they
would have no life at all (Gen 7.22; Job 27.3), and in whose **shadow** they
themselves would **live** among the nations, just as lesser creatures find protection in the shadow of a tree (Jdg 9.15; Dan 4.20–22).

But those who seek protection in the **shadow** of any human being will
be put to shame (Isa 30.1–3; Ezek 31.17). When Jerusalem was invaded by
the Babylonians, Zedekiah, the last king of Judah, was **captured** by the
conquerors and taken in chains to Babylon (Jer 39.1–7). Only the **shadow**
of the Lord will provide true and lasting protection from all distresses
(Isa 25.4–5; Psa 91.1–16; 121.5–7; 17.8–9; 36.7; 57.1; 63.7; Mark 4.30–32).

> **The breath of our nostrils.** Our King—the King of kings—"is
> our life" (Col 3.4); "in Him we live and move and are" (Acts
> 17.28). His **breath** *(rwḥ)* in our nostrils gives life to us (Gen 2.7;
> Psa 104.29–30; Job 33.4). In the same way, although on a lesser
> scale, a lesser king was the **breath** of his people's **nostrils**—
> a term used especially in ancient Egypt (Williams, "Some
> Egyptianisms in the Old Testament," 93–94), where the king
> was regarded as "the breath of all nostrils, by whom people
> breathe" (BAe VIII 24.7). "What is a person's life, when no
> breath comes out from the mouth of his lord the king?" (EA

149.21–23). Their very lives depended on him: "in the light of a king's face is life," whereas "the fury of a king is messengers of death" (Prov 16.14–15; cf. Est 7.3; 2 Sam 18.3).

The LORD's anointed one. This is the reading of all Hebrew copies, and in ancient times it was evidently also the reading of the LXX, because it is found in the Ethiopic and Arabic versions (both of which were translated from the LXX). However, all existing manuscripts of the LXX read "the anointed Lord" (*christos kurios* instead of *christos kuriou*), and that influenced some of the early English translations ("Christ the Lord," DRCV). The textual history of the phrase is discussed in Assan-Dhôte 275–76, 184–85.

Has been captured in their pits. The same expression is used to describe the capture of Zedekiah's predecessors Jehoahaz (by the Egyptians, Ezek 19.4; 2 Kgs 23.33–34) and Jehoiakim (by the Babylonians, Ezek 19.8–10; 2 Chr 36.5–6).

We said, "In his shadow we will live." The king's **shadow** should have sheltered his people from harm (cf. Isa 4.6; 25.4; Dan 4.20–22; Song 2.3). Some commentators have argued that a prophet would not say this about an unrighteous king like Zedekiah, and therefore that the verse must be either looking back on the death of the righteous king Josiah two decades earlier, or else foretelling the death of Christ—or both (Hrabanus 1229–30; Castro 983–87; Costa 258–64; del Rio 216–19). But God's people were required to respect even a very unrighteous king and to **live** submissively under his rule, because he was still **the LORD's anointed one** (1 Sam 26.11, 16, 23; Matt 22.21; cf. Rom 13.1–5). Even during the final days of the Babylonian siege, Zedekiah still had the power to shelter his people from disaster so that they might **live** among their enemies; and Jeremiah urgently entreated him to do so (Jer 38.17, 20).

4.21 Be glad† and be joyful†, daughter of Edom,
    dwelling in *the* land of Uz;
against you† also *the* cup will pass;
        you† will be filled with strong drink, and you† will make yourself
        naked.

4.22 Your[†] iniquity has been finished, daughter of Zion;
    He will not continue to exile you[†];
He has attended to your[†] iniquity, daughter of Edom;
    He has uncovered *what is* over your[†] sins.

The people of **Edom** were the Israelites' very closest relatives, since they were descendants of Jacob's twin brother Esau. Yet, age after age, Edom kept "pursuing his brother with the sword, and destroyed his own compassions; and his anger tore continually, and he kept his fury perpetually" (Amos 1.11). When Jerusalem was destroyed, the Edomites "stood opposite," behaved as the invaders did ("like one of them," Obad 11), and "cried out, 'Lay it bare, lay it bare, even to its foundation!'" (Psa 137.7). They "were joyful at the inheritance of the house of Israel, because it was a desolation" (Ezek 35.15).

Jerusalem (**Zion**) was rightly punished for her **iniquity.** But now the prophet foretells that the same thing would happen to **Edom.** She **also** would receive punishment for her **iniquity,** for her **sins.** The **cup** of the LORD's anger, which Jerusalem had drunk (Isa 51.17; Ezek 23.31–34), would now **pass** to her. She **also** would drink it, and **be filled with strong drink;** her people would "drink and stagger and be crazed from the face of the sword that I am sending among them" (Jer 25.15–17, 21)—the same experience that Jerusalem underwent (Jer 25.18). In that spiritually intoxicated condition, she would **make** herself spiritually **naked** (cf. Hab 2.15), so that the shame of her **sins** was openly **uncovered** (Jer 49.10; cf. Rev 3.18; 16.15)—again like Jerusalem (see the comments on 1.8; Jer 13.26; Ezek 16.37–39). When we humans sin, we often seek to conceal our sins (John 3.19–20). But everything that humans may try to conceal is inescapably exposed by the Lord. "God will bring every deed into judgment, with every hidden thing, whether good or evil" (Ecc 12.14; Heb 4.13; 1 Cor 4.5; Eph 5.13).

The punishment of the Edomites would be permanent, and final. He told them: "I will make you lasting desolations, and your cities will not be inhabited" (Ezek 35.9; Jer 49.17–18). They were a "people against whom the LORD is indignant to lasting time" (Mal 1.3–4).

The punishment of Jerusalem, however, would not be permanent. The LORD would **not continue to exile** her. "Thus has the LORD God of Israel said about this city, of which you are saying, 'It has been given into the hand of the king of Babylon...': I will gather them out of all of the countries where I drove them in My anger… and I will make them return to this place, and I will make them dwell in confidence" (Jer 32.36–37). And He would go even beyond that. "I will make a new covenant with the house of Israel… and I will forgive all their iniquity, and I will no longer be mindful of their sin" (Jer 31.31–34)—a promise that has now come to pass through Jesus (Heb 8.6–12; 10.15–17).

We must not think that these Edomites were the only people in history destined by God for eternal punishment. Nor must we think that these Israelites were the only people to whom God ever offered forgiveness of sins. In any and every age, the same two alternatives are before us. "I have set before you life and death, blessing and curse. Then choose life in order that you will live" (Deut 30.19). Those who choose the curse "will go away into lasting punishment, but the righteous ones into lasting life" (Matt 25.41, 46; John 3.36).

> **Be glad, and be joyful.** Not an approval of Edom's attitude, but an acknowledgement of Edom's refusal to repent of his unkindness to his brother Israel—somewhat like the acknowledgements of disobedience elsewhere in the Scriptures: "he who will hear, let him hear; and he who will refuse, let him refuse" (Ezek 3.27); "the unrighteous one, let him still do unrighteousness" (Rev 22.11); "fill up then the measure of your fathers" (Matt 23.32).
>
> **The land of Uz.** The homeland of Job (Job 1.1), listed among the foreign nations surrounding Israel (Jer 25.20).
>
> **Your iniquity has been finished.** The term **iniquity** (*'wn)* sometimes describes a sinful act, sometimes the punishment for that act (see the comments on v 6). In v 13 it had the former meaning; here it has the latter. Jerusalem was punished sufficiently by the **exile** that had been imposed on her; the LORD would not add any further penalties on top of it. "Her iniquity has been pardoned… for she has received from the LORD's hand double for all her sins" (Isa 40.2).
>
> **He has attended** [*pqd*] **to your iniquity.** Forms of Hebrew *pqd* ("visit," KJV) are translated by forms of Greek *episkeptomai* ("oversee," "watch over") in the New Testament Scriptures (e.g., Psa 8.4 ≡ Heb 2.6). The act can be either positive or negative: God "attends to" or "visits" His faithful servants with salvation

(Psa 106.4; Luke 1.68), but evildoers with punishment (Isa 26.21; Psa 89.30–32).

Your iniquity has been finished [*tm*].... **He has attended** [*pqd*]... **He has uncovered** [*glh*]. All three verbs are Qaṭal forms, presenting the actions as already past, presumably because they have already been determined in the will of God (see the notes on 3.52–63; Joosten 207–08; Rogland, *Alleged Non-Past Uses of Qatal in Classical Hebrew*, §3.4.5).

Exile... uncovered. These are two forms (Hiphʻil and Piʻel) of the same Hebrew word *(glh);* for the sense of the Piʻel, see the notes on 2.14. The LORD "will not continue to remove" Zion into exile; instead, He has now "removed what is over" Edom's sins. The former removal **has been finished;** the latter will last forever.

LAMENTATIONS 5

Summary

The whole of this chapter is an extended prayer to the LORD. In fact, many of the ancient manuscripts in Greek, Syriac, and Latin give it a special heading: "A Prayer" (or "Prayer of Jeremiah"; cf. Geneva). Still, it is essentially similar in structure to its four predecessors: its main body (vv 1–18) is predominantly a description of the sufferings of the people, and its conclusion (vv 19–22) carries the principal address to the LORD.

Verses 1–18 entreat Him to see what has happened to the people of Judah. Slaves are ruling over them, and their houses have been given to strangers. Even their leaders and elders have been killed and dishonored. They are hungry for food, and have to pay even for water and wood. Mount Zion is desolate and uninhabited. These woes have happened because of their sins and those of their fathers.

The final verses (19–22) entreat the LORD, who has rejected the people and been extremely wrathful against them, to return them to Himself and to renew their days.

5.1 Be mindful†, LORD, of what has come to be for us;
  look† and see† our reproach.

The people of Judah have suffered **reproach** *(ḥrph)* from their enemies (3.30, 61)—that is, their enemies have mocked them and dishonored them (Jer 24.9; Zep 2.8; Psa 44.13–16; 79.4; 69.19–20; 102.8; Isa 37.23). Righteous people are reproached falsely (Matt 5.11), but these people were reproached justly, because of their sins (Dan 9.16, 8). Their reproach was appointed by the LORD Himself: "I have made you a reproach to the nations and a mockery to all the lands" (Ezek 22.4). Now the prophet humbly confesses the sins that have caused this (vv 16, 7), and appeals to the LORD to **see** their reproach (as in 1.11, 20; 3.49–50) and **be mindful** of it (as in Psa 74.18, 22; cf. Lam 3.19).

5.2 Our inheritance has been turned over to strangers,
      our houses to aliens.

All the households of Israel had been given their **inheritance** in the land by the LORD (Deut 4.21; Psa 135.12; Num 26.53–56; Acts 13.19). But He had warned them that if they disobeyed Him, it would be taken away from them and given to **strangers** and **aliens**: "you will build a house, but you will not dwell in it" (Deut 28.30). In particular, those who robbed other people of property would themselves be deprived of their property (Amos 5.11). Now that punishment had come to pass (Jer 6.12; Ezek 7.20–24; Zep 1.13).

Under the new covenant, God's people are not promised an earthly inheritance, but a spiritual one: "the kingdom prepared for you from the foundation of the world" (Matt 25.34). Those who do the deeds of the flesh "will not inherit the kingdom of God" (Gal 5.19–21; 1 Cor 6.9–10; Eph 5.5; cf. Heb 12.14–17); it will be taken away from them, and given to those who bear fruit pleasing to God (Matt 21.33–43).

5.3 We have become orphans *with* no father;
      our mothers *have become* like widows.

The LORD had warned the men of Israel that, if they ill-treated orphans or widows, their own children and wives would become **orphans** and **widows** (Exod 22.22–24). This too had now come to pass (Jer 15.8; 18.21).

> **We have become orphans... our mothers have become like** [*k-*] **widows.** The *k-* in the second half could apply to both halves ("We have become [like] orphans... our mothers like widows"), as in Song 5.11–12 ("His head is fine gold... His eyes are like [*k-*] doves"); cf. IBHS §11.4.2b. In that case, the passage could be speaking about the population as a whole: they have been left desolate, with no support or help, like widows or

orphans (see the comments on 1.1). On the other hand, the *k-* could perhaps be emphatic ("We have become orphans... our mothers are indeed widows"; cf. HCSB), although that meaning is uncommon in Hebrew (possible examples are discussed in GKC §118*x;* BDB 454, §1d).

5.4 Our waters *come* in exchange for silver;
   our pieces of wood come in exchange for a price.

In this time of affliction, it was hard to obtain even the most basic commodities, such as **water** (cf. 4.4) and **wood** (needed almost daily for baking and cooking, 1 Kgs 17.10–12, and from time to time for housing, Lev 14.45; Zec 5.4). The Lord had warned them that "in Jerusalem... they will eat bread by weight and in anxiety, and they will drink water by measure and in devastation, so that they will lack bread and water" (Ezek 4.16–17). During the Babylonian siege, food must have become desperately expensive (cf. 2 Kgs 6.25); by its end, "the famine was powerful in the city, and there was no bread for the people of the land" (Jer 52.6; cf. Jer 37.21). Even after the siege, food and water would have been in short supply (see the notes on 1.11), because the invaders were using both—and were controlling both. The enemy would "eat the fruit of your livestock and the fruit of your land, until you are destroyed," and would "leave you no grain, wine, or oil, the offspring of your herds or the young of your flocks, until he has destroyed you" (Deut 28.51). The people were reduced to seeking nourishment in the least rewarding places ("in the gravel," 3.16).

   The Lord blesses His faithful servants with spiritual food and drink that can always be obtained freely, "without silver and without price" (Isa 55.1–2; cf. Rom 3.24). Those who partake of that food and drink will never hunger and never thirst (John 6.35; 4.14). "Those who seek the Lord will not lack any good thing" (Psa 34.10). But to those "who forsake the Lord," He says: "Because I called, and you did not answer; I spoke, and you did not hear; and you did evil in My eyes, and chose what I did not delight in... behold, My servants will eat, but you will be hungry; behold, My servants will drink, but you will be thirsty" (Isa 65.11–13; cf. Luke 14.16–20, 24; 16.24–25).

In exchange for. Hebrew *b-*, "against"—as if one was being weighed in a balance "against" the other (4.2); cf. GKC §119*p*. See also the comments on v 9.

5.5 Upon our neck we have been pursued;
 we have wearied ourselves; no rest has been given to us.

The suffering people were **pursued** constantly (1.3, 6; 4.19) and became **wearied** ("without strength," 1.6; "ill all of the day," 1.13), with **no rest** (1.3; Jer 45.3). The LORD's enemies will "have no rest day and night" forever (Rev 14.11; Isa 57.20–21), whereas those who come to Him, and take His light yoke upon their necks, rest forever from all weariness (Matt 11.28–30). "He gives power to the weary one, and to the one who has no might, He increases strength. And the youths will be tired and weary, and the young men, stumbling, will stumble; but those who wait for the LORD will renew their strength; they will go up with wings like vultures; they will run and not be weary; they will walk and not be tired" (Isa 40.29–31).

> **Upon [***'l***] our neck we have been pursued.** This clause has been translated and explained in various ways:
>
> 1. The medieval Masoretic scribes construed *'l* as the preposition **on** (as in 1.14: "my transgressions… have come up on [*'l*] my neck"). This raises two main possibilities.
>
> 1a. Some versions describe the pursuers as pressing down on the neck (*'l* in a vertical sense, **upon,** as in 3.54; 2.10): "Oppressors trample on our servile necks" (Quarles); "our necks are under persecution" (KJV). Many ancient Egyptian illustrations show Pharaohs putting their feet on the necks of their prostrate enemies. Similarly, when the Israelites defeated the kings of Canaan, "they put their feet on [*'l*] their necks" (Josh 10.24). But now the situation was reversed. The Israelites themselves were defeated; they themselves were trodden underfoot (1.15; cf. Mic 5.5). The Hebrew word *rdp* (**pursued**) does not necessarily imply that someone is physically running after someone else; it can describe any kind of persecution (e.g., Psa 119.161; Jer 15.15; 17.18; Job 19.22; cf. BDB 922, §1f).
> In German and Dutch, someone who is harass-

ing someone else is said to be "sitting on his neck." Many German and Dutch Bibles use that idiom as an equivalent to the Hebrew expression here. *Unsere Verfolger sitzen uns im Nacken* (ELB) ≡ *Wij worden op de nek gezeten door onze verfolgers* (NBG). In English the MLB, translated by Gerrit Verkuyl, uses the same expression: "Our pursuers now sit on our necks." (Verkuyl's first language was Dutch, and he evidently did not realize that "sit on one's neck" is not an English idiom.)

1b. Some versions describe the pursuers as pressing close behind the neck (*'l* in a horizontal sense, "against," as in Lev 1.5): "Our pursuers are at our necks" (NASB), i.e., "at our heels" (NIV). This is possible, although there is no other evidence that Hebrew used the expression "pursued against the neck" in that way.

In practical terms, the difference between 1a and 1b is not very great. Whichever way the scene is pictured, the pursuers are pressing close and harassing their victims.

2. Alternatively, *'l* could be construed as the noun "yoke" (often mentioned in connection with the **neck,** because that was where the yoke was worn: 1.14; Deut 28.48; etc.). Again this raises two main possibilities.

2a. If **pursued** means "persecuted" (as in option 1a), then the meaning might be that the neck yoke is itself a persecution: "[by] the yoke of our neck we have been persecuted," i.e., "continually burdened" (Blayney 406). The victims are in its grip and cannot escape (cf. Deut 28.48; Jer 28.14).

2b. Some commentators (e.g., Gottlieb 69) have held that **pursued** *(rdp)* might mean "driven hard." If so, the present clause might mean "we are being driven hard [by] the yoke of our neck" (like farm animals pulled by a yoke, forcing them to perform excessively hard labor). *Rdp* can indeed mean "driven" in Syriac (SL 1438–39), but there is no evidence that it could have that meaning in Hebrew.

3. Some have assumed that the text is faulty, and should have *'l* twice: "With a yoke [*'l*] on [*'l*] our necks we are hard driven" (NRSV). But this has no significant advantage

over option 2; and there is no evidence that any Hebrew manuscript ever had *'l* twice here. Some (e.g., NRSV mg) have claimed that the ancient Greek translator Symmachus worked from such a manuscript, since his rendering was *zugos kata ton trachēlou hēmon...* ("a yoke against our neck..."). However, it is more likely that Symmachus had the same Hebrew text as the existing copies, and simply construed *'l* as "yoke" instead of "on" (Blayney 406), adopting option 2.

5.6 We have given *our* hand to Egypt,
    to Assyria, to be filled with bread.

Deprived of food and drink (v 4), the people of Judah were desperate **to be filled with bread,** and even reached out for help to remote foreign nations like **Egypt** and **Assyria**—regardless of God's commands concerning those nations. The Israelites were specifically, and repeatedly, commanded to put no trust in Egypt or Assyria (Jer 2.18, 36; Hos 7.11; 12.1); whereas, in the time of Jeremiah, they were specifically, and repeatedly, commanded to "bring your necks under the yoke of the king of Babylon, and serve him and his people, and live" (Jer 27.12; 21.9; 38.2).

> **We have given our hand.** In the Scriptures, giving one's **hand** to someone was generally a sign of agreement or acceptance (Ezra 10.19; Ezek 17.18; Gal 2.9). Some have suggested that it could also be a description of begging ("we hold out our hands... just to get enough bread," JB), but there is no Scripture support for that.
>
> **Assyria.** The Assyrian empire had been replaced by the Babylonian (Jer 50.17–18), but the term **Assyria** was still applied to some or all of the Mesopotamian region for centuries afterwards (Ezra 6.22). In Jeremiah's time, people in Judah were still looking for help from that direction, as well as from **Egypt** (Jer 2.18). During the final siege of Jerusalem, some of the people "fell away to the Chaldeans" and saved their lives by doing so (Jer 38.19, 2); afterwards, some fled to Egypt in the vain hope that they would "not hunger for bread" there (Jer 42.14; 43.5–7). There is no need to think that these were the only regions where help was sought; in-

deed, "perhaps Egypt and Assyria are to be understood more generally, meaning simply that [the Israelites] were turning in all directions for help—as we might say 'to east and west'" (Aalders 112).

To be filled with bread. This comes just after a reference to the costliness of basic commodities (v 4; see also v 9) and therefore presumably refers to the same thing—the hardships during and after the Babylonian siege (not Israel's pacts with Egypt and Assyria in earlier generations).

5.7 Our fathers have sinned; they are not;
we ourselves have borne *the* burden of their iniquities.

The current generation was suffering (bearing a **burden**) not only because of their own sins (v 16), but also because of the **iniquities** of previous generations (their **fathers**). That was exactly what Moses had warned: if the Israelites departed from the LORD, they would be afflicted by foreign nations "because of your iniquities, and also because of your fathers' iniquities" (Lev 26.39; Isa 65.6–7; Dan 9.16). True, people are held guilty and condemned by God only for their own sins, never for anyone else's sins (Ezek 18.20; Rom 2.6–9; 14.12; 2 Cor 5.10). But they may suffer the consequences of previous generations' sins (Exod 20.5). (The children in the wilderness suffered hardship for forty years because of their fathers' sins, Num 14.33, even though they themselves had no knowledge of those sins, Deut 1.39.) So the inhabitants of Judah in Jeremiah's time reaped the consequences of what they themselves had done (when they refused to heed the LORD's word and submit to Nebuchadnezzar, Jer 25.8–11; 27.12–17; 38.17–23), and also reaped the consequences of what previous generations had done—above all in the time of Manasseh, whose abominations became so great that captivity could no longer be avoided (at most, it could only be temporarily delayed; 2 Kgs 21.11–15; 23.26–27; 24.3–4; Jer 15.4).

> **Fathers.** The word can include any or all previous generations of ancestors (Jer 7.22; 31.32; 35.6; etc.).
>
> **They are not.** That is, they "are no more" (NASB), as in Jer 31.15.

5.8 Slaves have ruled over us;
     there is no *one* delivering from their hand.

It "is not desirable… for a servant to rule over leaders" (Prov 19.10; 30.21–22; Ecc 10.5–7). In the past Jerusalem had been a "ruling woman" ("princess"), a "great one among the nations" (see the comments on 1.1). But Moses had warned the people that, if they disobeyed the Lord, "the stranger who is among you will go up higher and higher, and you yourself will go down lower and lower; he will lend to you, and you will not lend to him; he will be the head, and you will be the tail" (Deut 28.43–44). In the time of Hezekiah, the king of Babylon himself had sent a gift *(mnḥh)* to the king of Judah (2 Kgs 20.12). But now the king of Babylon had taken away all "the treasures of the king, and of his leaders" (2 Chr 36.18). Jerusalem was in the **hand** of people who would have been her **slaves** in the great days of her kingdom. And if God appoints something, **no one** can deliver from it (Psa 127.1; 107.10–12).

That has been our own situation in relation to sin. We ought to "rule over it" (Gen 4.7; Psa 119.133); but we have enslaved ourselves to it, letting it rule over us (John 8.34). And neither we, nor anyone else on earth, can deliver us from the hand of our sins; only God can do that (Rom 7.23–8.4; 6.12–23).

5.9 We are bringing in our bread in exchange for our soul,
     because of *the* face of *the* sword *in* the wilderness.

5.10 Our skin has become hot like an oven
     from *the* face of *the* raging of hunger.

The scarcity of **bread** was so great (see the comments on vv 6, 4) that the inhabitants of Jerusalem were risking their lives (their **soul**) in order to get it. And even if their lives were spared, they still had to suffer the ravages of **hunger**—which, in some respects, were even greater torments than a rapid death (see the comments on 4.9).

> **In exchange for.** Hebrew *b-*, as in v 4 (see the comments there). David's mighty men went through the Philistine army to get water "in exchange for their souls," i.e., "at the risk of their lives" (2 Sam 23.17). Adonijah asked to marry Abishag the Shulam-

mite "in exchange for his soul": when he made that request, he traded away his life in exchange for it (1 Kgs 2.23).

The sword [*ḥrb*] in the wilderness. The word *ḥrb* could be construed in two ways.

1. The medieval Masoretic scribes construed it as *ḥereb*, **sword** (which is undoubtedly its meaning elsewhere in Lamentations: 1.20; 2.21; 4.9). During the Babylonian invasion, the main danger from the **sword** was outdoors— "out on the street" (1.20) and, especially, "in the country-side" outside the city (Jer 14.18; 6.25).

2. Alternatively, *ḥrb* could be construed as *ḥōreb*, "dryness" or "drought" (as in Jer 50.38; Hag 1.11; Jdg 6.37–40; characteristic of a **wilderness,** Psa 106.9; Isa 50.2). On this view, the search for **bread** risked one's life because of "the dryness of the wilderness" (Calvin 636/502). Among the punishments for disobedience foretold by Moses was drought, so that "your strength will be brought to an end in vain, for your land will not give its produce" (Lev 26.19–20 ≡ Deut 28.23–24). This too came to pass in the time of Jeremiah (Jer 14.1–6).

Our skin *(ḥrbnw).* The singular form **skin** is strange, because its verb is unambiguously plural *(-w);* a precise rendering would be "Our skin have become...." Perhaps **skin** is here treated as a collective noun, and takes a plural verb for that reason (Renkema 436–37/607–08)—although it takes a singular verb everywhere else in the Hebrew Scriptures (including Lam 4.8). Or perhaps the plural suffix **our** *(-nw)* has prompted the choice of a plural verb (ATD 374)—although the same suffix seems to be followed by a singular verb in every grammatically comparable passage elsewhere (including "Our inheritance has been turned over," v 2). Our Lord does not always abide by human rules of grammar (as any page of the book of Revelation in Greek will show), and we cannot expect always to understand why He does not (cf. Isa 55.8–9).

Has become hot *(nkmrw,* a Niph'al form of *kmr).* In the present passage, several renderings have been suggested:

1. **Has become hot.** Nearly all other Scriptural forms of *kmr* refer to the rousing of compassion (Hos 11.8; Gen 43.30; 1 Kgs 3.26); these are usually taken to mean "grow warm

and tender" (BDB 485; cf. HALOT 2.481–82). In the present context, a reference to heat would also fit the mention of an **oven.** Hunger itself would not cause the **skin** to **become hot,** but it would make the person more susceptible to infection (plague, often connected in the Scriptures with hunger: "the one who is in the city, hunger and plague will devour him," Ezek 7.15). In that case, the **skin** would **become hot** with the fever of the infection; indeed, the term **raging** could possibly mean "fever" (NKJV).

2. "Is shriveled up" (NAB). This is certainly a common effect of starvation, but it derives only from renderings in the LXX and Syriac Peshitta—and neither of those translators seemed to have a sound knowledge of the meaning of *kmr,* because each of them provided two different renderings of it. No evidence in favor of the translation "is shriveled up" can be found in the Scriptures themselves.

2. "Was black" (KJV). A possibly related form, *kmrwr,* may mean "darkness" (Job 3.5). But no ordinary consequence of hunger would be likely to darken the skin.

5.11 They have afflicted women in Zion,
    virgins in *the* cities of Judah.

5.12 Leaders have been hanged by their hand;
    faces of elders have not been honored.

5.13 Young men have borne *the* grinding;
    youths have stumbled with wood.

5.14 Elders have ceased from *the* gate,
    young men from their music.

5.15 *The* gladness of our heart has ceased;
    our dancing has been turned to mourning.

The disaster has stricken all sections of the community: the **women** (2.20; 4.10) and **virgins** (1.4, 15, 18; 2.10, 21), the **young men** (1.15, 18; 2.21) and **youths** (2.21), the **elders** (1.19; 2.10, 21; 4.16) and **leaders** (1.6; 2.2, 9). And the troubles mentioned are merely a few specific examples of far more extensive ones. (When the prophet says that **leaders** were **hanged** and **elders** were **not... honored,** he does not mean that elders were never hanged and leaders were always honored.) "The king of the Chaldeans… had no compassion on young man or virgin, old man or aged"; "all" alike were given into his hand (2 Chr 36.17). Some were killed and **hanged;** others were forced into hard labor (**grinding** grain, carrying **wood**). In times of peace, **elders** would sit at the **gate** delivering judgment (see the comments on 2.9); but now they were silent (2.10). In times of prosperity, **music** (a sign of **gladness,** v 15; Jas 5.13) would be heard from the **young men;** but now, in a time of **mourning,** they too were silent (Ezek 26.13; Isa 24.7–8).

Not only the earthly Jerusalem, but the whole world, and everything in it, is passing away (1 Jn 2.15–17). Only in the heavenly Jerusalem is there everlasting gladness and justice, and no affliction, mourning, or death at all (Rev 21.1–22.5; 7.9–17). No enemy can ever take that away (John 16.22).

> **They have afflicted.** A common Hebrew word, *'nh*, which is applied to many different hardships, including famine (1 Kgs 8.35), ill-treatment of the powerless (Exod 22.22–23; Psa 94.5–6; 140.12), oppressive slavery (Exod 1.11–12; 3.7; Deut 26.6), imprisonment (Psa 105.18), and rape (2 Sam 13.14)—all of which would have afflicted Jerusalem's **women** and **virgins** at this time ("her virgins are grieved," 1.4; "have gone into captivity," 1.18; "have fallen by the sword," 2.21).

> **Leaders have been hanged.** After offenders had been killed, their bodies were sometimes hung up in public (by Israelites: Deut 21.22–23; Josh 8.29; 10.26; 2 Sam 4.12; by Philistines: 2 Sam 21.12). Hanging was also practiced from early times by the Babylonians (CH 21; 227), although their procedures could have differed in some respects. "Accursed of God is one who is hanged" (Deut 21.23); this is the punishment that our Lord bore for our sins (Gal 3.13). A number of the most important people in Judah (including the king's sons, the high priest, and the second priest) were put to death by the Babylonians after Jerusalem had been captured (2 Kgs 25.7, 18–21).

> **By their hand** presumably means "by the hand of the enemies" (as in v 8), not that the victims were suspended by their own hands (which is not the meaning of death or punishment **by** someone's **hand** elsewhere in the Scriptures; cf. Ezek 28.10; Josh 20.9).

Young men have borne. The subject of the verb is not the enemies ("They took the young men," KJV) but the **young men** themselves (as shown by the parallel in the next line: **youths have stumbled**).

Have borne. Like English "bear," Hebrew *nś'* can refer either to lifting up something physically (as in Jer 10.5) or to enduring something emotionally (as in Jer 10.19), or both (as in Isa 46.1). Here both aspects would be applicable.

The grinding. Forms of Hebrew *ṭhn* describe the task of **grinding** grain for food (Num 11.8), a job often assigned to people of lowly status (Isa 47.2), such as Samson in prison (Jdg 16.21). This particular form, *ṭhwn,* occurs nowhere else, so it is impossible to tell whether it is an infinitive describing the activity ("to grind," KJV), or a noun describing either the place of grinding ("at the grinding mill," NASB) or the implement of grinding ("a millstone," Rotherham). But that question does not significantly affect the meaning of the passage.

Music. Hebrew *ngn* describes instrumental music; it is distinguished from "sing" (Psa 68.25; Ezek 33.32) and is applied to David's playing on the lyre (1 Sam 16.16–18, 23). Nowadays music and dancing are usually regarded as forms of worldly entertainment. Such practices were known in ancient times too (e.g., "the music [*ngynwt*] of the drinkers of strong drink," Psa 69.12; the dance of Herodias's daughter, Mark 6.22). But under the old covenant, both instrumental **music** and **dancing** were also authorized and commanded as acts of worship in praise to God (Psa 33.3; 150.3–5; 149.3; 2 Chr 29.25); those commands have not been repeated under the new covenant. At the time of the Lamentations, the praise had been turned into **mourning** (1.4; cf. Amos 8.10; Jer 6.26). Nevertheless, the LORD had already promised that He would restore His people from their captivity. "Then the virgin will rejoice in the dance, and the young men and the old men together; and I will turn their mourning into gladness, and I will comfort them and make them rejoice, out of their sorrow" (Jer 31.13; cf. Psa 30.11).

5.16 *The* crown *from* our head has fallen;
    woe to us, for we have sinned!

A **crown** was worn by kings (2 Sam 12.30; Ezek 21.25–26) and, at least occasionally, by important officials (Est 8.15); the term is also applied to a condition of honor, a "crown of excellence" (Prov 4.9; 16.31). The Lord's people were themselves to be a "crown of excellence" in His hand (Isa 62.3). But at this time, both Israel's kingship and her honor had **fallen** (see the comments on 1.1, 8; 2.9; 4.20).

None of Jerusalem's woes had happened by chance, or unjustly. All of them were fully deserved, because she had **sinned:** "The Lord—He is righteous; for against His mouth I have rebelled" (1.18; see the comments on 1.8; 3.42). Daniel too, in his prayer at the end of the period of punishment, humbly acknowledged both the justice of the punishment and the extent of the sin: "We have not entreated the face of the Lord our God, turning from our iniquity and gaining understanding in Your truth; and the Lord God has kept watch over the evil and brought it upon us; for the Lord our God is righteous in all His works that He has done; and we have not hearkened to His voice" (Dan 9.13–14).

Unless we confess our sins and turn from them in the way God has appointed, the inevitable consequence is **woe.** "Woe to the wicked! It will be evil for him, for the reward of his hands will be done to him" (Isa 3.11; Hos 7.13; Matt 18.7; 11.21).

Under the old covenant, it was necessary for God's people to confess that they had **sinned,** before those sins could be forgiven: "The one who covers up his transgressions will not prosper; but the one who confesses and forsakes them has obtained compassion" (Prov 28.13). "If they turn their heart around in the land where they were taken captive, and they turn around and make entreaty to You in the land of their captivity, saying, 'We have sinned, we have done wrong, and we have done wickedness,' and they turn back to You with all of their heart and all of their soul... and pray toward their land... then hear from heaven, the place of Your dwelling, their prayer and their entreaties, and do justice for them, and forgive Your people who sinned against You" (2 Chr 6.37–39). The same principle applies for God's people under the new covenant today: "If we confess our sins, He is faithful and righteous to forgive us the sins, and to cleanse us from all unrighteousness" (1 Jn 1.9).

5.17 Because of this our heart has become ill,
   because of these *things* our eyes have become dark,

5.18 because of *the* mountain of Zion, which has become desolate;
   jackals have walked in it.

Many centuries earlier, Moses had warned the Israelites that, if they departed from the LORD, He would give them "a trembling heart and failing eyes" (Deut 28.65). Now these things were happening. **Because of** the **desolate** state of Jerusalem (see 1.4, 13), the people were suffering both inwardly and outwardly: their **heart** had **become ill** (see 1.13, 22) and their **eyes** had **become dark**—an expression meaning that they were unable to see (Psa 69.23; their eyes had "come to an end," 2.11). "The city that was great with people" (1.1) had now become so **desolate** that it was inhabited by wild animals such as **jackals** (Jer 9.11)—a punishment that was also inflicted on heathen nations who did not serve the LORD (Assyria: Zep 2.13–15; Babylonia: Isa 13.19–22; 14.22–23; Edom: Isa 34.11–15).

> **Has become desolate** *(šmm)*. The word-form here could be construed either as an adjective, "desolate" (as in Dan 9.17), or as a verb, **has become desolate** (cf. 4.5). The meaning is not affected.
>
> **Jackals.** Hebrew *šw'l* usually—perhaps always—describes the active and gregarious jackal rather than the shy and solitary fox (cf. Jdg 15.4; Psa 63.10; Tristram, *Natural History of the Bible*, 110–11, §2).

5.19 You†, LORD, to lasting time You† are seated;
   Your† throne *is* to generation and generation.

"From lasting time and until lasting time," the LORD is God (Psa 90.2–5). He is "the Alpha and the Omega, the first and the last, the beginning and the end" (Rev 1.8; 22.13). Moreover, He is **seated** on His **throne** forever, "in every generation and generation" (Psa 145.13; 146.10). No one ever takes that away from Him; He is always King: "His dominion will be a lasting dominion that will not pass away, and His kingship will not be destroyed" (Dan 7.14). From His throne in the heavens, He "judges the world in righteousness" (Psa 9.7–8; 89.14), seeing all (Psa 11.4–7) and ruling over all (Psa 103.19; 47.8).

The LORD had promised that there would come a time when Jerusalem herself would be His throne, and people of all nations would gather there. "At that time they will call Jerusalem 'The throne of the LORD,' and all nations will be gathered to her" (Jer 3.17). He also promised that David's throne would last forever: "I will establish your seed to lasting time, and build up your throne to generation and generation" (Psa 89.4). After the Babylonian conquest, it might have seemed that those promises had failed. Jerusalem and all the other cities of Judah lay desolate and uninhabited (Jer 44.2, 6), the kingship had been taken away from David's lineage, and the last king's sons had been killed (Jer 52.10). Yet all those promises have now been fulfilled through Jesus, the Son of David. "The Lord God will give Him the throne of David His father, and He will be King over the house of Jacob to lasting time, and there will be no end of His kingdom" (Luke 1.32–33). His kingdom is for "all the nations" (Matt 28.19; Luke 24.47; Mark 11.17), and all those who have come to it have gathered at Jerusalem: "you have come to Mount Zion, and to the city of the living God, the heavenly Jerusalem... and to Jesus" (Heb 12.22–24; Acts 15.14–18). The Lord has set up the words of His servants, and completed the counsel of His messengers (Isa 44.26); not one word of all His good promises has fallen (cf. 1 Kgs 8.56).

5.20 Why are You† forgetting us to enduring time;
    why are You† forsaking us to length of days?

The people of Jerusalem had forgotten the LORD "for days without any number at all" (Jer 2.32; 3.21; 13.25; 18.15), and had forsaken Him for "broken cisterns that hold no water" (Jer 2.13, 17, 19; 9.13). Therefore, in recompense, He had justly forgotten and forsaken them: "The prophets who prophesy falsehood... reckon to make My people forget My name.... Therefore, behold, I also, forgetting, will forget you, and I will cast away you and the city that I gave you" (Jer 23.26–27, 39; 12.7; cf. Deut 31.16–17). They deserved that punishment, because they had sinned (v 16; 1.18; see the comments on 1.8). Nevertheless, they could lawfully appeal to the LORD and ask **why** their punishment should remain unaltered forever (**to enduring time... to length of days**), since His authority would remain unaltered forever (**to lasting time... to generation and generation, v 19**). That question would be asked not only on earth, but also in heaven: "The angel of the LORD answered and said, 'LORD of hosts, how long will You not have compassion on Jerusalem and the cities of Judah, with whom You have been angry these seventy years?' And the LORD answered the angel... with good words, words of comfort" (Zec 1.12–13).

God's people today may lawfully ask Him similar questions (Luke 18.7–8; Rev 6.10). Indeed, in the psalms that He has appointed for His people to sing (under the new covenant as well as the old: Eph 5.19 ≡ Col 3.16), He has repeatedly provided us with words to ask Him such questions (Psa 79.5; 74.1, 10, 19; 44.23–24; 77.7–9; 89.46; 13.1–2). Even if we are suffering justly because of our sins (1 Pet 2.20; 4.15), we may still, while confessing our sins (v 16), ask Him to set a limit to our deserved sufferings, and not allow them to continue to the utmost. Those who are suffering unjustly (1 Pet 2.19; 4.16) may also present such requests to Him—as Jesus Himself did on the cross (Psa 22.1–2 ≡ Matt 27.46). "I know, LORD, that not to a person belongs his way; it does not belong to a man who walks to direct his steps. Discipline me, LORD, but in justice; not in Your anger, lest You reduce me to nothing" (Jer 10.23–24).

5.21 Return† us, LORD, to Yourself†, and let us be returned;
     renew† our days as before;

5.22 even though, rejecting, You† have rejected us;
     You† have been wrathful against us, as far as extremely *so*.

Whenever the LORD's people sin, they need to confess their sins to Him (see the comments on v 16). But merely confessing one's sins is not enough. Judas confessed his sin (Matt 27.3–4), yet he was not saved (John 17.12; cf. 2 Cor 7.10). It is also necessary to forsake one's sins (Prov 28.13) and **return to** the LORD with all one's heart and soul (2 Chr 6.37–38). "Let us search our ways, and let us search them out, and let us return to the LORD" (Lam 3.42). That was the teaching of the old covenant (Isa 55.6–7), and it is also the teaching of the new (Acts 8.22).

However, when we have defiled ourselves with sin, we ourselves are unable to **return to** Him, even when we seek to do so. Our sin has separated us from Him, so that He cannot look on us or hear us (Isa 59.1–2). He must inevitably continue to be **wrathful against** us and **reject** us. And "who can say, 'I have made my heart clean, I have been pure from my sin'?"

(Prov 20.9). Only He Himself can overcome that barrier, cleansing our sins through the blood of His Son, and thus restoring us to Himself (1 Jn 1.9, 7). Jesus said, "No one is able to come to Me, unless it should be given to him by the Father" (John 6.65).

We have His promise that He will indeed **return to** Himself all those who seek it: "everyone who asks receives" (Matt 7.7–11). "Come near to God, and He will come near to you" (Jas 4.8). Only those who are unwilling to return to Him will not be returned (Matt 23.37).

The LORD did indeed **return** the people of Jerusalem to Himself and "restore the restoration of the land, as it was at first" (Jer 33.11). But at the time described in the Lamentations, that was still in the future. At that time, they were still **rejected,** and the LORD was still extremely **wrathful against** them—as He continued to be, until the appointed seventy years had been completed ("with whom You have been angry these seventy years," Zec 1.12–13; Jer 29.10; 2 Chr 36.21; Dan 9.2). Again and again the Scriptures remind us how terrible it is to lie under the wrath of God, how desperately we need salvation from it, and how impossible it is for us to escape unless His good pleasure is to remove it. We must never think that our sins are trivial things, or that their defilement will disappear of its own accord, or by any effort of our own. "God's anger is revealed from heaven on all irreverence and unrighteousness of people" (Rom 1.18; Eph 5.6 ≡ Col 3.6), and until a person has had his sins cleansed and forgiven, "the anger of God abides on him" (John 3.36; Rom 2.5). We can be "saved from the anger" only by Him, and only through the means He has appointed—the blood of His Son (Rom 5.9; 1 Thes 1.10).

> **Even though** *(ky 'm)*. This is a common Hebrew expression, but even in ancient times different translators held different views about its meaning in the present passage. The main options are as follows:
>
> 1. "For if thou hast utterly rejected us, [then] great indeed has been thy anger against us" (NEB). However, a "for if…" clause is generally followed by *w-* or some other term signifying "then…" (JM §176*d*), as in 3.32. Here there is no such term. Moreover, **You have been wrathful against us** is not a consequence of **You have rejected us** but another way of stating the same point.

2. "Unless Thou hast utterly rejected us, [and] art exceedingly angry with us" (NASB). However, this would require a preceding negative clause (GKC §163*c;* JM §173*b*), as in Isa 55.10–11.

3. "But thou hast utterly rejected us; thou art very wroth with us" (KJV). However, this too would require a preceding negative clause (GKC §163*a;* JM §172*c*), as in Psa 1.1–2, 4.

4. "Or hast thou utterly rejected us? Art thou exceedingly angry with us?" (RSV). But nowhere else does *ky 'm* introduce a question.

5. "Even though you have indeed rejected us and have been exceedingly angry at us" (House 454, 470–72). This option has been challenged because "the proposed syntactic sequence—prayer to God in the main clause, accompanying circumstances in the subordinate clause, linked by 'even though'—would have no parallel in the psalms of lament" (Westermann 179/218). But that would not be surprising (many undisputed phenomena of Hebrew syntax "have no parallel in the psalms of lament"), and at any rate each of the *components* of this sequence can be found elsewhere in the Scriptures: a prayer to God with "accompanying circumstances in the subordinate clause" occurs in Psa 89.50–51, and *ky 'm* meaning "even though" occurs in Isa 10.22 and Amos 5.22. On the whole, therefore, this option seems to pose less difficulty than any of those listed above.

Rejecting, You have rejected us *(m's m'stnw).* See the notes on "Weeping, she is weeping" (1.2). Here the repetition emphasizes a contrast (JM §§123 *g, i*)—the contrast between this clause and the preceding appeal to the Lord ("You have indeed rejected us," NAB; "truly, You have rejected us," NJPS). Perhaps it may also stress the extent of the rejection ("thou hast utterly rejected us," KJV), corresponding to **as far as extremely** in the next clause; but this is less in keeping with Biblical Hebrew usage (see JM §123*j*). The clause does not necessarily indicate that the rejection is either complete or irrevocable.

BIBLIOGRAPHY

Texts

De Rossi, Giovanni Baptista. *Variae lectiones Veteris Testamenti.* 4 vols. Parma: Regio Typographeo, 1784–1788.

_____. *Scholia critica in V. T. libros.* Parma: Regio Typographeo, 1798.

Elliger, Karl, and Wilhelm Rudolph (general eds.). *Biblia Hebraica Stuttgartensia.* Stuttgart: Deutsche Bibelstiftung, 1977.

Freedman, David Noel, Astrid B. Beck, and James A. Sanders (eds.). *The Leningrad Codex: A Facsimile Edition.* Grand Rapids, MI: Eerdmans, 1998.

Goshen-Gottstein, M. H. (ed.). *The Aleppo Codex.* Part 1. *Plates.* Jerusalem: Magnes, 1976.

Kennicott, Benjamin (ed.). *Vetus Testamentum Hebraicum.* 2 vols. Oxford: Clarendon, 1776–1780.

Schäfer, Rolf (ed.) "Lamentations." In *Biblia Hebraica Quinta: Megilloth.* Stuttgart: Deutsche Bibelgesellschaft, 2004. 54–72, 113*–136*.

Ulrich, Eugene (ed.). *The Biblical Qumran Scrolls: Transcriptions and Textual Variants.* Leiden: Brill, 2009.

Ancient Versions

Albrektson, Bertil. *Studies in the Text and Theology of the Book of Lamentations, with a Critical Edition of the Peshitta Text.* Lund: Gleerup, 1963.

Field, Frederick (ed.). *Origenis Hexaplorum quae supersunt.* 2 vols. Oxford: Clarendon, 1875.

Sperber, Alexander (ed.). *The Hagiographa.* The Bible in Aramaic. Leiden: Brill, 1968.

Weber, Robert (general ed.). *Biblia Sacra iuxta vulgatam versionem.* 2nd ed. Stuttgart: Württemburgische Bibelanstalt, 1975.

Ziegler, Joseph (ed.). *Jeremias, Baruch, Threni, Epistula Jeremiae.* Septuaginta. 3rd ed. Göttingen: Vandenhoeck & Ruprecht, 2006.

English Versions (in Chronological Order)

The Bible and Holy Scriptures. (Geneva Bible.) Geneva: Rowland Hall, 1560.

The Holy Bible… Newly Translated out of the Originall Tongues. (King James Version.) London: Robert Barker, 1611.

_____. *Newly Translated out of the Original Tongues.* (Ed. Benjamin Blayney.) 2 vols. Oxford: Oxford UP, 1769.

_____. *The Cambridge Paragraph Bible of the Authorized English Version.* Ed. F. H. Scrivener. 2nd ed. Cambridge, England: Cambridge UP, 1873.

Sions Elegies. Paraphrased by Francis Quarles. London: W. Stansby, 1624.

"The Lamentations of Jeremy." Tr. John Donne. (First published 1633.) In *The Divine Poems of John Donne.* Ed. Helen Gardner. Oxford: Clarendon, 1952. 35–48.

A Paraphrase vpon the Divine Poems. By George Sandys. London: John Leggatt, 1638.

The Holy Bible, Translated from the Latin Vulgat. (Ed. Richard Challoner. Douai-Rheims-Challoner Version. 1749–1750.) 2nd ed. 5 vols. N. p., 1763–1764.

The Septuagint Version of the Old Testament. Tr. Launcelot Charles Lee Brenton. 2 vols. London: Bagster, 1844.

The Holy Bible... Translated Literally from the Original Tongues. (Tr. Julia E. Smith.) Hartford, CT: American Publishing Company, 1876.

The Holy Bible... Newly Edited by the American Revision Committee. (American Standard Version.) New York: Nelson, 1901.

The Emphasized Bible. Tr. Joseph Bryant Rotherham. (1872–1902.) 4 vols. Cincinnati: Standard Publishing, 1916.

The Holy Scriptures According to the Masoretic Text. (JPS Version.) Philadelphia, PA: Jewish Publication Society of America, 1917.

The Holy Bible: Revised Standard Version. New York: Nelson, 1952.

The Modern Language Bible: The New Berkeley Version. Ed. Gerrit Verkuyl. (1959.) 2nd ed. Grand Rapids, MI: Zondervan, 1969.

The Jerusalem Bible. London: Darton, Longman & Todd, 1966.

The New English Bible. Oxford and Cambridge, England: Oxford UP and Cambridge UP, 1970.

The New American Bible. Paterson, NJ: St. Anthony Guild, 1970.

New American Standard Bible. La Habra, CA: Creation House, 1971.

"A Literal Translation of the Bible." Tr. Jay P. Green, Sr. (1976.) In *The Interlinear Hebrew-Greek-English Bible.* 2nd ed. 4 vols. Wilmington, DL: Associated Publishers & Authors, 1985.

The Holy Bible: New International Version. Grand Rapids, MI: Zondervan, 1978.

The Holy Bible: The New King James Version. Nashville, TN: Nelson, 1982.

The New Jerusalem Bible. London: Darton, Longman & Todd, 1985.

Tanakh: The Holy Scriptures: The New JPS Translation. Philadelphia, PA: Jewish Publication Society of America, 1985.

The Revised English Bible. Oxford and Cambridge, England: Oxford UP and Cambridge UP, 1989.

The Holy Bible: New Revised Standard Version. New York: Oxford UP, 1989.

Tanach: The Stone Edition. Ed. Nosson Scherman. Brooklyn, NY: Mesorah, 1996.

The Holy Bible: English Standard Version. Wheaton, IL: Crossway, 2001.

Holy Bible: Holman Christian Standard Bible. Nashville, TN: Broadman & Holman, 2004.

Other Modern Language Versions (in Chronological Order)

Biblia: das ist die gantze Heilige Schrift Deudsch. Tr. Martin Luther. Wittenburg: Hans Lufft, 1545.

La Biblia… Revista… por Cypriano de Valera. (Versión Reina-Valera.) Amsterdam: Lorenzo Jacobi, 1602.

La Sacra Bibbia tradotta in lingua Italiana. Tr. Giovanni Diodati. 2nd ed. Geneva: Pierre Chouet, 1641.

Biblia, dat is de gantsche H. Schrifture… door last der Hoogh Mog Heeren Staten Generael der Vereenighde Nederlanden. 2nd ed. Amsterdam: Ravesteyn, 1657.

La Sainte Bible. Tr. David Martin. Revised by Pierre Roques. 2 vols. Basel: Im-Hoff, 1744.

La Sainte Bible. Tr. Jean Frédéric Ostervald. 2nd ed. Neuchâtel: Boyve, 1744.

Библия… в русском переводе. (Russian Synodal Version.) Moscow: Синодальная типография, 1876.

La Sainte Bible. (Version Darby Française.) The Hague: Blommendaal, 1885.

La Santa Biblia… Versión de Cipriano de Valera… Revisada. (Revised by the British and Foreign Bible Society.) Madrid: Sociedad Bíblica Británica y Estranjera, 1909.

Bijbel: Vertaling 1951 in opdracht van het Nederlands Bijbelgenootschap. Amsterdam: Nederlandsch Bijbelgenootschap, 1951.

La Santa Biblia… Revisada por Cipriano de Valera (1602); otras revisiones: 1862, 1909 y 1960. (Revised by the American Bible Society.) Asunción: Sociedades Bíblicas en América Latina, 1960.

La Sainte Bible: Nouvelle Version Segond révisée. (Bible à la Colombe.) Paris: Alliance Biblique Universelle, 1978.

La Biblia de las Américas. Anaheim, CA: Foundation Publications, 1986.

La Sacra Bibbia… La Nuova Diodati: Revisione 1991. Brindisi: La Buona Novella, 1991.

Elberfelder Bibel. (Revidierte Elberfelder Bibel, 3rd ed.) Wuppertal: R. Brockhaus, 2006.

Zürcher Bibel 2007. (Neue Zürcher Bibel.) Zurich: Verlag der Zürcher Bibel, 2007.

La Bible… Segond 21. Geneva: Société Biblique de Genève, 2007.

Biblia Textual. (Tr. Sociedad Bíblica Iberoamericana.) Nashville, TN: Holman, 2010.

Secondary Sources

Aalders, G. C. *De Klaagliederen.* Korte Verklaring der Heilige Schrift. Kampen: Kok, 1925.

Adeney, Walter F. *The Song of Solomon and the Lamentations of Jeremiah.* Expositor's Bible. London: Hodder & Stoughton, 1895.

Albertus Magnus. "In Threnos Jeremiae commentarii." (Thirteenth century.) In *Opera omnia.* Vol. 18. Ed. Auguste Bornet. Paris: Vivès, 1893. 243–353.

Assan-Dhôte, Isabelle, and Jacqueline Moatti-Fine. *Baruch, Lamentations, Lettre de Jérémie.* La Bible d'Alexandrie. Paris: Cerf, 2005.

ben Isaac, Solomon (Rashi). (Commentary on Lamentations. Eleventh century.) In תוליגמ שמח רפס. Ed. Menachem Cohen. Mikra'ot Gedolot Haketer. Ramat Gan, Israel: Bar-Ilan UP, 2012.

Bergmann, Eugenio (ed.). *Codex Hammurabi Textus Primigenius.* 3rd ed. Rome: Pontifical Biblical Institute, 1953.

Blayney, Benjamin. *Jeremiah and Lamentations.* (1784.) Ed. James Nichols. London: Tegg, 1836.

Böttcher, Friedrich. *Ausführliches Lehrbuch der hebräischen Sprache.* Ed. Ferdinand Mühlau. 2 vols. Leipzig: Barth, 1866–1868.

Botterweck, G. Johannes, Helmer Ringgren, and Heinz-Josef Fabry (eds.). *Theological Dictionary of the Old Testament.* Vols. 1–15. Grand Rapids, MI: Eerdmans, 1974–2006.

Brown, Francis, S. R. Driver, and Charles A. Briggs. *A Hebrew and English Lexicon of the Old Testament.* Oxford: Clarendon, 1907.

Calvin, John. "Praelectiones in Lamentationes Ieremiae." (1563). In *Ioannis Calvini Opera quae supersunt omnia.* Vol. 29. Ed. Wilhelm Baum, Eduard Cunitz, and Eduard Reuss. Corpus Reformatorum. Brunswick: Schwetschke, 1889. 505–646. (ET: "Prelections… on the Lamentations of Jeremiah." In *Commentaries on the Book of the Prophet Jeremiah and the Lamentations.* Vol. 5. Tr. John Owen. Edinburgh: Calvin Translation Society, 1850. 299–518.)

——————. *Sermons sur les livres de Jérémie et des Lamentations.* Ed. Erwin Mülhaupt. Supplementa Calviniana. Geneva: Droz, 1971.

Castro, Christoforo a. *Commentariorum in Ieremiae prophetas, Lamentationes, et Baruch.* Paris: Sonnius, 1609.

Costa de Andrada, Sebastianus a. *Commentarii in Threnos et Orationem Ieremiae prophetae.* Lyon: Cardon, 1609.

del Rio, Martinus. *Commentarius litteralis in Threnos.* Lyon: Cardon, 1608.

Dobbs-Allsopp, F. W. *Lamentations.* Interpretation. Louisville, KY: John Knox, 2002.

Ewald, Heinrich. *Die Psalmen und die Klaglieder.* 3rd ed. Göttingen: Vandenhoeck & Ruprecht, 1866. (ET: *Commentary on the Psalms.* Vol. 2. Tr. E. Johnson. London: Williams & Norgate, 1881.)

Fuerst, Julius. *A Hebrew and Chaldee Lexicon to the Old Testament.* Tr. Samuel Davidson. 5th ed. London: Williams & Norgate, 1885.

Gerlach, Ernst. *Die Klagelieder Jeremiä.* Berlin: Hertz, 1868.

Gordis, Robert. *The Song of Songs and Lamentations.* New York: Ktav, 1974.

Harris, R. Laird, Gleason L. Archer, and Bruce K. Waltke (eds.). *A Theological Wordbook of the Old Testament.* 2 vols. Chicago: Moody, 1980.

Harrison, R. K. *Jeremiah and Lamentations.* Tyndale Old Testament Commentaries. London: Inter-Varsity Press, 1973.

Hillers, Delbert R. *Lamentations.* Anchor Bible. 2nd ed. Garden City, NY: Doubleday, 1992.

House, Paul R. "Lamentations." In *Song of Songs/Lamentations.* Word Biblical Commentary. Nashville, TN: Nelson, 2004. 267–479.

Hrabanus Maurus. "Commentaria in Jeremiam." (Ninth century.) In *Patrologia Latina* 111. Ed. J.-P. Migne. Paris: Migne, 1852. 793–1272.

Humphries, John A. *The Books of Jeremiah and Lamentations.* Truth Commentaries. Bowling Green, KY: Guardian of Truth, 2003.

Ibn Ezra, Abraham. (Commentary on Lamentations. Twelfth century.) In מישורים פירוש רשע מינש סע מגיולת שמח. Warsaw: Lewin-Epstein, 1924.

Jenni, Ernst, and Claus Westermann (eds.). *Theological Lexicon of the Old Testament.* Tr. M. E. Biddle. 3 vols. Peabody, MA: Hendrickson, 1997.

Joosten, Jan. *The Verbal System of Biblical Hebrew.* Jerusalem: Simor, 2012.

Joüon, Paul. "Notes de critique textuelle (suite)." *Mélanges de la Faculté Orientale, Université Saint-Joseph* 6 (1913): 64–211.

_____ and Takamitsu Muraoka. *A Grammar of Biblical Hebrew.* 2nd ed. Rome: Pontifical Biblical Institute, 2006.

Kaiser, Otto. "Die Klagelieder." In H.-P. Müller, Otto Kaiser, and J. A. Loader, *Das Hohelied, Klagelieder, Das Buch Ester.* 4th ed. Alte Testament Deutsch. Göttingen: Vandenhoeck & Ruprecht, 1992. 91–198.

Kaiser, Walter C., Jr. *Grief and Pain in the Plan of God: Christian Assurance and the Message of Lamentations.* Fearn, Ross-Shire: Christian Focus, 2004.

Kautzsch, Emil (ed.). *Gesenius' Hebrew Grammar.* Revised by A. E. Cowley. 2nd ed. Oxford: Clarendon, 1910.

Keil, Carl Friedrich. *Biblischer Commentar über den Propheten Jeremia und die Klagelieder.* Biblischer Commentar über das Alte Testament herausgegeben von Carl Friedr. Keil und Franz Delitzsch. Leipzig: Dörffling & Franke, 1872. (ET: *The Prophecies of Jeremiah.* Vol. 2. Tr. James Kennedy. Edinburgh: T. & T. Clark, 1874.)

Koehler, Ludwig, Walter Baumgartner, and J. J. Stamm. *The Hebrew and Aramaic Lexicon of the Old Testament.* Ed. M. E. J. Richardson. 5 vols. Leiden: Brill, 1994–2001.

König, Friedrich Eduard. *Historisch-kritisches Lehrgebäude der hebräischen Sprache.* 3 vols. Leipzig: Hinrichs, 1881–1897.

_____. *Stilistik, Rhetorik, Poetik in Bezug auf die biblische Litteratur.* Leipzig: Dieterich, 1900.

Knudtzon, J. A. *Die El-Amarna Tafeln.* 2 vols. Aalen: Zeller, 1915.

Laetsch, Theo. *Bible Commentary: Jeremiah.* St. Louis, MO: Concordia, 1952.

Lapide, Cornelius a. *Commentarius in Ieremiam prophetam, Threnos, et Baruch.* Antwerp: Nutius, 1621.

Liddell, H. G., and Robert Scott. *A Greek-English Lexicon.* Revised by Henry Stuart Jones. 9th ed. (1940.) With revised Supplement. Oxford: Clarendon, 1996.

McDaniel, Thomas F. "Philological Studies in Lamentations." *Biblica* 64 (1968): 27–53, 199–220.

Mackay, John L. *Lamentations.* Mentor Commentary. Fearn, Ross-Shire: Christian Focus, 2008.

Nägelsbach, C. W. Eduard. "Die Klagelieder." In *Der Prophet Jeremia und dessen Klagelieder.* Theologisch-homiletisches Bibelwerk... von J. P. Lange. Bielefeld: Velhagen & Klasing, 1868. 1–78. (ET: "The Lamentations of Jeremiah." Tr. and ed. William H. Hornblower. In *The Book of the Prophet Jeremiah.* Lange's Commentary on the Holy Scriptures. New York: Scribner, 1871. 1–196.)

Origen. "Die Klageliederkommentar." (Third century.) In *Origenes Werke.* Vol. 3. Ed. Erich Klostermann, revised by Pierre Nautin. Die Griechischen Christlichen Schriftsteller der ersten drei Jahrhunderte. 2nd ed. Berlin: Akademie, 1983. 233–79.

Parry, Robin A. *Lamentations.* Two Horizons Old Testament Commentary. Grand Rapids, MI: Eerdmans, 2010.

Payne Smith, Robert. "Lamentations." In *The Holy Bible.* Vol. 5. Ed. F. C. Cook. (Speaker's Commentary.) London: Murray, 1875. 577–606.

Provan, Iain W. *Lamentations.* New Century Bible Commentary. New Century Bible Commentary. Grand Rapids, MI: Eerdmans, 1991.

Renkema, Johan. *Klaagliederen.* Commentaar op het Oude Testament. Kampen: Kok, 1993. (ET: *Lamentations.* Tr. Brian Doyle. Historical Commentary on the Old Testament. Leuven: Peeters, 1998.)

Salters, R. B. *A Critical and Exegetical Commentary on Lamentations.* International Critical Commentary. London: T. & T. Clark, 2010.

Sanctius, Gaspardus. *In Ieremiam prophetam commentarii.* Lyon: Cardon, 1618.

Sandman, Maj. *Texts from the Time of Akhenaten.* Bibliotheca Aegyptiaca VIII. Brussels: Fondation Égyptologique de la Reine Élisabeth, 1938.

Sokoloff, Michael. *A Syriac Lexicon.* Winona Lake, IN, and Piscataway, NJ: Eisenbrauns and Gorgias, 2009.

Streane, A. W. *The Book of the Prophet Jeremiah, together with the Lamentations.* Cambridge Bible for Schools and Colleges. Cambridge, England: Cambridge UP, 1889.

Theodoret of Cyrrhus. "Explanatio in Threni." (Fifth century.) In *Patrologia Graeca* 81. Ed. J.-P. Migne. Paris: Migne, 1864. 779–806. (ET: "Commentary on the Book of Lamentations." In *Commentaries on the Prophets*. Vol.1. Tr. R. C. Hill. Brookline, MA: Holy Cross Orthodox Press, 2006. 181–95.)

Tregelles, Samuel Prideaux (ed.). *Gesenius' Hebrew and Chaldee Lexicon to the Old Testament Scriptures*. 2nd ed. London: Bagster, 1857.

Tristram, H. B. *The Natural History of the Bible*. London: S. P. C. K., 1867.

VanGemeren, Willem A. (ed.). *New International Dictionary of Old Testament Theology and Exegesis*. 5 vols. Grand Rapids, MI: Zondervan, 1997.

Waltke, Bruce K., and M. O'Connor. *An Introduction to Biblical Hebrew Syntax*. Winona Lake, IN: Eisenbrauns, 1990.

Westermann, Claus. *Die Klagelieder: Forschunggeschichte und Auslegung*. Neukirchen-Vluyn: Neukirchener Verlag, 1990. (ET: *Lamentations: Issues and Interpretation*. Tr. Charles Muenchow. Minneapolis, MN: Fortress, 1994.)

Williams, Ronald J. "Some Egyptianisms in the Old Testament." In *Studies in Honor of John A. Wilson*. Chicago: University of Chicago Press, 1969. 93–98.

Wordsworth, Christopher. *The Holy Bible*. Vol. 5. *Isaiah, Jeremiah, Lamentations, and Ezekiel*. London: Rivingtons, 1871.

Xirouchakis, Stavros M., and Giorgos Andreou. "Foraging Behaviour and Flight Characteristics of Griffon Vultures *Gyps fulvus* in the Island of Crete, Greece." *Wildlife Biology* 15 (2009): 37–52.

Evan and Marie Blackmore have published eighteen previous volumes. Their most recent publications have been La Rochefoucauld: *Collected Maxims and Other Reflections* (Oxford World's Classics), *Leviticus* (Truth Commentaries), and *Between Malachi and Jesus: Writings from Maccabean and Roman Times* (DeWard). Their work has received the American Literary Translators' Association Prize and the Modern Language Association Scaglione Prize for Literary Translation.

Also by the Blackmores

Between Malachi and Jesus
Writings from Maccabean and Roman Times

The last 300 years before Christ are little known to Bible readers nowadays. Yet during that time God was doing wonderful works in preparation for the coming of His Son.

It was an age of terrible persecutions—some of the worst ever endured by God's people. The government imposed laws that were contrary to God's commands. Many professed believers were only too willing to live like the rest of the world. Yet this was also a time of shining lights in the darkness. Some people stood firm in spite of the persecutions, and laid down their lives gladly without any visible reward. They did not live to see it, but their deeds were helping to pave the way for the Messiah. Step by step, the Lord's great plan was unfolding.

In this book you will read that story—told not at second hand, but by some of the very people who remained faithful in the crisis. The volume contains fresh modern English renderings of these enthralling documents, with a full commentary from the Scriptures. Maps, charts, and timelines guide the reader through each phase of the struggle. In addition, 1 Maccabees is newly edited in Greek (with parallel English translation), and the Psalms of Solomon in parallel Greek and Syriac (with English translations of both). A final chapter shows how the prophecies of Daniel and other Old Testament prophets were being fulfilled during this time.

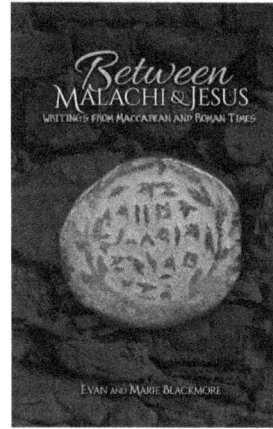

"Evan and Marie Blackmore's Between Malachi and Jesus *is an extraordinarily useful and insightful book. … This masterpiece belongs on the shelf of all who have interest in the time leading up to the emergence of Christianity and Rabbinic Judaism. I recommend this book enthusiastically!"*

Craig A. Evans
Payzant Distinguished Professor of New Testament
Acadia Divinity College, Nova Scotia